HIPPOCRENE |

LAO BASIC COURSE

Warren G. Yates
Souksomboun Sayasithsena

HIPPOCRENE BOOKS
New York

First published by the Foreign Serivce Institute, U.S. Government Printing Office, 1970.

Hippocrene paperback edition, 1995.

For information, address:
HIPPOCRENE BOOKS, INC.
171 Madison Avenue
New York, NY 10016

ISBN 0-7818-0410-8

Printed in the United States of America.

TABLE OF CONTENTS

xiv

INTRODUCTION

This is the first of two volumes designed to teach spoken Lao to English speakers. Some dialect of Lao is spoken and understood by approximately three million persons in Laos and about ten million in Thailand. The Lao presented in this book is the Vientiane dialect, which is used in all governmental communications. It is spoken in the central part of Laos by approximately 2,000,000 persons and is understood throughout the Kingdom of Laos and in Northeast Thailand.

The material in this text is in the form of a series of 85 'cycles' in the 'microwave' format originated by Dr. Earl W. Stevick of the FSI, and first used in two 'modules' of a course in Swahili.[1] The description of the microwave format that follows is based on these two texts. Each 'unit' of a microwave course is called a cycle and consists of two 'phases' In the first phase (M-phase) the student learns a small amount of the language and in the second phase (C-phase) he puts it to use. The diagram below illustrates this:

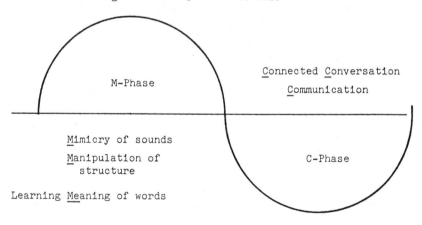

M-Phase

Connected Conversation
Communication

Mimicry of sounds
Manipulation of
structure

C-Phase

Learning Meaning of words

ONE CYCLE

(Footnote on next page)

The term 'microwave' (a very short wave) emphasizes the short span of time between the presentation of new material and its actual use in real communication.

The teaching methods[2] used with the M-phase and C-phase may vary a great deal and the teacher should feel free to use the one that seems most effective to him. 'The sentences in the M-phase are provided with cue words and they may be done like substitution drills, but other types of drill such as mimicry drills, transformation drills, translation drills, etc., should also be used whenever they seem appropriate.

In the C-phase the instructor should exert himself to the fullest extent possible to make everything that is said in class be 'real communication'. Communication can occur only if this condition is met: One person is giving information that another person doesn't have but is interested in having. The C-phase will normally consist of questions and answers, which may be joined together to form short conversational exchanges. In the beginning this will be the limit of the student's capacity. Later on short narrations will be possible and normal. If the students are going to be interested in what is being said it follows that they may wish to have some control over what is being talked about. The instructor should encourage this. This may mean any of several things, depending on the nature of the class and their spirit of independence, etc. It may mean only that the instructor supplies new vocabulary items

---

[1] Swahili: An Active Introduction, General Conversation and Swahili: An Active Introduction, Geography ed. by Earl W. Stevick, Foreign Service Institute, Department of State, Washington, D.C., 1966

[2] More explicit and detailed suggestions for teaching microwaves are included in Notes to Teachers at the end of the Introduction. Specific advice for full exploitation of the material in each cycle is given in each cycle. All of these suggestions are given in the Lao language for the benefit of Lao teachers who may not understand English very well.

to be used in patterns already learned or it may mean that
additional grammatical patterns and vocabulary items may have
to be taught. In either case the instructor should allow the
student to have a major voice in what is taught. The instructor
should be thoroughly familiar with the materials contained in
this text so that he may readily skip about when the student's
interest leads him to do so. Each cycle forms an independent
unit so that taking the cycles out of sequence will not cause
any problems that can not be easily dealt with. This text
should be looked upon as an aid to teaching and not as a
complete course of instruction.

It will normally require from 250 to 300 hours in class
to complete this text. A student who has done well in this
part of the course should be able to perform all of the following
things: order a simple meal, ask for a room in a hotel, ask and
give street directions, tell time, handle travel requirements and
expressions of politeness plus some of the following: introduce
people to each other, discuss his work, give autobiographical
information, and discuss current events.

<u>Notes</u> <u>To</u> <u>Students</u>

1) Listen carefully and imitate as closely as you can
what the instructor says. Be prepared to try to
improve what you say if the instructor doesn't
approve of it. Keep in mind that in the beginning
of language study you will probably have rather
poor ability to monitor your own efforts. The
closer your sounds resemble English the farther
they will be from Lao.

2) You should always know the meaning of anything you
say without trying to put a literal word-for-word
English translation on it. For example, sŷa kh3j
sĭi faa means 'My shirt is blue' but a word-by-word
translation of this would be 'shirt I color sky.'
All you need to know is what a Lao would say if he
wanted to tell you that his shirt was blue.

3) The material presented to you in each cycle is very
limited both in content and grammatical form. You
will not find it difficult to learn the meanings,
to pronounce the sentences, or to understand the

grammatical structure presented, but you should keep in mind that you will not only be expected to do the things referred to above, but you will be expected to know how to use these sentences in 'communicative' situations, i.e. situations in which you are telling someone else something he doesn't know, but needs or wants to know.

4) The 'Notes' that accompany each cycle contain information of several different kinds: (a) description of the grammatical structure in the cycle, (b) information about the meanings and uses of words, and (c) descriptions of situations in which words are used. This information should help you understand better what is being taught in the cycle. You should study it outside of class after you have learned to use the material in the cycle.

5) The 'Application' should be done after completion of all other parts of the cycle. It provides an opportunity for you to test your knowledge of different aspects of the cycle such as grammatical structure, vocabulary, etc.

6) The Lao use a writing system which is historically related to that used for Sanskrit. At a later stage in the course you will be asked to learn to read it, but it would impose an undue hardship on you in the beginning to have to learn it, so a special transcription has been devised. It is, however, provided only as an aid to memory. You will learn correct pronunciation by imitating your teacher, being corrected, and trying again, but not by reading. Although all the symbols used in the special transcription are explained in the chart that follows, it will be helpful to keep the following conventions in mind: (a) Vowel length is indicated by doubling the vowel symbol, and (b) The pitch contour on a syllable is indicated by a symbol above the vowel.

EXPLANATION OF THE SPECIAL TRANSCRIPTION
USED IN THIS TEXT

Symbol	Usual English Letter	Approximate Pronunciation
b	b	similar to English b in buy
p	p (after s)	like the p in spy (no puff of air after it)
ph	p	like p in pie
d	d	similar to English d
t	t (after s)	like the t in sty (no puff of air after it)
th	t	t as in tie
k	k (after s)	like the k in ski (no puff of air after it)
kh	k	k as in kite
c	...	somewhat like j in jet
l	l	l as in long
m	m	m as in me
h	h	h as in hen
f	f	f as in fun
s	s	s as in see
n	n	n as in need
ŋ	-ng	like -ng in sing
nj	-ny	as in canyon
w	v	as in vet
j	y	as in yet
i	i	i as in sip
ii	ee	ee as in see

e	e	e as in pet
ee	ay	a as in date
ɛ	a	a as in cat
ɛɛ	a	a as in fan
y	u	somewhat like u in sugar
yy	...	nothing like it in English
ə	uh	like a in Cuba
əə	...	similar to British pronunciation of sir
a	u	somewhat like u in fun
aa	ah	a as in father
u	oo	oo as in look
uu	ou	like oo in boot
o	o	o as in cone but shorter
oo	o	o as in so
ɔ	...	....
ɔɔ	aw	aw as in law
ia, ua, iw, ew, eew, ɛw, uj, ooj, ya, yaj, and uaj		have no counterparts in English
aw	ow	ow as in cow
aaw	ow	like ow above but longer
aj	y	y as in my
aaj	y	like y in my but longer
ɔj	oy	oy as in boy
ɔɔj	oy	like oy as in boy but longer

xx

TONES IN LAO

There are six tones in Lao. The pitch contours, names, and symbols for them are illustrated below:

	khaa	khāā	khàa	khǎa	kháaw	khâw
Pitch Contour						
Names	LOW	MID	HIGH FALLING	LOW RISING	HIGH	LOW FALLING
Symbol	NO MARK	—	\	V	/	∧

ບົດແນະນຳສຳລັບນາຍຄຣູ   (Notes to the Teacher)

ບົດຮຽນມາສາລາວແຕ່ລະບົດຍັງຢູ່ໃນປຶ້ມຕ່ວນປະກອບດ້ວຍສອງພາກດ້ວຍກັນຄື ພາກ M ແລະພາກ C
ຈຶ່ງແຕ່ລະພາກອາດຈະປະກອບດ້ວຍຫລາຍຕອນ. ຢູ່ໃນພາກ M ຕາມຫົມມະຄາຕອນໜຶ່ງຈະສອນກາມຖາມ
ແລະອິກຕອນໜຶ່ງຈະສອນກາມຕອບຄຳຖາມ ຈຶ່ງໃນພາກໜຶ່ງອາດຈະມີດ້ວຍກັນຫລຳຍຕອນ. ສອນພາກ C ກໍ
ແມ່ນກາມຝຶກຫັດສ້ວຫຮຽນມາແລ້ວຢູ່ໃນພາກ M ຄືນໂດຍນັກຮຽນເອງ. ໝາຍຄວາມວ່າ ນັກຮຽນຈະຖຶກ
ປ່ອຍໃຫ້ຖາມກັນພາຍໃຕ້ກາມຄວບຄຸມຂອງນາຍຄຣູ.

ເມື່ອວລາສອນພາກ M ແຕ່ລະຕອນທ່ານຈະໃຫ້ນັກຮຽນເປີດປຶ້ມໄວ້ກໍໄດ້ແລະຈຶ່ງແບ່ງກາມສອນອອກ
ຖານອອກຄ້ວຍ: (1) ເວົ້າແຕ່ລະໂຍກໃຫ້ນັກຮຽນຟັງດ້ວຍຄວາມໄວຫົມມະດາ. (2) ໃຫ້ນັກຮຽນ
ເວົ້າຄຳສຽງຕົມເສັງຍຶດຂອງຕາມຫ່ານໄຫລຮຽນແລະຖຶກສ້ວງ ພ້ອມທັງໃຫ້ຂະເຈົ້າຮູ້ຄວາມໝາຍຂອງມັນ.
(3) ໃຫ້ນັກຮຽນເວົ້າປໂຍກຕາມຫ່ານຈົນລຶ້ງ ແລະຖຶກສ້ວງ ພ້ອມທັງໃຫ້ຂະເຈົ້າຮ້ວາຂະເຈົ້າເວົ້າຕຶວ່ຍ.
ຖ້າວ່າປໂຍກທີ່ສອນຫາກຍາວເກີນໄປ ກໍຈຶ່ງແບ່ງສອນຕໍ່ລະນ້ອຍຄ້ວຍກາມເລີ່ມຕົ້ນແຕ່ທາຍປໂຍກກ່ອນໄປ.

ທ່ານຈະຕ້ອງຄ່ຽວຄັດຄັດກາມອອກສຽງຂອງນັກຮຽນ ຖ້າຂະເຈົ້າເວົ້າຕຶວ່ຍບຸຍຖຶກກໍຈຶ່ງພຍາຍາມຈຸ່ອຍ
ແກ້ໄຂໃຫ້ມັນຖຶກ. ຖ້າຫາກບ່ຽບຖຶກກໍຈຶ່ງໃຫ້ນັກຮຽນເຕັ້ນອາລາວເວົ້າຕຶວ່ຍຜຶດໂດຍກາມເວົ້າຕາມສ້ວງທີ່
ຜຶດຂອງລາວໃຫ້ລາວຟັງກ່ອນ ແຕ່ຢ່າໃຫ້ລາວເວົ້າສ້ວງທີ່ຜຶດຕາມ; ໃຫ້ລາວມີດຟັງສ້ຽງກ່ອນ. ຕໍ່ໄປກໍທ່ອຍ
ສ້ວງທີ່ຜຶດກັບກາມອອກສຽງທີ່ຖຶກໃຫ້ລາວໜ້ວຈິນລາວຮູ້ແລະໄດ້ຍຶນຄວາມແຕກຕ່າງກັນ ແລ້ວຈຶ່ງໃຫ້ລາວເວົ້າ
ຕາມສ້ວງທີ່ຖຶກຈຶນປັ່ນທຶມໃຈຂອງທ່ານ.

ພາກ C ແມ່ນສຳລັບໃຫ້ນັກຮຽນຕັດໃຈສ້ວທີ່ຂະເຈົ້າຮຽນມາໃນພາກ M . ຈຶ່ງແຕ່ງໃຫ້ນັກຮຽນຜຶ່
ໜຶ່ງເປັນ A ແລະຜຶ່ໜຶ່ງເປັນ B ແລ້ວໃຫ້ຂະເຈົ້າສົມທະນາກັນພາຍໃຕ້ກາມນຳຂອງນາຍຄຣູ. ເຫດທີ່ແຕ່ລະ
ຕອນຂອງພາກ C ມັນສັ້ນ ຫລືເປັນພຽງແຕ່ຄ້ວຢ່າງຕ່ຳ ນັ້ນກໍໝ່ອນວ່າ ຢາກປ່ອຍໂອກາດໃຫ້ນາຍຄຣູຫຳ
ກາມຝຶກຫັດນັກຮຽນໂດຍບໍ່ຂອບເຂດຈຳກັດ. ໝາຍຄວາມວ່ານາຍຄຣູຈະເລືອກໃຊ້ຄຳສັ່ງຄຳໃດຈາກບົດ
ຮຽນກ່ອນໆທີ່ນັກຮຽນຮຽນມາແລ້ວມາໃຊ້ເປັນກັນກໍໄດ້ຕິວ່ມັນ. ດັ່ງນັ້ນ ມັນຈຶ່ງເປັນສ້ວສຳຄັນຢ່າງຍ້ງທີ່ນາຍຄຣູ
ຈະຕ້ອງເອາໃຈໃນຈຸດປະສິງອັນນັ້ນ.

ຕລົງຈາກກາມສອນພາກ C ຢ່າງພໍເໝິກໃຈແລ້ວ ຖ້າຫາກທ່ານຕົມວ່າມີເຄ່ອງຫຳຈະສົມທະນາ
ກັນໄດ້ກໍໃຫ້ສົມທະນາກັນໂລດ. ແຕ່ໃນຕອນຄົນບ້ວມຈຶ່ງພານັກຮຽນຝຶກຫັດເວົ້າຫລາຍໆສ້ຽງກ່ອນ ຄໍໄປຈ່ອ

ໃຈເວລາສິນທະນາຕລາຍຍ້ອນ ຊິ້ງໃນການສົນທະນານີ້ ມາຍຕຣຈະຕ້ອງເຮັດໃຫ້ນັກຣຽນໄດ້ມີໂອກາດເວົ້າ
ຕລາຍກວ່າຕົນ. ຢ່າປ່ອຍໃຫ້ຂະເຈົ້ານັ່ງຟັງແຕ່ຂອງຂອງທ່ານແຕ່ຝ່າຍດຽວ.

ກົມງທ່ານຄວນແຕ່ງແຕ່ງຂອງຍົນປະກອບເຕົ່ອນັ້ງ ໂດຍອາສັຍຄ່າສັຍທີ່ນັກຣຽນໄດ້ຮຽນມາແລ້ວ. ຈິ່ງ
ແຕ່ງແຕ່ງທັກຊ້ອຂຂອງກັບວຽກການຍົນແຕ່ຈິ່ງຂອງນັກຣຽນ; ຄືກ້າຕາກວ່າ ຂະເຈົ້າເປັນນັກການທຸດກໍຈິ່ງ
ພຍາຍາມແຕ່ງແຕ່ງທັກຊ້ອຂຂອງໄປໃນຕາງວຽກຍ້ານການເມືອງ. ຖ້າຂະເຈົ້າເປັນນັກຕນາກອນກໍໃຫ້ແຕ່ງ
ແຕ່ງທັກຊ້ອຂຂອງກັບການພັທນາສ້າງສາ ຕລິການປຸກຝັງແລະລ້ຽງສັດ. ຫ້ວນກໍເພື່ອຍ່ອຍໃຫ້ນັບຍາກາດຍູ່
ໃນຕາງຣຽນມີຊຸດຊຸອາຍຽນ.

xxiii

GREETING CYCLE

A. Repeat each utterance after the instructor.

B. Give a complete sentence that includes the cue word that the instructor will give you.

C. Be sure you understand the meaning of each sentence.

M-1

sábaaj	sábaaj	to be well, comfortable	
dii	sábaajdii	good, well	Hello! Hi!

M-2

bɔɔ	sábaajdii bɔɔ?	(question word)	How are you? [Good morning, good afternoon, good evening, etc.]
càw	càw sábaajdii bɔɔ?	you	How are you?

M-3

khɔ̃ɔpcaj	sábaajdii khɔ̃ɔpcaj	thank you	Fine, thank you.
khɔ̃j	khɔ̃j sábaajdii khɔ̃ɔpcaj	I, me	I'm fine, thank you.
...dee?	càw dee?	and { what, how about...?	And you?

C-1

A. sábaajdii	A. Hello.	[Hi, good morning, etc.]
B. sábaajdii	B. Hello.	[Hi, good morning, etc.]

1

C-2

A. sábaajdii bɔɔ?   A. How are you?
B. sábaajdii khɔɔpcaj, càw dee?   B. Fine, thank you, and you?
A. khɔj sábaajdii khɔɔpcaj   A. I'm fine, thank you.

C-3

A. càw sábaajdii bɔɔ?   A. How are you?
B. khɔj sábaajdii khɔɔpcaj,   B. I'm fine, thank you, and you?
   càw dee?
A. khɔj sábaajdii khɔɔpcaj   A. I'm fine, thank you.

NOTES

1) A Lao sentence has two parts: a Subject and a Predicate.

Subject	Predicate
càw	sábaajdii
'You	are well, fine.'

2) The Subject is a Noun Phrase. A Noun Phrase is a (1) Noun plus modifiers, determiners, etc. or (2) a Noun Substitute (pronoun, etc.).

Noun Phrase

càw
'you'

3) The Predicate is a Verb Phrase. A Verb Phrase is a Verb (or Verbs) with optional preverbal elements and postverbal complements.

Verb Phrase

sábaajdii
'(is/are) well, fine'

2

4) The Subject (NP) precedes the Predicate (VP), thus a Sentence (S) can be written in this way:

$$S \longrightarrow NP + VP$$

which means 'A sentence consists of a Noun Phrase preceding a Verb Phrase'.

5) A Sentence can be changed into a question by the addition of a question word (Q), thus S + Q.

NP	+	VP	+	Q
càw		sábaajdii		bɔɔ
(you		[are] well		Question)

'Are you well?'

APPLICATION

1. khɔ̃j is probably the _____ of the sentence khɔ̃j sábaajdii
   (a) predicate   (b) subject   (c) question word   (d) none
   of these.

(All answers are at the bottom of the page.)

2. In the sentence sábaajdii bɔɔ, sábaajdii is (a) subject
   (b) question word   (c) predicate   (d) none of these.

3. In the sentence càw sábaajdii bɔɔ, bɔɔ is (a) the question word
   (b) predicate   (c) subject   (d) none of these.

4. càw sábaajdii bɔɔ is (a) a statement   (b) a question
   (c) a command   (d) none of these.

5. bɔɔ càw sábaajdii is (a) a question   (b) a statement
   (c) a command   (d) none of these.

Answers: 1b, 2c, 3a, 4b 5d

3

6. khɔ̌j sábaajdii is (a) a command (b) a question (c) a statement (d) none of these.

7. sábaajdii is (a) a Noun Phrase (b) a Verb Phrase (c) a question word (d) none of these.

8. bɔɔ is (a) a Verb Phrase (b) Noun Phrase (c) question word.

9. In càw sábaajdii bɔɔ , càw is (a) Noun Phrase (b) Verb Phrase (c) question.

10. In khɔ̌j sábaajdii, khɔ̌ɔpcaj, càw dee, dee means something like (a) you (b) but (c) ...how about (you) (d) it has no meaning.

CYCLE 1.

M-1

pâakkaa	an nìi mɛɛn pâakkaa	pen	This is a pen.
tó?	an nìi mɛɛn tó?	table	This is a table.
tāŋ-ìi	an nìi mɛɛn tāŋ-ìi	chair	This is a chair.
pỳm	an nìi mɛɛn pỳm	book	This is a book.
cìa	an nìi mɛɛn cìa	paper	This is paper.

M-2

njǎŋ	an nìi mɛɛn njǎŋ?	what(?)	What is this?
nàn	an nàn mɛɛn njǎŋ?	that	What is that?
fǎa	an nàn mɛɛn fǎa	wall	That is a wall.

C-1

| njǎŋ | A. an nìi mɛɛn njǎŋ? | A. What is this? |
| pâakkaa | B. an nìi mɛɛn pâakkaa | B. This is a pen. |

Answers: 6c, 7b, 8c, 9a, 10c

4

C-2

njǎŋ   A.   an nàn mɛɛn njǎŋ?   A.   What is that?

tāŋ-lì   B.   an nàn mɛɛn tāŋ-lì   B.   That is a chair.

ເມື່ອສອນ ໄຊເກີລ ມີແລວ ຫານລອງຖາມສະບາຍນັກຣຽນຫານຄືບຫຼກ! ຂະເຈົ້າສາມາດຖາມສະບາຍ
ຫານຄືນໄດຣຽນຄືຍ? ຖ້າຫາກວ່າຍັງບໍລຽນກໍໃຫ້ຫານຈົ່ງຫາຂະເຈົ້າຫັດເວົ້າອີກແລວ.

NOTES

1) The Verb Phrase may consist of a Verb (V) with a Noun Phrase
complement, thus VP ⟶ V + NP.

     Verb   +   NP

     <u>mɛɛn</u>   pâakkaa

     'is   (a) pen'

The following sentence is an example of the copula verb <u>mɛɛn</u>
followed by NP complement:

     NP   +   V   +   NP

     <u>annìi</u>   <u>mɛɛn</u>   pâakkaa

     'This   is   (a) pen.'

2) The NP <u>an nìi</u> is made up of a Noun <u>an</u> plus a determiner <u>nìi</u>. <u>an</u>
belongs to a special class of nouns that serve as substitutes
for other nouns. They are called 'classifiers.' <u>an</u> can be
used as a substitute for any inanimate noun (pen, chair,
etc.). <u>an nìi</u> means 'this' or 'this one'.

3) <u>tāŋ lì</u>, <u>tó</u>ʔ, <u>pâakkaa</u> and other nouns like this (things that
can be counted) have no number indication in Lao, so they
may refer to one or more than one thing according to the
construction they occur in.

5

4) njǎŋ 'what?' is a question word substitute. It substitutes for all inanimate nouns and for some other nouns in questions. Observe the following example:

	NP	V (copula)	NP	
Question:	an nìi	mɛɛn	njǎŋ	
	(this	is	what)	'What's this?'
Response:	an nìi	mɛɛn	tó?	
	'This	is	(a) table.'	

njǎŋ is in the same position in the sentence as the word it replaces. (NOTE: This is not the case with English what.

> What is this?
>
> This is a book.)

5. mɛɛn 'be' is used to indicate the identification of things in the example given. It has other uses, but is much more restricted in use than 'be' in English.

APPLICATION

In the sentence an nìi mɛɛn pâakkaa.

1. an nìi is (a) predicate   (b) subject   (c) Noun Phrase complement   (d) Verb Phrase.

2. mɛɛn is (a) Noun Phrase   (b) question   (c) Verb (d) complement of the verb.

3. pâakkaa is (a) Verb Phrase   (b) Noun Phrase complement of mɛɛn   (c) question   (d) predicate.

Answers: 1b, 2c, 3b

6

In the sentence an nìi mɛɛn njǎŋ

4. njǎŋ refers to (a) an animate noun   (b) the Verb Phrase
   (c) an inanimate noun.

5. mɛɛn is (a) a copula verb   (b) it is used to identify the
   subject   (c) it is a Noun Phrase   (d) it is none of these.

6. an is a classifier and refers to things, not people.   True
   or false?

7. nìi (a) means 'this'   (b) it is a Noun Phrase   (c) it is
   a determiner   (d) it precedes the classifier.

8. taŋ lì may mean (a) 'a chair'   (b) 'chair'   (c) 'the chair'
   (d) 'chairs'   (e) 'the chairs'   (f) any of these.

CYCLE 2

M-1

khɔj	an nìi mɛɛn pâakkaa khɔj	I, me	This is my pen.
càw	an nìi mɛɛn pâakkaa càw	you	This is your pen.
láaw	an nìi mɛɛn pâakkaa láaw	he, she	This is his(her) pen.
phùakháw	an nìi mɛɛn pâakkaa phùakháw	we (all)	This is our pen.
phùakkhɔj	an nìi mɛɛn pâakkaa phùakkhɔj	we	This is our pen.
phùakcàw	an nìi mɛɛn pâakkaa phùakcàw	you (pl.)	This is your pen.
khácàw	an nìi mɛɛn pâakkaa khácàw	they	This is their pen.

Answers: 4c, 5a-b, 6true, 7a and c, 8f

7

M-2

sǒɔdam	an nìi mɛɛ̄n sǒɔdam phǎj?	pencil	Whose pencil is this?
sǒɔkhǎaw	an nìi mɛɛ̄n sǒɔkhǎaw phǎj?	chalk	Whose chalk is this?
mûak	an nìi mɛɛ̄n mûak phǎj?	hat	Whose hat is that?
sŷa-fǒn	an nìi mɛɛ̄n sŷa-fǒn phǎj?	raincoat	Whose raincoat is this?
khán-hōm	an nìi mɛɛ̄n khán-hōm phǎj?	umbrella	Whose umbrella is this?

Supplement to Cycle 2

M-1 khǒɔthòot   Excuse me. Pardon me. 'I'm sorry!'
                     'I apologize.'

    bɔɔ̄ pen njǎŋ   It's O.K., Sure! That's all right! It does
                     not matter!

    khɔɔ̀pcaj   Thank you.

    bɔɔ̄ pen njǎŋ   You are welcome. Don't mention it.

njǎŋ   A. khǒɔthòot, an nìi mɛɛ̄n njǎŋ? Excuse me, what is this?

pâakkaa   B. an nìi mɛɛ̄n pâakkaa.   This is a pen.

           A. khɔɔ̀pcaj   Thank you.

           B. bɔɔ̄ pen njǎŋ   You are welcome.

ໂດຍະນໍເມນໂດຍະຫຼັກການຈະຕອງກຳກັບນຳການອອກສຽງຂອງນັກຮຽນຢ່າງໃກ້ຊິດ ກ່ອນຫຼະເຈົ້າ
ຈະເກີດຄວາມເຄີຍຊິນກັບການເວົ້າຕລິການອອກສຽງຕໍເຜີດພາດ.

8

C-1

(pâakkaa)	A.	an nîi mɛɛn pâakkaa phăj?	(pen)	Whose pen is this?
(khɔ̆j)	B.	an nîi mɛɛn pâakkaa khɔ̆j	(I)	This is my pen.

ການປ່ອຍປະລະເລີຍຕໍ່ການອອກສຽງອອງນັກຣຽນໃນຊັ້ນນີ້ ຈະເປັນການສ້າງນິໄສຕາໃຫແກ່ທ່ານເອງໃນ
ພາຍຫນ້າ. ສະນັ້ນ "ຢ່າເສັຽຕຍາປົກຂຽມາ!" ຈົ່ງຄອຍແນມນຳນັກຣຽນຂອງທ່ານຢ່າງໃກ້ຊິດ!

C-2

(njăŋ)	A.	an nîi mɛɛn njăŋ?	(what)	What is this?
(mûak)	B.	an nîi mɛɛn mûak	(hat)	This is a hat.
(phăj)	A.	an nîi mɛɛn mûak phăj?	(who)	Whose hat is this?
(láaw)	B.	an nîi mɛɛn mûak láaw	(he)	This is his/her hat.

NOTES

1) The NP may consist of N + NP in which the second noun or [1] Noun substitute stands in the relationship of 'possessor' to the main or 'head' noun, as in this example:

Noun	+	NP (Possessor)
pâakkaa		khɔ̆j
pen		I
'my pen'		

---

[1] The term 'possessor' implies a varied set of structural and semantic relationships besides simple ownership in Lao just as it does in English.

9

2) phǎj 'who, whose, whom' is a question word substitute. It substitutes only for animate nouns and noun substitutes in questions.

Noun   +   NP (Possessor)

pâakkaa   láaw
pen   he
'his pen'

pâakkaa   phǎj
pen   who
'whose pen'

phǎj occupies the same position in the sentence as the noun it substitutes for.

3) Since the form of the pronoun does not change in Lao (like English I ,me, my, mine, etc.) its structural relationship is determined by the kind of construction it is in, thus:

(a) As subject of a sentence

khɔ̂j sábaajdii

I   am fine.

(b) As 'possessor' after the 'head' noun

pâakkaa khɔ̂j
pen   my
'my pen'

4) Although sex distinctions are not indicated in the Lao pronoun, number distinctions are:

Singular	Plural	
khɔ̂j 'I'	phùak khɔ̂j	'we'
	phùak háw	'we'

10

càw   'you'   phùak càw   'you (plural)'
láaw   'he, she'   khácàw   'they'

Both phùak háw and phùak khɔ̂j mean 'we'. phùak háw is used
when the speaker wishes to include the hearer in his reference.
phùak khɔ̂j is used when he does not wish to include the hearer.

None of these pronouns may be used to refer to inanimate object
objects, thus láaw does not mean 'it' and khácàw does not
refer to 'they' for objects.

APPLICATION

1. In the NP pỳm càw, càw can be translated as (a) you   (b) yours,
   (c) your   (d) none of these.

2. In the NP sɔ̆ɔdam khácàw, khácàw means (a) they   (b) their
   (c) theirs   (d) none of these.

3. In the NP mûak láaw, láaw means (a) him   (b) her   (c) she
   (d) his   (e) all of these   (if) none of these.

4. In the NP pâakkaa khɔ̂j, khɔ̂j means (a) I,   (b) my   (c) me
   (d) mine.

5. In the NP tó?·phùakcàw, phùakcàw means (a) one male person
   (b) more than one person   (c) one female person.

6. In the NP cìa phǎj, phǎj (a) is a question word, (b) means
   'what?'   (c) means 'whose'   (d) has no meaning.

7. càw pâakkaa means (a) my pen   (b) your pen   (c) his pen
   (d) it has no meaning.

8. Translate the following NP into English: (a) sɔ̆ɔdam phǎj
   (b) mûak láaw   (c) tāŋ lì càw   (d) cìa khɔ̂j   (e) pỳm khácàw
   (f) pâakkaa phùakcàw   (g) sŷa fǒn phǎj   (h) tó?phuakháw

Answers: 1c, 2b, 3b and d, 4b, 5b, 6a and c, 7d, 8whose pencil,
          his/her hat, your (sg.) chair, my paper, their book,
          your (pl.) pen, whose raincoat, our table.

11

CYCLE 3

M-1

hóoŋkaan	nìi mēēn hóoŋkaan bɔɔ?	office building	Is this an office building?
hɔ̌ɔŋkaan	nìi mēēn hɔ̌ɔŋkaan bɔɔ?	office	Is this an office?
hóoŋhían	nìi mēēn hóoŋhían bɔɔ?	school	Is this a school?
hóoŋmɔ̌ɔ	nìi mēēn hóoŋmɔ̌ɔ bɔɔ?	hospital	Is this a hospital?
hóoŋsǎaj	nìi mēēn hóoŋsǎaj bɔɔ?	post office	Is this a post office?

M-2

tálâat	mēēn lɛ̀ɛw, nìi mēēn tálâat	market	Yes, this is a market.
hóoŋhɛ́ɛm	mēēn lɛ̀ɛw, nìi mēēn hóoŋhɛ́ɛm	hotel	Yes, this is a hotel.
hàan aahǎan	mēēn lɛ̀ɛw, nìi mēēn hàan aahǎan	restaurant	Yes, this is a restaurant.
komtamlûat	mēēn lɛ̀ɛw, nìi mēēn komtamlûat	police station	Yes, this is the Police Station.
khàaj thāhǎan	mēēn lɛ̀ɛw, nìi mēēn khàaj thāhǎan	military base	Yes, this is the military base.

12

C-1

hóoŋhéɛm   A.   nìi mɛ̄ɛn hóoŋhéɛm   hotel   A.   Is this a hotel?
            bɔɔ?

         B.   mɛ̄ɛn lɛ̀ɛw, nìi mɛ̄ɛn   B.   Yes, this is a
            hóoŋhéɛm   hotel.

ຈິງໃຫ້ນັກຮຽນຂອງທ່ານຊຸມໃສ່ສ່ວຍຂອງຕ່າງໆ ແລວຖາມແລະຕອບກັນ.

C-2

pỳm   A.   an nìi mɛ̄ɛn pỳm càw bɔɔ   book   A.   Is this your book?
     B.   mɛ̄ɛn lɛ̀ɛw, an nìi mɛ̄ɛn   B.   Yes, this is my
         pỳm khɔ̌j   book.

ໃນຕອນນີ້ເຈົ້ນຄ່ອກັນ ໃຫ້ນັກຮຽນຖາມແລະຕອບກັນວ່າອັນໃດແມ່ນຂອງຜູ້ໃດ.

C-3   A.   an nìi mɛ̄ɛn pỳm phǎj,   A.   Whose book is this?   Is
         pỳm càw bɔɔ?   it yours?
     B.   mɛ̄ɛn lɛ̀ɛw, an nìi mɛ̄ɛn   B.   Yes, this is my book.
         pỳm khɔ̌j

ນັກເຈົ້ນຄ່ອກັນກັຍ (1) ແລະ (2) ກ່ອນຕໍ່ທ່ານຈະເປິດສອນຫນ້າຕໍ່ໄປ ຕ່ານລອງ
ພຍາຍາມປະຄົດເຄື່ອງໃດເຄື່ອງນ່ວຍຍ່າງສັນງ ແລວລ້ຳສູ່ນັກຮຽນຟັງ ໂດຍອາໃສ
ຄ່ຳຮັບຕຮຽນມາແກຕໍ່ນ ແລວໃຫ້ສ່ວງເກດເບ່ງວ່ານັກຮຽນຂອງທ່ານເຂົ້າໃຈດີຕໍ່ລຍ.

13

NOTES

1) One type of Noun Compound is composed of Noun + Noun, in which the second noun stands in a 'modifier' relationship to the first or head noun. The following are examples:

        Noun   +   Noun ('Modifier')

    1)   hàan   aahǎan

         shop   food

            'restaurant'

    2)   hóoŋ   mǒɔ

         building   medical doctor

            'hospital'

    3)   khàaj   thāhǎan

         camp   military persons

           'camp, fort'

    4)   sŷa   fǒn

         clothing   rain

           'raincoat'

Another type of Noun Compound is made up of Noun + Verb and is similar to a Sentence:

        Noun   +   Verb

    1)   sǒɔ   dam

         stick   black

           'pencil'

    2)   khán   hōm

         instrument to shade

           'umbrella'

2) n̄i means 'here, this, this one' when it occurs alone. It
   may also occur after the classifier as a determiner, as in
   an n̄i 'this, this one'.

3) Observe the relationship between a question with mɛɛn bɔɔ and
   its affirmative response:

   Question: NP + mɛ̄ɛn +   NP   + bɔ́ɔ
              n̄i   mɛɛn   hóoŋmɔ̌ɔ   bɔɔ

   Affirmative
   Response: mɛ̄ɛn   lɛ̀ɛw

   Both the Subject NP and the Complement NP are usually absent
   in the response; however, the response may contain a complete
   confirmation after the mɛɛn lɛ̀ɛw response, as follows:

   Question: n̄i mɛ̄ɛn hóoŋmɔ̌ɔ bɔɔ?
   Response: mɛ̄ɛn lɛ̀ɛw , n̄i mɛɛn hóoŋmɔ̌ɔ

APPLICATION

1. In the Noun Compound sɣ̂a fɔ̌n , sɣ̂a is (a) the head noun,
   (b) the modifier of fɔ̌n (c) the classifier (d) none
   of these.

2. In the Noun Compound hàan aahǎan, aahǎan is (a) the head noun,
   (b) the modifier (c) a question word (d) none of these.

3) In the Noun Compound hóoŋ hían, hían is (a) a Noun, (b) a verb
   (c) VP (d) none of these.

4. khán hǒm is (a) a NP (b) VP (c) S (d) Noun Compound
   (e) none of these (f) all of these.

5. dam sɔ̌ɔ means (a) black stick (b) pencil (c) pen (d) it
   is meaningless.

Answers: 1a, 2b, 3b, 4a and d, 5d

6. 'Fort' is translated into Lao, as (a) sȳa thāhǎan   (b) khàaj thāhǎan   (c) hóoŋ thāhǎan   (d) khàaj aahǎan   (e) thāhǎan khàaj.

7. 'Raincoat' is translated into Lao as (a) fǒn sȳa   (b) fǒn mɔ̌ɔ   (c) sȳa fǒn   (d) sȳa pỳm   (e) sȳa fǒn.

8. A correct response to the question nìi mɛ̄ɛn hóoŋmɔ̌ɔ bɔɔ is
(a) lɛ̀ɛw   (b) lɛ̀ɛw bɔɔ   (c) mɛ̄ɛn lɛ̀ɛw   (d) mɛ̄ɛn   (e) mɛ̄ɛn bɔɔ   (f) mɛ̄ɛn lɛ̀ɛw, nìi mɛ̄ɛn hóoŋ mɔ̌ɔ

9. If you wanted to find out if something was a book, what would you say?

10. If you wanted to find out if a certain umbrella belonged to a particular person, what would you say?

CYCLE 4

M-1

tálâat	khácàw si paj tálâat	market	They are going to the market.
hóoŋhían	khácàw si paj hóoŋhían	school	They are going to school.
hóoŋsǎaj	khácàw si paj hóoŋsǎaj	post office	They are going to the post office.
hóoŋmɔ̌ɔ	khácàw si paj hóoŋmɔ̌ɔ	hospital	They are going to the hospital.
komtamlûat	khácàw si paj komtamlûat	police	They are going to the police station.

Answers: 6b,   7c,   8c,d,f,   9(an) nìi mɛ̄ɛn pỳm bɔɔ,   10(an) nìi mɛ̄ɛn khán hǒm càw bɔ̄ɔ   (or)   (an) nìi mɛ̄ɛn khán hǒm phǎj

M-2

càw	càw si paj sǎj?	you	Where are you going?
láaw	láaw si paj sǎj?	he, she	Where is he going?
phùakháw	phùakháw si paj sǎj?	we	Where are we going?
phùakcàw	phùakcàw si paj sǎj?	you (pl.)	Where are you going?
khácàw	khacàw si paj sǎj?	they	Where are they going?

M-3

hóoŋ-síinée	càw si paj hóoŋ-síinée bɔɔ?	theatre	Are you going to the theatre?
wāt	càw si paj wāt bɔɔ?	temple	Are you going to the temple?
hàan-khǎaj-kêəp	càw si paj hàan-khǎaj-kêəp bɔɔ?	shoe store	Are you going to the shoe store?
hàan sɤ̌əm-sǔaj	càw si paj hàan-sɤ̌əm sǔaj bɔɔ?	beauty-parlor	Are you going to the beauty parlor?
hóoŋkaan-pháasǐi	càw si paj hóoŋkaan-pháasǐi bɔɔ?	custom house	Are you going to the custom house?
hóoŋphím	càw si paj hóoŋphím bɔɔ?	printing office	Are you going to the printing office?

M-4

paj	paj	to go	Yes, I'm going.
bɔɔ	bɔɔ paj.	no	No, I am not going.

17

C-1

A.　càw si paj hàan khǎaj-
　　kêəp bɔɔ?

B.　paj, khɔ̂j si paj hàan-
　　khǎaj kêəp

A.　Are you going to the
　　shoe store?

B.　Yes, I am going to the
　　shoe store.

C-2

A.　càw si paj hóoŋkaan-
　　pháasǐi bɔɔ?

B.　bɔ̄ɔ, bɔ̄ɔ paj

A.　Are you going to the
　　custom house?

B.　No, I'm not going.

C-3

láaw　　A.　láaw si paj sǎj?

hóoŋhían　B.　láaw si paj
　　　　　　hóoŋhían

he, she　A.　Where is he going?

school　　B.　He is going to
　　　　　　school.

ຢ່າໃຫ້ເດັກໃຫມ່ອົນອິກ ແຕ່ພຍາຍາມໃຫ້ນັກຣຽນເວົ້າປໄຍກທີ່ກຳລັງຮຽນຢູ່ໃຫຄວງ.

C-4

A.　càw si paj hóoŋsǎaj
　　bɔɔ?

B.　mɛ̄ɛn lɛ̀ɛw, khɔ̂j si
　　paj hóoŋsǎaj

A.　Are you going to the
　　post office?

B.　Yes, I'm going to the
　　post office.

ຢ່າລືມວ່າເມື່ອນັກຣຽນເວົ້າທີ່ຍ່ ຂະເຈົ້າຈະຕອງເວົ້າຄອຍຄວາມເຂົ້າໃຈ.

18

NOTES

1) Verbs of motion frequently have locative (place word) complements.

NP   +   Pre-V + V (motion) + Loc

  khácàw   si   paj   tálâat

  they   { will   go
     { are   going   (to the) market

No relational word is necessary between the verb of motion and the place expression.

2) sǎj 'where' is a question word that stands in a substitute relationship with locatives:

Question: càw si paj sǎj ?   'Where are you going?'

Response: khôj si paj tálâat   'I'm going to the market.'

si is a pre-verb used to indicate future action here.

3) mɛɛn lɛɛw is an acceptable affirmative response to any question with bɔɔ as the question word.

   Question: càw si paj hóoŋsǎaj   Are you going to Post
        bɔɔ?   Office?

Affirmative
  Response: mɛɛn lɛɛw, (khôj si   Yes, (I'm going to the
       paj hóoŋsǎaj)   Post Office).

The confirmation part of the response is optional, although fairly common.

19

APPLICATION

1. In the sentence <u>láaw si paj tálâat</u>, the action (a) has already taken place   (b) will take place in the future   (c) takes place regularly   (d) is taking place at present   (e) it's impossible to tell when the action takes place.

2. In the sentence <u>khácàw si paj hóoŋmɔ́ɔ</u>, <u>hóoŋmɔ́ɔ</u> is (a) NP, (b) VP   (c) locative   (d) all of these.

3. In the sentence above, <u>si paj</u> is (a) a pre-verb + V   (b) NP   (c) VP   (d) the predicate.

4. Which of the following is a possible response to the question <u>paj săj</u> ? : (a) <u>paj tálâat</u>   (b) <u>hóoŋsăaj</u>   (c) <u>mɛ̄ɛn lɛ̀ɛw</u> (d) <u>paj pym</u>   (e) <u>khɔ̂j si paj</u>.

5. Which of the following is a correct response to the question <u>phùakcàw si paj komtamlûat bɔɔ</u> : (a) <u>si paj</u>   (b) <u>càw bɔɔ</u> (c) <u>paj lɛ̀ɛw</u>   (d) <u>mɛ̄ɛn lɛ̀ɛw</u>, <u>phùakhǎw si paj komtamlûat</u> (f) <u>paj</u>   (g) All except <u>b</u> are possible answers.

CYCLE 5

M-1

càw si paj hóoŋhían mɛ̄ɛn bɔɔ?	You are going to school aren't you?
an nìi mɛ̄ɛn pâakkaa mɛ̄ɛn bɔɔ?	This is a pen, isn't it?
láaw si paj khàaj-thāhǎan mɛ̄ɛn bɔɔ?	He's going to the military base, isn't he?
láaw si paj hàan aahǎan mɛ̄ɛn bɔɔ?˙	He is going to the restaurant, isn't he?
nìi mɛ̄ɛn komtamlûat mɛ̄ɛn bɔɔ?	This is the police station, isn't it?

Answers: 1b and d,   2a and c,   3a,   4a,   5g

M-2

bɔ̄ɔ mɛ̄ɛn, láaw si bɔ̄ɔ paj hóoŋhéɛm,	No, he is not going to the hotel.
láaw. si paj nàan aahǎan	He is going to the restaurant.
bɔ̄ɔ mɛ̄ɛn, an nìi bɔ̄ɔ mɛ̄ɛn pỳm,	Nɔ, this is not a book.
an nìi mɛ̄ɛn cìa	This is paper.
bɔ̄ɔ mɛ̄ɛn, khɔ̀j si bɔ̄ɔ paj hóoŋkaan,	No, I'm not going to the office building.
khɔ̀j si paj hóoŋsǎaj	I'm going to the Post Office.
bɔ̄ɔ mɛ̄ɛn, nìi bɔ̄ɔ mɛ̄ɛn hóoŋhéɛm	No, this is not the hotel.
nìi mɛ̄ɛn hàan aahǎan	This is the restaurant.

C-1

(hàan aahǎan)	A. láaw si paj hàan aahǎan, mɛ̄ɛn bɔ̄ɔ?	restaurant	He is going to the restaurant isn't he?
	B. bɔ̄ɔ mɛ̄ɛn, láaw si paj hóoŋhéɛm	hotel	No, he is going to the hotel.

ໃນເວລາສອນນັກຮຽນ ໃຫ້ພະຍາຍາມເວົ້າຄ່ອຍຄວາມໄວສົມຄວນ ຢ່າເວົ້າຊ້າເກີນໄປຈົນຜິດທໍ່ມະດາ.
ນັກຮຽນຈະຕ້ອງຕັດຝ່ຽແລະເອົາໃຈການເວົ້າຢ່າງທໍ່ມະດາຕາມຄຮອນໄປ.

C-2

| (tó?) | A. | an nìi mɛ̄ɛn tó?,
mɛ̄ɛn bɔ̄ɔ? | table | This is a table,
isn't it? |
| (tāŋ lì) | B. | bɔ̄ɔ mɛ̄ɛn, an nìi
mɛ̄ɛn tāŋ lì | chair | No, this is a
chair. |

ຕລ້ວຈາກນັ້ງເບິ່ງນັກຮຽນຂອງທ່ານເວົ້າພາສາລາວແລ້ວ ທ່ານຄົດວ່າຄົນລາວຕາມຈຸນນະບົດ ຕລົຫຼ
ທ່ຽວບລວງກັບສຽຂອງນັກຮຽນຂອງທ່ານຈະສາມາດເຂົ້າໃຈຂະເຈົ້າບໍ?

C-3

| (hɔ̄ɔŋkaan) | A. | nìi mɛ̄ɛn hɔ̄ɔŋkaan,
mɛ̄ɛn bɔ̄ɔ? | office | This is an office,
isn't it? |
| (hɔ̄ɔŋhían) | B. | bɔ̄ɔ mɛ̄ɛn, nìi bɔ̄ɔ
mɛ̄ɛn hɔ̄ɔŋkaan,
nìi mɛ̄ɛn hɔ̄ɔŋhían | classroom | No, this is not
an office. This
is a classroom. |

ໝາຍເຫດ: "ບໍ່ແມ່ນ" ແມ່ນຄຳຕອບຕໍ່ຄຳຖາມທີ່ໃຊ້ "ແມ່ນບໍ?" ຕໍ່ກັນນັ້ນ; ບໍ່ແມ່ນຕໍ່ຄຳຖາມຄວຍຄໍ່ວ່າ
"ບໍ?". ເຊັ່ນ: "ເຈົ້າສິໄປບໍ?" "ບໍ, ບໍໄປ"; "ເຈົ້າສິໄປແມ່ນບໍ?" "ບໍ່ແມ່ນ, ຜູ້ນນ້ສິໄປ."

NOTES

1) mɛ̄ɛn bɔ̄ɔ can be attached to any statement (S + mɛ̄ɛn bɔ̄ɔ).
The usual affirmative response is mɛ̄ɛn lɛ̀ɛw with or without
confirmatory statement. The usual negative response is bɔ̄ɔ
mɛ̄ɛn plus a Statement of the actual facts.

  Question: láaw si paj hàan aahǎan, mɛ̄ɛn bɔ̄ɔ?

  Affirmative
  Response: mɛ̄ɛn lɛ̀ɛw, (láaw si paj hàan aahǎan)

  Negative
  Response: bɔ̄ɔ mɛ̄ɛn, láaw si paj hóoŋhéɛm

APPLICATION

1. Which of the following responses is a correct negative response to láaw si paj hàan aahǎan, mɛ̄ɛn bɔɔ? (a) bɔ̄ɔ, (b) bɔ̄ɔ mɛ̄ɛn, (c) bɔ̄ɔ paj (d) bɔ̄ɔ hàan aahǎan (e) bɔ̄ɔ mɛ̄ɛn, láaw si paj hóoŋhɛɛm.

2. Which of these sentences is correct (a) láaw bɔ̄ɔ si paj hóoŋhían (b) láaw si bɔ̄ɔ paj hóoŋhían, (c) láaw si paj bɔ̄ɔ hóoŋhían (d) láaw bɔ̄ɔ paj si hóoŋhían.

3. Which of these sentences is correct (a) nìi mɛ̄ɛn bɔ̄ɔ hóoŋhɛɛm, (b) nìi bɔ̄ɔ mɛ̄ɛn hóoŋhɛɛm (c) hóoŋhɛɛm bɔ̄ɔ nìi (d) bɔ̄ɔ nìi mɛ̄ɛn hóoŋhɛɛm.

4. Disagree with this statement: láaw si paj hóoŋkaan.

5. Disagree with this sentence: an nìi mɛ̄ɛn pỳm

6. Translate the following sentences into English (a) khácàw si paj hɔ̀oŋkaan (b) khɔ̂j si bɔ̄ɔ paj tálâat (c) phùakcàw si paj hàan aahǎan, mɛ̄ɛn bɔ̄ɔ? (d) càw si bɔ̄ɔ paj komtamlûat, mɛ̄ɛn bɔɔ? (e) láaw si paj khàajthāhǎan (f) càw si paj sǎj (g) phùakhǎw si bɔ̄ɔ paj hooŋmɔ̌ɔ (h) càw si paj hóoŋhɛɛm, mɛ̄ɛn bɔɔ?

Answers: 1b and e, 2b, 3b, 4láaw si bɔ̄ɔ paj hóoŋkaan, 5an nìi bɔ̄ɔ mɛ̄ɛn pỳm, 6(a) They're going to the the office. (b) I'm not going to the market. (c) You're going to the restaurant, aren't you? (d) You're not going to the Police Station, are you? (e) We're not going to the army post. (f) Where are you going? (g) We're not going to the hospital. (h) You're going to the hotel, aren't you?

23

CYCLE 6

M-1

súksŏmbuun	khɔ̌j sɣ̄y súksŏmbuun	Souksomboun	My name is Souksomboun.
mālíican	khɔ̌j sɣ̄y mālíican	Malichanh	My name is Malichanh.
láaw	láaw sɣ̄y mālíican	she	Her name is Malichanh.
khón phūu nìi	khɔ́n phūu nìi sɣ̄y mālíican.	this person	This person's name is Malichanh.
náaj khúu khɔ̌j	náaj khúu khɔ̌j sɣ̄y mālíican	my teacher	My teacher's name is Malichanh.

M-2

càw	càw sɣ̄y njǎŋ?	you	What's your name?
nāk hían phūu nìi	nāk hían phūu nìi sɣ̄y njǎŋ?	this student	What's this student's name?
thāhǎan phūu nìi	thahǎan phūu nìi sɣ̄y njǎŋ?	this serviceman	What's this serviceman's name?
tamlûat phūu nàn	tamlûat phūu nán sɣ̄y njǎŋ?	that policeman	What's that policeman's name?
khâalàatsākaan phūu nàn	khâalàatsākaan phūu nàn sɣ̄y njǎŋ?	that government official	What's that government official's name?

24

C-1

càw   A.   càw s̄yȳ njǎŋ?   you   What's your name?

          B.   khɔ̀j s̄yȳ...   My name is...

C-2

nākhían   A.   nākhían càw s̄yȳ...   your   Your student's name

càw   mɛ̄ɛn bɔɔ?   student   is..., isn't it?

          B.   bɔɔ mɛ̄ɛn, nākhían   No, my student's

              khɔ̀j s̄yȳ...   name is...

ເວລາຝຶກຫັດຍິດໂຕພຍາຍາມໃຊ້ຊື່ແຫຼ່ວວດຄົນທີ່ຕົນພັນຢູ່ ຫຼືຊື່ໃດຜູ້ວທີ່ຖຶກຄົນຮູ້ຈັກ ຕລອດຫົວຊຸຍນາຍ ຂອງຍຸກຄົນສາຄົນຕ່າງໆ. ປ່າລົມກັນໄປໃຈດາໃທີ່ຣຽມມາແລວວໃຫຫລາຍຫີສຸດເຕ່າທີ່ຈະຫລາຍໄດ.

NOTES

1) The verb s̄yȳ 'to be named' requires an <u>animate</u> noun (or noun substitute) as a subject and a personal name as complement:

         NP   +   s̄yȳ   +   NP

         láaw   s̄yȳ   mālíican

         'She   is named   Malichanh.'

A further restriction in this type of sentence is that the name must be appropriate (in terms of sex) to the subject. <u>Malichanh</u> is a female name; <u>Souksomboun</u> is a male name.

The Noun Complement of s̄yȳ may be replaced by njǎŋ in questions:

Question: càw <u>s̄yȳ</u> njǎŋ   'What's your name?'

Response: khɔ̀j <u>s̄yȳ</u> khámdɛɛŋ   'My name's Khamdaeng.'

25

2) Since Lao nouns are not marked for <u>number</u> or for the definite:
indefinite category, the Noun Phrase is marked only if it
contains a Classifier Phrase. If it contains Classifier+
Determiner, it is marked as <u>definite</u> (not generic). Compare
the marked and unmarked examples below:

Generic: thāhǎan   '(a) soldier'
                                'soldiers'

Definite: thāhǎan phūu nìi   'This soldier'

<u>phūu</u> is a classifier for <u>human</u> nouns. It is used only in the
singular. <u>nìi</u> is a determiner. It refers to something near
the speaker. <u>phūu nìi</u> is one type of classifier phrase. <u>nàn</u>
is also a determiner. It refers to something not near the
speaker.

APPLICATION

1. A possible answer to the question càw sȳy njǎŋ is (a) khɔ̌j
mɛ̄ɛn komtamlûat (b) khɔ̌j sȳy hɔ̌ɔŋkaan (c) khɔ̌j sȳy mālíican
(d) khɔ̌j bɔ̄ɔ sȳy.

2. Which of the following sentences is correct Lao: (a) náaj
khúu láaw sȳy súksɔ̌mbuun (b) láaw sȳy nākhían (c) tɔ́ʔ sȳy
njǎŋ (d) pâakkaa sȳy tāŋ lì (e) láaw mɛ̄ɛn mālíican.

3. Translate the following NP into English: (a) nākhían phūu nìi
(b) thāhǎan phūu nìi (c) khâalàatsākaan phūu nàn (d) tamlûat
phūu nàn (e) khón phūu nìi (f) náaj khúu phūu nàn.

4) Match the questions with correct answers:

(a) càw sȳy njǎŋ?   (a) mɛ̄ɛn lɛ̀ɛw

(b) láaw sȳy Peter, mɛ̄ɛn bɔ̄ɔ?   (b) khɔ̌j si paj tálâat

(c) annìi mɛ̄ɛn tɔ́ʔ bɔ̄ɔ?   (c) khɔ̌j sȳy mālíican

(d) càw si paj sǎj?   (d) mɛ̄ɛn lɛ̀ɛw, annìi mɛ̄ɛn tɔ́ʔ

Answers: 1c, 2a, 3this student, this serviceman, that govern-
          ment official, that policeman, this person, that
          teacher 4a/c, b/a, c/d, d/b

CYCLE 7

M-1

sǔuŋ	láaw sǔuŋ bɔɔ?	to be tall, high	Is he tall?
ŋáam	láaw ŋáam bɔɔ?	to be pretty	Is she pretty?
tùj	láaw tùj bɔɔ?	to be fat	Is he fat?
cɔ̄ɔj	láaw cɔ̄ɔj bɔɔ?	to be skinny	Is she skinny?
tām	láaw tām bɔɔ?	to be short, low	Is he short?
dii	láaw dii bɔɔ?	to be good	Is he good?

M-2

dii	láaw pen khón dii mɛ̄ɛn bɔɔ?	good	He is a good person, isn't he?
cajdii	láaw pen khón cajdii mɛ̄ɛn bɔɔ?	kind	He is a kind person, isn't he?
sūa	láaw pen khón sūa mɛ̄ɛn bɔɔ?	bad	He is a bad person, isn't he?
kàahǎan	láaw pen khón kàahǎan mɛ̄ɛn bɔɔ?	courageous	He is a courageous person, isn't he?
dú?mān	láaw pen khón dú?mān mɛ̄ɛn bɔɔ?	studious	He is a studious person, isn't he?
sálâat	láaw pen khón sálâat mɛ̄ɛn bɔɔ?	intelligent	He is an intelligent person, isn't he?

27

M-3

khěɛŋhéɛŋ	láaw pen khon khěɛŋhéɛŋ lǎaj	strong	He is a very strong person.
ɔ̄ɔn-ɛɛ	láaw pen khón ɔ̄ɔn-ɛɛ lǎaj	weak	He is a very weak person.
caj-ɔ̄ɔn	láaw pen khón caj-ɔ̄ɔn lǎaj	softhearted	He is a very soft-hearted person.
cajkhěɛŋ	láaw pen khón cajkhěɛŋ lǎaj	hardhearted	He is a very hard-hearted person.
khîikhàan	láaw pen khón khîikhàan lǎaj	lazy	He is a very lazy person.

C-1

A. láaw sǔuŋ bɔɔ?   A. Is he tall?

B. sǔuŋ   B. Yes, he is.

C-2

A. láaw pen khón (dú?mān) A. He is a (studious) person,
   mɛ̄ɛn bɔ̄ɔ?   isn't he?

B. mɛ̄ɛn lɛ̀ɛw, láaw pen   B. Yes, he is a very (studious)
   khón (dú?mān) lǎaj   person.

_____

ອະວົງຢ່າງປ່ອຍໃຫ້ນັກຮຽນໃຈຄ້ວາ "ເປັນ" ຢູ່ຕໝາຄ້ວຶ່ເສຄ. ເປັນຄຳວ່າ:"ລາວເປັນອອນແອ" ຫລື
"ລາວເປັນຍຄ້າມ ດ້ວນ. ນັກຮຽນມັກໃຈຄ້ນຜຄປ່ສເມ ຫ້ວງເນື່ອງມາຈາກພາສາພມເນື່ອງຂອງຂະເຈ້າ.

28

CYCLE 8

M-1

súphàap	khón phūu nìi súphàap lǎaj	to be polite	This person is very polite.
sálâat	khón phūu nìi sálâat lǎaj	intelligent	This person is very intelligent.
ŋōō	khón phūu nìi ŋōō lǎaj	stupid	This person is very stupid.
ùan	khón phūu nìi ùan lǎaj	fat	This person is very fat.
cɔ̄ɔj	khón phūu nìi cɔ̄ɔj lǎaj	skinny	This person is very skinny.
dìi	khón phūu nìi dìi lǎaj	good	This person is very good.
sǔuŋ	khón phūu nìi sǔuŋ lǎaj	tall, high	This person is very tall.
tìa	khón phūu nìi tìa lǎaj	short (height)	This person is very short.
tām	khón phūu nìi tām lǎaj	short (height)	This person is very short.

M-2

phūu-njín	phūu-njín phūu nàn pen khón ŋáam	woman	That woman is a pretty person.
phūu-sǎaw	phūu-sǎaw phūu nàn pen khón ŋáam	unmarried woman	That unmarried woman is a pretty person.
nākhían njíŋ	nākhían njíŋ phūu nàn pen khón ŋáam	girl student	That girl student is a pretty person.

29

léekhǎanū- ... kaan	léekhǎanūkaan phūu nàn pen khón ŋáam	secretary	That secretary is a pretty person.
phūubāaw	phūubāaw phūu nàn pen khón ŋáam	unmarried man	That unmarried man is handsome person.
sáaj-nūm	sáaj-nūm phūu nàn pen khón ŋáam	young man	That young man is a handsome person.

M-3

phȳan càw	phȳan càw phūu nàn pen khón cāŋdaj?	your friend friend	What sort of person is that friend of yours?
khâalàatsā- kaan	khâalàatsākaan phūu nàn pen khón cāŋdaj?	government official	What sort of person is that government official?
náaj-thāhǎan	náaj-thāhǎan phūu nàn pen khón cāŋdaj?	military officer	What sort of person is that military officer?
náaj-tamlûat	náaj-tamlûat phūu nàn pen khón cāŋdaj?	police officer	What sort of person is that police officer?
khón-sōŋ- nǎŋšy̌y	khón-sōŋ-nǎŋšy̌y phūu nàn pen khón cāŋdaj?	mailman	What sort of person is that mailman?
náaj-pháasǎa	náaj-pháasǎa phūu nàn pen khón cāŋdaj?	interpreter	What sort of person is that interpreter

C-1

A. phūū njíṇ phūū nìi ṇáam bɔɔ?

B. láaw ṇáam lǎaj

A. Is this woman pretty?

B. She is very pretty.

C-2

A. sáaj-nūm phūū nàn pen khón cāṇdaj?

B. láaw pen khón sǔuṇ.

A. What, sort of person is that young man?

B. He is a tall person.

ຈົ່ງພຍາຍາມໃຈຣຸຍພາຍຕາາວງປະກອບໃນການສອນ ຈຶ່ງຈະເປັນການຊ່ອຍໃຫ້ວຣກອອງທານເບົ້າລົ້ວອິກ. ທານຄວນເປີດເບຶ່ງບົດຣຽນຕໄປກ່ອນໄມ່ວຄ່ອານສອນ ແລວຫາວຕາສ່ວທ່ະຊ່ອຍໃນການສອນໄວ.

NOTES[1]

1) Words like sǔuṇ 'tall', dii 'good' are called **stative** verbs (Vₛ). They function as the Main Verb (MV) in sentences describing the state or condition of something or someone.

NP + V_S

láaw   sǔuṇ

'He (is) tall.'

Since words having similar meanings are adjectives in English, 'be' must be added in translation.

2) The following are transformations of the sentence láaw sǔuṇ (NP + Vₛ):

Negative statement:	láaw bɔɔ sǔuṇ	'He isn't tall.'
Affirmative question:	láaw sǔuṇ bɔɔ?	'Is he tall?'
Affirmative response:	sǔuṇ	'Yes, he is.'
Negative response:	bɔɔ sǔuṇ (lǎaj)	'No, not (very) tall.'

---

[1] These notes and the application are for use with cycles 7 and 8.

31

3) Stative verbs may also function as modifiers of NP:

NP   +   V$_s$

khón   khîikhàan
(person   lazy)
'lazy person'

4) NP of the type above often occur in sentences with pen as the copula verb:

NP   +   pen   +   NP

láaw   pen   khón sálâat
'He's   an intelligent person.'

mɛɛn bɔɔ may be added to form a question.

5) lǎaj occurs after V$_s$ as an intensifier: sǔuŋ lǎaj 'very tall', etc.

6) Both khɛ̌ɛŋhɛ́ɛn 'strong, powerful' and ɔɔn ɛɛ 'weak, frail, feeble' refer to physical strength.

7) Both tìa and tǎm may be used to refer to the shortness of a person, but tǎm is usually used in referring to objects.

8) cāŋdaj 'what kind of, what sort of' is used with khón to inquire about a person's personal traits or physical features:

Question: láaw pen khón cāŋdaj?   What sort of person
                                    is she?'

Answer: láaw pen khón ŋáam   She's a very pretty
           lǎaj   person.'

Answer: láaw ŋáam lǎaj   She's very pretty.'

32

LAO BASIC COURSE

APPLICATION

1. In the sentence càw súphàap, súphàap is (a) NP, (b) VP,
   (c) Q (d) V_s (3) none of these.

2. ŋōo lǎaj is probably (a) a question (b) a negative statement,
   (c) an affirmative response (d) a negative response.

3. dii bɔ̄ɔ is probably (a) a negative statement (b) a question
   (c) NP (d) negative response (e) none of these.

4. Which of these sentences has an error in it? (a) càw bɔ̄ɔ tìa
   (b) láaw bɔ̄ɔ pen sálâat (c) khɔ̌j cɔ̄ɔj (d) khón phūu nìi ŋōo
   lǎaj.

5. Translate the following sentences into Lao: (a) What sort of
   person are you? (b) That young man is very skinny. (c) That
   friend of yours is stupid, isn't he? (d) I'm not a very
   courageous person. (f) She's not very fat. (g) Is she tall?

6. In the sentence khón phūu nìi ŋōo lǎaj, phūu is (a) a noun
   (b) a verb (c) V_s (d) classifier (e) determiner.

7. In the NP khón cɔ̄ɔj, cɔ̄ɔj is (a) NP (b) V_s (c) Q (d) modifier
   of khón (e) none of these.

8. In the VP dii lǎaj, lǎaj is (a) NP (b) VP (c) negative
   (d) intensifier of dii.

Answers: 1b and d, 2c, 3b, 4b, 5(a) càw pen khón cāŋdaj
   (b) sáaj nūm phūu nàn cɔ̄ɔj lǎaj (c) phȳan càw phūu
   nàn ŋōo, mɛ̄ɛn bɔɔ (d) khɔ̌j bɔ̄ɔ pen khon kàahǎan.
   lǎaj (e) láaw bɔ̄ɔ tùj (ùan) lǎaj (f) láaw sǔuŋ bɔ̄ɔ,
   6a and d, 7b and d, 8d.

33

CYCLE 9

M-1

<u>améelīkan</u>	càw pen khón améelīkan, mɛ̄ɛn bɔɔ?	American	Are you an American?
<u>láaw</u>	càw pen khón láaw, mɛ̄ɛn bɔɔ?	Laotian·	Are you a Laotian?
<u>tháj</u>	càw pen khón tháj, mɛ̄ɛn bɔɔ?	Thai	Are you a Thai?
<u>khámĕen</u>	càw pen khón khámĕen, mɛ̄ɛn bɔɔ?	Cambodian	Are you a Cambodian?
<u>aŋkít</u>	càw pen khón aŋkít, mɛ̄ɛn bɔɔ?	Englishman	Are you an Englishman?
<u>ciin</u>	càw pen khón ciin, mɛ̄ɛn bɔɔ?	Chinese	Are you a Chinese

M-2

<u>améelīkan</u>	mɛ̄ɛn lɛ̀ɛw, khɔ̂j pen khón améelīkan.	American	Yes, I am an American.
<u>njīipūn</u>	mɛ̄ɛn lɛ̀ɛw, khɔ̂j pen khón njīipūn	Japanese	Yes, I am a Japanese.
<u>wîatnáam</u>	mɛ̄ɛn lɛ̀ɛw, khɔ̂j pen khón wîatnáam	Vietnamese	Yes, I am a Vietnamese.
<u>phāmàa</u>	mɛ̄ɛn lɛ̀ɛw, khɔ̂j pen khón phāmàa	Burmese	Yes, I am a Burmese.
<u>fálāŋ</u>	mɛ̄ɛn lɛ̀ɛw, khɔ̂j pen khón fálāŋ	French	Yes, I am a Frenchman.
<u>jeelāmán</u>	mɛ̄ɛn lɛ̀ɛw, khɔ̂j pen khón jeelāmán	German	Yes, I am a German.

34

C-1

(aŋkít)   A. càw pen khón (aŋkít),   Englishman A. Are you an
               mɛ̄ɛn bɔɔ?   (Englishman)?

            B. mɛ̄ɛn lɛ̀ɛw, khɔ̂j pen   B. Yes, I am an
               khón (aŋkit).   Englishman.

ເນື່ອນັກຣຽນເວົ້າຊ້ອງປະເທດຕ່າງໆໄດ້ດີແລ້ວ ຖ້າຫາກທ່ານເຕັ້ມວ່າໃຈເປັນທ່ານຈະບອກຊື່ປະເທດ
ອັນໃຫຊະເຈົ້າອກກໍໄດ້. ມີຊ້ວຫາງແມວໃດທີທ່ານຈະປະດິດເຊື່ອງໃຫມ່ອນໄດ້ອກບໍ?

C-2

(náajkhúu) A. (náajkhúu) phūū nàn   teacher   A. Is that (teacher)
               pen khón aŋkít,   an Englishman?
               mɛ̄ɛn bɔɔ?

(améelĪkan) B. bɔ̄ɔ mɛ̄ɛn, náajkhúu   American   B. No, that
               phūū nàn bɔ̄ɔ pen   teacher is
               khón aŋkít.   not an
                                                       (Englishman).
               láaw pen khón   He is an
               (améelĪkan).   (American).

ຜູ້ຊ້ອມຕົວວ່າທ່ານຈະເປັນຄົນທີ່ດີວ່ລັດຕໍການອອກສຽງຊ້ອງນັກຣຽນ. ນັກຣຽນບາງຄົນອາດຈະບໍ່ກລ້າໄລ,
ແຕ່ທ່ານຢ່າໄດ້ຕົກຖອຍ. ຄຣູຕດຈະຕ້ອງບເປັນຄົນອ່ອນຫຽ ຫາຍລຸນມາທ່ານຈະບໍ່ມີຄວາມກັນແຕນວງໃຈ.

35

NOTES

1) The Noun khón 'person' + Name of Country is used to refer to nationals of any country.

Noun   +   Noun

khón   láaw

Person   Laos

'a Laotian'

2) pen 'be' is a copula verb (like mɛ̄ɛn) and occurs only in constructions of this type: NP + pen + NP.

NP   +   pen   +   NP

càw   pen   khón láaw

'You are a Lao'.

3) Sentences with pen as the linking verb can be converted to questions by adding mɛ̄ɛn bɔɔ.. mɛ̄ɛn bɔɔ is normally used when asking for confirmation of a fact. The response follows the usual pattern.

Statement:	càw pen khón tháj	'You are a Thai.'
Question:	càw pen khón tháj, mɛ̄ɛn bɔɔ?	'Are you a Thai?'
Affirmative Response:	mɛ̄ɛn lɛ̀ɛw, (khɔ̀j pen khón tháj)	'Yes, I'm Thai.'
Negative Response:	bɔ̄ɔ mɛ̄ɛn, khɔ̀j pen khón láaw	'No, I'm a Lao.'

36

APPLICATION

1. Answer the following questions with the correct information:
   (a) càw sȳȳ njǎŋ? (b) càw pen khón láaw, mɛ̄ɛn bɔɔ?

2. Translate the following NP: (a) khón aŋkít (b) thāhǎan phūū nìi (c) khácàw (d) khón ciin (e) khòn láaw phūū nìi

3. In the NP nākhían phūū nàn, phūū is (a) NP, (b) determiner, (c) a classifier (d) a question word (e) it refers to people.

4. What would you say to find out if a serviceman you saw was a German?

5. In answer to a question you say that your teacher is English.

6. You are asked if you are a Thai. You say that you are not, but that you are an American.

CYCLE 10

M-1

sáhárāt	khɔ̄j máa câak sáhárāt	U.S.A.	I'm from the USA.
améelīka	améelīka		
páthèet	khɔ̄j máa câak páthèet	Laos	I'm from Laos.
láaw	láaw		
páthèet	khɔ̄j máa câak páthèet	Thailand	I'm from Thailand.
tháj	tháj		
páthèet	khɔ̄j máa câak páthèet	Vietnam	I'm from Vietname.
wîatnáam	wîatnáam		

Answers: 1.Give factual information. 2(a)Englishman (b)this serviceman (c)they (d)a Chinese (e)this Lao 3(c and e) 4thāhǎan phūū nàn pen khón jeelāmán, mɛ̄ɛn bɔɔ 5náaj khúu khɔ̄j pen khón aŋkít, 6bɔ̄ɔ mɛ̄ɛn, khɔ̄j bɔ̄ɔ pen khón tháj, khɔ̄j pen khón améelīkan

| páthèet ciin | khɔ̀j máa câak páthèet ciin | China | I'm from China. |
| páthèet aŋkít | khɔ̀j máa câak páthèet aŋkít | England | I'm from England. |

M-2

càw	càw máa câak páthèet daj?	you	What country are you from?
khón fálāŋ	khón fálāŋ máa câak páthèet daj?	French-man	What country are Frenchmen from?
nākhían phūu nìi	nākhían phūu nìi máa câak páthèet daj?	this student	What country is this student from?
khón phūu nàn	khón phūu nàn máa câak páthèet daj?	that person	What country is that person from?
náajkhúu phūu nàn	náajkhúu phūu nàn máa câak páthèet daj?	that teacher	What country is that teacher from?

C-1

| (khón améelīkan) | A. khón améelīkan máa câak páthèet daj? | Americans | A. What country are Americans from? |
| (sáhárāt améelīka) | B. khón améelīkan máa câak sáhárāt améelīka | the U.S.A. | B. Americans are from the U.S.A. |

ຖ້າຫາກຫາກມີແຜນທີ່ໂລກມາໃຊ້ປະກອບກັບການສອນຍິ່ງຄຣູນນ ກໍ່ຈະເປັນການດີຍ້ງ ເພາະນອກຈາກທີ່
ຢູ່ໃນບົມມົນລວ ຫານຂາດຈະບອກຊ່ຍານເມ່ອວຕ່າວງໃຫ້ນັກຣຽນອົກກໄດ້. ຫານນັກຣຽນຫານແຜນທີ່ເບິ່ງດຸ!

C-2

(sǎj) A. càw máa câak sǎj? where Where are you from?

(pátheet B. khɔ̀j máa câak pátheet Laos I'm from Laos.
láaw) láaw?

ໃຕ້ນັກຮຽນຫາມຈູ້ອະປ໋ວັດຫຍ້ອອງຫານແລະຂອງກັນແລະກັນເບ້ງດ! ໃນການຝຶກດັນອະເຈົ້າອາດຈະ
ຄວງການດຳໃຫມ່ເປັນບາງຄຳ ຫານລອງຈອຍຂະເຈົ້າເບ້ງ! ແຕ່ຢ່າລົນວ່ານແນນການລ່ມລັນເຕົ່ານັນ.

NOTES

1) The Main Verb (MV) may be composed of two or more individual
   verbs in a series. The verb <u>máa</u> 'to come' (like <u>paj</u> 'to go'
   and other verbs of motion) may be followed by verbs showing
   direction of motion (like câak '(to move) away from').

NP   MV   NP (Loc)

<u>khɔ̀j</u> <u>máa</u> <u>câak</u> <u>sáhárat</u> <u>améelīka</u>

'I come
   came from the United States..
  am coming

Since there is no time indication in this sentence, <u>máa</u> may
refer to present, past, or future time.

2) <u>daj</u> 'which' is a question word substitute. It substitutes
   for the determiners (<u>nìi</u>, <u>nàn</u>), for names, and some other
   nouns.

Question: <u>pátheet</u> <u>daj</u>? 'Which country?

Response 1: <u>pátheet</u> <u>ciin</u> 'China'

Response 2: <u>pátheet</u> <u>nìi</u> 'This country.'

39

APPLICATION

1. In the sentence, khɔ̌j máa câak páthèet láaw, máa câak is (a)
   (a) NP (b) VP (c)MV (d) Q (e) determiner.

2. In the sentence above, páthèet láaw is (a) VP (b) Q (c) NP
   (d) Locative (e) S.

3. In the sentence above, the action is (a) in the past (b) the
   future (c) in progress. (d) none of these.

4. nākhían phūu nìi refers to (a) one person (b) two persons
   (c) more than two (d) it is unclear.

5. In the Vb máa câak, câak is (a) NP (b) V (c) preposition
   (d) VP.

6. In the Noun Compound sáhárāt améelīka, sáhárāt probably means
   (a) country (b) America (c) United States (d) nation
   (e) none of these.

7. China is translated into Lao as (a) ciin (b) ciin páthèet
   (c) páthèet ciin (d) phūu ciin.

8. 'This teacher of mine' would be translated into Lao as:
   (a) náaj khúu càw nìi (b) náaj khúu phūu nìi khɔ̌j (c) náaj
   khúu khɔ̌j phūu nìi (d) náaj khúu càw phūu nìi.

Answers: 1c, 2c and d, 3a and c, 4a, 5b, 6c, 7c, 8c

CYCLE 11

M-1

n.ýaŋ wíaŋcan	Vientiane
mýaŋ wíaŋcan juu sǎj?	Where is Vientiane?
khǔεŋ séedoon	Sedone province
khǔεŋ séedoon juu sǎj?	Where is the province of Sedone?
mýaŋ wòosíŋtan	Washington
mýaŋ wòosíŋtan juu sǎj?	Where is Washington?
rāt mínísóotàa	Minnesota
rāt mínísóotàa juu sǎj?	Where is the State of Minnesota?
rāt kháalíifòoníá	California
rāt khálífóoníá juu sǎj?	Where is the State of California?
bàan sǐikháj	Sikhay village
bàan sǐikáj juu sǎj?	Where is the village of Sikhay?
khǔεŋ húaphán	Houa Phan Province
khǔεŋ hǔaphán juu sǎj?	Where is the province of Houa Phan ?
bàan kən	Ban Keun village
bàan kən juu sǎj?	Where is the village of Ban Keun ?

M-2

mýaŋ wíaŋcan	The city of Vientiane
mýaŋ wíaŋcan juu náj pátheet lǎaw	The city of Vientiane is in Laos.
khǔɛŋ séedoon	The province of Sɛdone.
khǔɛŋ séedoon juu náj pátheet lǎaw	The province of Sedone is in Laos.
mýaŋ wɔ́ɔsíŋtan	Washington, D.C.
mýaŋ wɔ́ɔsíŋtan juu náj sáhàrāt améelīkaa	Washington, D.C. is in the United States of America.
bàan sǐikháj	The village of Sikhay
bàan sǐikháj juu náj mýaŋ wíaŋcan	The village of Sikhay is in Vientiane.
rāt khálífɔɔnía	State of California
rāt khálífɔɔnía juu náj sáhárāt améelīkaa	The State of California is in the U.S.A.
mýaŋ sájŋɔ̄ɔn	Saigon
mýaŋ sájŋɔ̄ɔn juu náj pátheet wǐatnáam	Saigon is in Vietnam.
khǔɛŋ hǔaphán	Houa Phan
mýaŋ sámnÿa juu náj khǔɛŋ hǔaphán	Sam Neua is in the province of Houa Phan.

C-1

(bàan náathɔ́ɔŋ)	The village of Nathong.
A. bàan náathɔ́ɔŋ juu sǎj?	Where is the Nathong village?
(mýaŋ phóonhóoŋ)	The city of Phonhong.
B. bàan náathɔ́ɔŋ juu náj mýaŋ phóonhóoŋ	The village of Nathong is .in the city of Phonhong.
(mýaŋ phóonhóoŋ)	The city of Phonhong.
A. mýaŋ phóonhóoŋ juu sǎj?	Where is the city of Phonhong?
(khǔɛŋ wíaŋcan)	The province of Vientiane.
B. mýaŋ phóonhóoŋ juu náj khǔɛŋ wíaŋcan	The city of Phonhong is in the province of Vientiane.
(khǔɛŋ wíaŋcan)	The province of Vientiane.
A. khǔɛŋ wíaŋcan juu sǎj?	Where is the province of Vientiane?
(pátheet láaw)	Laos.
B. khǔɛŋ wíaŋcan juu náj pátheet láaw	The province of Vientiane is in Laos.

_____

ຈິ່ງໃຈແຜນທີ່ປະເທດລາວ ແລວໃຫ້ນັກຮຽນຊຸແລະບອກຊື່ບານແລະເມືອງຕ່າງໆເບິ່ງໆ! ຂະເຈົາບອກ
ໄດຢ່າງຖືກຕອງແລະຢ່າງວ່າຍດາຍບໍ?
_____

43

C-2

(hóoŋhían càw)	your school
A. hóoŋhían càw juu sǎj?	Where is your school?
(mýaŋ áalíŋtán)	Arlington
B. hóoŋhían khɔ̌j juu náj mýaŋ áalíŋtán	My school is in Arlington.
(mýaŋ áalíŋtán)	Arlington
A. mýaŋ áalíŋtán juu sǎj?	Where is Arlington?
(rāt wɔ̀əcíinía)	Virginia
B. mýaŋ áalíŋtán juu náj rāt wɔ̀əcíinía	Arlington is in the State of Virginia.
(rāt wɔ̀əcíinía)	Virginia
A. rāt wɔ̀əcíinía juu sǎj?	Where is the State of Virginia?
(sáhárāt améelīkaa)	The U.S.A.
B. rāt wɔ̀əcíinía juu náj sáhárāt améelīkaa	The State of Virginia is in the United States.

ຕາມລອງອະທິບາຍກາມແບ່ງລະບຽບການປົກຄອງຢູ່ໃນປະເທດລາວຢ່າງຫຍໍ້ໆໄດ້ນັກຣຽນຕາມເຂົ້າໃຈ
ເບົ້ງດຸ! ເປັນຕົ້ນວ່າດ້ວນ: ຢູ່ໃນປະເທດລາວ, ຫລາຍໆດອບດິໆທີ່ປະກອບດ້ວຍຈຳນວຈະກັນຍ່າງນ້ອຍ
ສິບຄົນຂນໄປ ຈະກ່ວຍ້າມບ້ວຍໄດ້; ຫລາຍຍ່ານໂຮມກັນເຂົ້າເປັນຕາແສ່ງ; ຫລາຍຕາແສ່ງໂຮມ
ກັນເຂົ້າເປັນເມືອງ; ຫລາຍເມືອງໂຮມກັນເຂົ້າເປັນແຂວງ ແລະ ຫລາຍແຂວງໂຮມກັນເຂົ້າເປັນ
ປະເທດ. ອະວັຍຍ່າງເຫລົ້ງເຂົ້າໄປຈິນເກີນຄວາມສາມາດຂອງນັກຣຽນທີ່ຈະເຂົ້າໃຈໄດ້ ເໝາະມັນຈະ
ເປັນການເສັຽເວລາເປົ່າໆ.

44

NOTES

1) This sentence type may be used to indicate geographical location:

   NP   +   júū   +   LOC

   m̈yaŋ sámnÿa   júū   náj khŭɛŋ hŭaphán
   'Sam Neua is located in the province of Hona-phan.'

2) The verb júū 'to be located in' is followed by Locatives (LOC). The term 'locative' refers to place e xpressions. It includes NP, Prep. + NP, and Adverbs of Place.

3) In questions LOC is replaced by săj 'Where (at)?'

4) bàan 'village', m̈yaŋ 'city', and khŭɛŋ 'province' are all political and administrative divisions in Laos.

APPLICATION

1. Answer these questions giving correct information: (a) m̈yan wíaŋcan júū săj (b) m̈yaŋ sájŋɔ̃ɔn júū náj pátheet wíatŋaam, mɛ̃ɛn bɔɔ?

2. Provide a possible question to each of these answers: (a) bɔ̃ɔ mɛ̃ɛn, láaw sī paj hóoŋhéɛm. (b) khŭɛŋ pâaksée júū náj pátheet láaw. (c) mɛ̃ɛn lɛ̀ɛw, phùakháw pen khon njĪĪpūn. (d) sáharāt améelĪka.

3. Fill in the blanks with the correct word: (a)_____ wíaŋcan júū náj _____ láaw. (b) rāt níwjóok júū náj _____ améelĪkaa. (c) _____ naathɔɔŋ júū náj _____ phóonhóoŋ. (d) _____ wíaŋcan júū náj _____ láaw.

Answers: 1(a)júū náj pátheet‘láaw (b)mɛ̃ɛn lɛ̀ɛw 2(a)láaw sī paj hóoŋhían, mɛ̃ɛn bɔɔ (b)khŭɛŋ pâaksée júū săj (c)phùakháw pen khón njĪĪpūn, mɛ̃ɛn bɔɔ (d)láaw máa câak pátheet daj. 3(a)m̈yan/pátheet (b)sáharāt (c)bàan, m̈yaŋ (d)khŭɛŋ/pátheet

CYCLE 12

M-1

kin khâw	To have one's meal.
khɔ̀j kin khâw	I am having my meal.
hētwlak	To do work.
láaw hētwlak	He works.
āan nǎŋšy	To read (letters).
phùakháw āan nǎŋšy	We read.
khǐan nǎŋšy	To write (letters).
khácàw khǐan nǎŋšy	They write.
hían pháasǎa	To study language.
càw hían pháasǎa	You study language.
sɔ̌ɔn pháasǎa	To teach language.
náajkhúu sɔ̌ɔn pháasǎa	The teacher teaches language.
khúakin	To cook.
náaŋ mālíican khúakin	Malichanh cooks.

M-2

hēt	to do
càw hēt njǎŋ?	What are you doing?
sỳy	to buy
càw sỳy njǎŋ?	What are you buying?

46

bɔ̄ŋ   to look at

    càw bɔ̄ŋ njǎŋ?   What are you looking at?

hěn   to see

    càw hěn njǎŋ?   What do you see?

sɔ̀ɔkhǎa   to look for

    càw sɔ̀ɔkhǎa njǎŋ?   What are you looking for?

pɛɛŋ   to fix, repair

    càw pɛɛŋ njǎŋ?   What are you fixing?

C-1

    A. càw hēt njǎŋ?   What are you doing?

    B. khɔ̂j hētwìak.   I am working.

ເມື່ອຣຽນມາຮອດຈຸດໂລຍະນຸຜລວ ນັກຣຽນອາດຈະຖາມເອົາຄຳໃໝ່ອີກ. ປ່າຍອອກຄຳໃໝ່ໃໝແກ່ຈະຮ່າ
ຫລາຍເກີນໄປ! ຈົ່ງໃໝແຕ່ສະເພາະຄຳທີ່ເຫັນວ່າຈຳເປັນໃຈໃນປັດຈຸບັນເທົ່ານັ້ນ!

NOTES

1) __kin__ 'to eat', __hēt__ 'to do, work', and __āan__ 'to read' are action
   verbs that __require__ NP complements.

        NP   +   V   +   NP

        khɔ̂j   kin   khâw

       (I   eat   rice)

      'I'm having a meal.'

LAO BASIC COURSE

The NP complement can be replaced by njǎŋ in questions:

Question: càw hían njǎŋ   'What are you studying?'
Answer: khòj hían pháasǎa láaw   'Laotian.'

2) bēŋ means 'to look at (something or someone)'. hěn means 'to see, perceive'.

3) Both sɔ̀ɔk and hǎa separately mean 'to look for something'; sɔ̀ɔkhǎa has the same meaning. Combinations of two verbs with the same or similar meaning are very common in Lao.

4) khúakin is the usual verb compound for 'the cooking of food.'

5) In VP hēt wìak, wìak means 'work (in general)' and hēt means 'to do, make'. hēt wìak means 'to have a job' or 't. be working on something'.

APPLICATION

1. In the sentence láaw hēt wìak , wìak is (a) subject (b) VP (c) NP (d) complement to verb hēt.

2. A possible answer to the question càw hēt njǎŋ is (a) bɔ̄ɔ mɛ̄ɛn (b) bɔ̄ɔ hēt (c) khòj kin khâw (d) bɔ̄ɔ njǎŋ.

3. A possible answer to the question láaw hían njǎŋ would be (a) pháasǎa láaw (b) bɔ̄ɔ hían (c) láaw hían pháasǎa aŋkít (d) bɔ̄ɔ pen njǎŋ.

4. In the sentence náajkhúu sɔ̌ɔn pháasǎa, sɔ̌ɔn is (a) MV (b) Subject (c) NP complement (d) classifier.

5. Complete the following sentences: (a) láaw āan... (b) khòj paj hēt... (c) khácàw kin... (d) càw hían...

Answers: 1c and d, 2c, 3a and c, 4a, 5(a)nǎŋsɣ̌y (b)wìak (c)khâw (d)pháasǎa (láaw, etc.)

48

LAO BASIC COURSE

6. Translate the following sentences into English: (a) càw bēŋ
khán hōm bɔɔ (b) càw sɔɔkhǎa nɪǎŋ (c) láaw si pɛɛŋ hyan láaw
(d) khôɪ hěn thāhǎan phūū nàn (e) phúak háw syy mûak ɪūū
tálâat.

CYCLE 13

M-1

<u>kin</u>   eat

   háw si kin ɪūū sǎɪ?   Where are we going to eat?
   ɪūū nìi bɔɔ?   Here?

<u>nāŋ</u>   sit

   háw si nāŋ ɪūū sǎɪ?   Where are you going to sit?
   ɪūū nìi bɔɔ?   Here?

<u>lómkan</u>   chat

   háw si lómkan ɪūū sǎɪ?   Where are we going to chat?
   ɪūū nìi bɔɔ?   Here?

<u>thāaɪhùup</u>   take pictures

   háw si paɪ thāaɪhùup ɪūū   Were are we going to take
   sǎɪ?   pictures?
   ɪūū nìi bɔɔ?   Here?

<u>lìi</u>   hide

   háw si paɪ lìi ɪūū sǎɪ?   Where are we going to hide?
   ɪūū nìi bɔɔ?   Here?

Answer: 6(a)Are you looking at the umbrella? (b)What are you
looking for? (c)He will repair his house. (d)I see
that soldier. (e)We bought a hat at the market.

49

M-2

<u>kin</u>   eat

   bɔ̄ɔ, paj kin jūu hân thɔ̄ˀ   No. Let's go eat there.

<u>jyyn</u>   stand

   bɔ̄ɔ, paj jyyn jūu hân thɔ̄ˀ   No. Let's go stand there.

<u>thâa</u>   wait

   bɔ̄ɔ, paj thâa jūu hân thɔ̄ˀ   No. Let's go wait there.

<u>sûup jaa</u>   smoke

   bɔ̄ɔ, paj sûup jaa jūu hân thɔ̄ˀ   No. Let's go smoke there.

<u>sáwmȳaj</u>   rest

   bɔ̄ɔ, paj sáwmȳaj jūu hân thɔ̄ˀ   No. Let's go rest there.

C-1

   A. càw si sáwmyāj jūu sǎj?   A. Where are you going to rest?
       jūu nìi bɔɔ?   Here?

   B. bɔ̄ɔ, khɔ̀j si paj sáwmȳaj   B. No. I'm going to rest
       jūu hân   there.

C-2

   A. háw si thâa láaw jūu sǎj?   A. Where are we going to
                                        wait for him?
       jūu nìi bɔ̄ɔ?   Here?

   B. bɔ̄ɔ, paj thâa láaw jūu   B. No. Let's go wait for
       hân thɔ̄ˀ   him there.

ຄາວຈາ"ສີ"ບອກຄຳວປັດຈຸບັນມະການແລະອະນາຄິດການ ແຕ່"ໃດ"ບໍ່ໄດ້ບອກຄຳວອະຄິດການສເມີໄປ.

NOTES

1) After j$\overline{\text{uu}}$ or Verbs of Motion (paj, máa, etc.) nìi means 'here'; hân 'there'.

2) The particle th$\overline{\text{ɔ}}$ʔ occurs at the end of sentences which 'urge' or 'suggest' a particular course of action.

APPLICATION

1. Complete these sentences: (a) láaw b$\overline{\text{ɔɔ}}$ j$\overline{\text{uu}}$ hân. láaw j$\overline{\text{uu}}$...
   (b) j$\overline{\text{uu}}$ nìi bɔɔ? b$\overline{\text{ɔɔ}}$ j$\overline{\text{uu}}$... (c) j$\overline{\text{uu}}$...? j$\overline{\text{uu}}$ nìi bɔɔ?

2. Change the following statements into suggestions for action:
   (a) paj jyyn j$\overline{\text{uu}}$ hân... (b) paj kin khâw... (c) paj th$\overline{\text{aa}}$j hùup...

3. Complete the following sentences (Using the English cue word):
   (a) paj... j$\overline{\text{uu}}$ sǎj (hide) (b) háw si lómkan j$\overline{\text{uu}}$... (where?)
   (c) paj sáwmȳaj j$\overline{\text{uu}}$... th$\overline{\text{ɔ}}$ʔ (there). (d) b$\overline{\text{ɔɔ}}$ paj... j$\overline{\text{uu}}$ hân th$\overline{\text{ɔ}}$ʔ (wait) (e) ...nìi bɔɔ? (here?) (f) n$\overline{\text{aŋ}}$ j$\overline{\text{uu}}$ hân... (Let's...)

Answers: 1a nìi, 2b hân 1c sǎj   2a th$\overline{\text{ɔ}}$ʔ 2b th$\overline{\text{ɔ}}$ʔ 2c th$\overline{\text{ɔ}}$ʔ
3a lìi, 3b sǎj 3c hân 3d thâa 3e j$\overline{\text{uu}}$ 3f th$\overline{\text{ɔ}}$ʔ

51

CYCLE 14

M-1

phāk	to stay
láaw phāk jūū sǎj?	Where is he staying?
hētkaan	to work
láaw hētkaan jūū sǎj?	Where is he working?
tátphǒm	to have one's hair cut
láaw tátphǒm jūū sǎj?	Where did he have his hair cut?
thóorāsáp	to make a phone call
láaw thóorāsáp jūū sǎj?	Where did he make the phone call?
sōŋ thóorālèek	to send a cable
láaw sōŋ thóorālèek jūū sǎj?	Where did he send the cable?
lîn	to play
láaw lîn jūū sǎj?	Where is he playing?
fáŋ wīthānjū?	to listen to the radio
láaw fáŋ wīthānjū? jūū sǎj?	Where did he listen to the radio?

M-2

hýan khɔ̌j	My house.
láaw phāk jūu hýan khɔ̌j	He is staying in my house.
hàantátphǒm	The barber shop.
láaw tátphǒm jūu hàan tátphǒm	He has his hair cut at the barbershop.
dēn bàan	The yard of the house
láaw lîn jūu dēn bàan	He is playing in the yard of the house.
hɔ̌ɔŋ pásúm	The meeting room.
láaw fáŋ jūu hɔ̌ɔŋ pásúm	He listened to it in the meeting room.
hóoŋsǎaj	The Post Office.
láaw sōŋ thóorālèek jūu hóoŋsǎaj	He sent the cable at the Post Office.
tùuthóorāsáp sǎathǎarānā?	The public phone booth.
láaw thóorāsáp jūu tùu thóorāsáp sǎatháarānā?	He made a phone call at the public phone booth.

C-1

(phāk)	to stay
A. láaw phāk jūu sǎj?	Where is he staying?
(hóoŋhɛ́ɛm)	hotel
B. láaw phāk jūu hóoŋhɛ́ɛm	He is staying at a hotel.

"ຂອງກິນ ບໍ່ກິນ ມັນເນົ່າ - ຂອງເກົ່າ ບໍ່ເລົ່າ ມັນລືມ" ຈົ່ງພາກັນຮຽນໃຈຄ່ຳທີ່ຮຽນມາແລ້ວຄືນອີກ!

C-2

(phȳan càw)	Your friend.
A. phȳan càw jūu sǎj?	Where is your friend?
(hóoŋhéɛm)	Hotel
B. láaw jūu hóoŋhéɛm	He is at a hotel.
(phāk)	to stay
A. láaw phāk jūu hóoŋhéɛm bɔɔ?	Is he staying at the hotel?
(mɛ̄ɛn lɛ̀ɛw)	Yes.
B. mɛ̄ɛn lɛ̀ɛw, láaw phāk jūu hóoŋhéɛm	Yes, he is staying at the hotel.

ຕາມລອງປະຕິຄເຄ໌ອງໂດເຄ່ອງນ່ວຍນອກເບ່ງຖ! ເວ່າເຄ່ອງການແຕ່ງເຄ່ອງປະກອບບົດຮຽນນ ຖາ
ຕາກຕາມພຍາຍາມແຕ່ງໂອກອນກໍຈະເປັນການດີ. ເມ່ອໃຊ່ແລວຫານຈົງເກັບໄວ້ຄົດແປງໃຫ່ດາວຮຕນ໌າ.

NOTES

1) The Verb Phrase **jūu** + Locative is frequently combined with sentences to indicate location of some activity.

Sentence	+	jūu + LOC
láaw phāk		jūu hȳan khɔ̄j
'He is staying		at my house'.
láaw fáŋ wīthānjū?		jūu hɔ̄oŋ pásúm
'He listened to the radio		in the meeting room.'

sǎj can replace the Locative in this construction in questions:

| láaw phāk jūu sǎj ? | 'Where is he staying?' |
| láaw fáŋ wīthānjū?jūu sǎj ? | 'Where did he listen to the radio?' |

54

APPLICATION

1. In the sentence láaw phāk jūu hýan khɔ̌j, jūu hýan khɔ̌j is
   (a) Vb (b) NP (c) VP (d) N

2. In the above sentence, jūu is (a) NP (b) preposition (c) verb
   (d) locative (e) none of these.

3. In the above sentence, jūu hýan khɔ̌j indicates (a) subject
   (b) location (c) negative (d) none of these.

4. Complete the following sentences: (a)...jūu hàan tát phǒm
   (b) ̱láaw lîn...dēn bàan (c) láaw sɔ̌ŋ thóorāleek jūu...
   (d) láaw...wīthānjū?jūu sǎj (e) láaw...jūu hóoŋhɛɛm
   (g) khɔ̌j si...jūu tùu...sǎathāarānā?

5. Answer the following questions: (a) láaw lîn jūu sǎj....
   (b) láaw fáŋ wīthānjū?jūu sǎj? (c) càw hían pháasǎa láaw
   jūu sǎj? (d) láaw tát phǒm jūu sǎj? (e) láaw thóorāsáp
   jūu sǎj?

55

CYCLE 15

M-1

paj kinkhâw	to go to eat
láaw si paj kinkhâw jūu hàan aahǎan	He is going to eat at the restaurant.
máa hētkaan	to come to work
láaw si máa hētkaan jūu hóoŋkaan nǐi	He is coming to work in this office building.
máa pásúm	to come to attend the meeting
láaw si máa pásúm jūu hɔ̀ɔŋpásúm	He is coming to attend a meeting in the conference room.
paj thóorāsáp	to make a phone call
láaw si paj thóorāsáp jūu hɔ̀ɔŋkaan láaw	He is going to make a phone call in his office.
máa sɔ̀ɔkhǎa	come to look for
láaw máa sɔ̀ɔkhǎa càw jūu hóoŋhían	He came to look for you at school.
paj bə̄ŋ	go to look at
láaw paj bə̄ŋ khàajthāhǎan jūu rāt khālīfóonía	He went to see the military post in the State of California.

56

I-2

njǎŋ   what

  láaw si paj hēt njǎŋ jūū   What is he going to do at
  hàan tátphŏm?   the barbershop?

sǎj   where

  láaw si paj sōŋ thóorālèek   Where is he going to send
  jūū sǎj?   the cable?

njǎŋ, sǎj   what, where

  láaw si paj hēt njǎŋ jūū   Where is he going to do
  sǎj?   what?

njǎŋ   what

  láaw si máa hēt njǎŋ jūū   What is he coming to do
  nìi?   here?

njǎŋ   what

  láaw si paj hēt njǎŋ jūū   What is he going to do there?
  hân?

C-1

  A. càw si paj hēt njǎŋ jūū   What are you going to do
    hàan tátphŏm?   at the barbershop?

  B. khɔ̀j si paj tátphŏm   I am going to have my hair
                                      cut.

บักมีจุกปะสิๆที่จะใฑ์มักธຽมติดใจดๆว่า "ไข" ແລະ "มา" ยูตามาๆดๆก์ธิຽๆ. ຂະເจๆจุูຼຼลอยๆว่า ເວລາใกເຮๆຄว่าๆ "ຂอยไปກันເຂๆ" ແລະເວລາใกເຮๆຄว่าๆ "ຂอยมาກันເຂๆ".

57

C-2

A. càw sī paj sǎj?	Where are you going?
B. khɔ̌j sī paj hàan aahǎan	I am going to the restaurant.
A. càw sī paj hēt njǎŋ jūū hân?	What are you going to do there?
B. khɔ̌j sī paj kinkhâw	I am going to eat.

ຕົກສອຍຄວາມເຂົ້າໃຈໃນບົດຮຽນບົດນ້ອຍຂອງນັກຮຽນຂອງທ່ານເບິ່ງໆ! ຂະເຈົ້າໃຊ້"ໄປ"ແລະ"ມາ"ຖືກຕ້ອງບໍ?

NOTES

1) paj 'to go' and máa 'to come' may be followed by a VP indicating
   an activity (kin khâw, etc.). This may be followed by jūū + Loc
   indicating the location.

NP	+	sī paj	+	Activity	+	Location
láaw		sī paj		kin khâw		jūū hàan aahǎan
'He		is going		to eat		at the restaurant.'

This sentence is made up of 3 basic underlying sentences:

(1) láaw sī paj ....

(2) (láaw)   kin khâw

(3) (láaw)   jūū hàan aahǎan

In questions the VP indicating Activity can be replaced by
hēt njǎŋ 'do what?'; the VP of Location by jūū sǎj.

Statement:	láaw sī paj	kin khâw	jūū hàan aahǎan ?
Question (Activity):	láaw sī paj	hēt njǎŋ	(jūū hàan aahǎan)?
Question (Location):	láaw sī paj	kin khâw	jūū sǎj?

APPLICATION

1. In the sentence láaw si paj sòokhǎa pỳm láaw jūu hóoŋmɔ̌ɔ, sòokhǎa pỳm is a VP indicating (a) location (b) time (c) activity (d) actor (e) none of these.

jūu hóoŋmɔ̌ɔ is a VP indicating (a) purpose (b) location (c) subject (d) time.

si paj indicates (a) past time (b) future time (c) present time (d) indefinite time.

2. In the sentence láaw máa sòokhǎa càw jūu hóoŋhían the time of the action is probably (a) present (b) future (c) past (d) future or present.

3. What are the 3 underlying sentences of the following sentence: láaw si paj sōŋ thóorālèek jūu hóoŋsǎaj

(a) _____

(b) _____

(c) _____

4. Translate the following sentences into English: (a) láaw si si paj sòokhǎa pỳm càw (b) khɔ̌j paj bɘ̄ŋ wǐthanjǔʔjūu haan aahǎan (c) laaw si bɔɔ paj hēt wíak jūu myaŋ sajŋɔ̄ɔn (d) laaw maa hēt njǎŋ jūu hɔ̀ɔŋ pasum (e) càw si paj sy̌y syafɔ̌n jūu sǎj (f) phǎj máa lîn jūu dɘ̄n baan càw (g) phỹan khɔ̌j si paj sōŋ thóorāleek jūu hóoŋsǎaj.

CYCLE 16

M-1

máa nîi	Come here.
láaw si máa nîi	He is coming here.
paj hân	Go there.
láaw si paj hân	He is going there.
máa phìi	Come over here.
láaw si máa phìi	He is coming over here.
paj phùn	Go over there.
láaw si paj phùn	He is going over there.

C-1

A. láaw si máa nîi bɔɔ?   Is he coming here?

B. bɔɔ, láaw si paj hân   No. He is going there.

C-2

A. càw si paj phùn bɔɔ?   Are you going over there?

B. bɔɔ, khɔ̀j si máa phìi   No. I'm coming over there.

60

NOTES

1) Both n̂ĩ and phĩi refer to space near at hand, but n̂ĩ is more specific ('right here') and phĩi is more general ('over here'). n̂ĩ is more likely to be used in commands, such as máa n̂ĩ 'come here.'

2) hân means 'there'. phùn means 'way over there.'

APPLICATION

1. Complete the following sentences: (a) láaw si máa... (or) ... (b) láaw si paj... (or) ...

2. Translate the following sentences into Lao: (a) Come here. (Command).   (b) Go over there.   (c) Go way over there. (d) Come over here.

3. (a) What would you say if you wanted to indicate that something was in the same room with you but was about 8 feet away?

   (b) What would you say if you wanted someone to come over in your general area but not right close to you?

   (c) If you were asked where someone was, what would you say to indicate that he was a considerable distance away but still visible?

   (d) If you were asked where someone was, how would you indicate that he wasn't near you?

Answers: 1(a) n̂ĩ or phĩi (b)hân or phùn 2(a)máa n̂ĩ (b)paj hân (c)paj phùn (d)máa phĩi 3(a)jūu hân (b)máa phĩi (c)jūu phùn (d)(láaw) bɔɔ jūu n̂ĩ

CYCLE 17

M-1

sáthǎanthùut améelɪ̃kan — American Embassy

   càw hùu tháaŋ paj sáthǎan
   thùut améelɪ̃kan bɔɔ?

   Do you know the way to the
   American Embassy?

hýan láaw — his house

   càw hùu tháaŋ paj hýan
   láaw bɔɔ?

   Do you, know the way to his
   house?

hóoŋ síinée nìi — this movie house

   càw hùu tháaŋ paj hóoŋ
   síinée nìi bɔɔ?

   Do you know the way to this
   movie house?

hàan tátphǒm — barbershop

   càw hùu tháaŋ paj hàan
   tátphǒm bɔɔ?

   Do you know the way to the
   barbershop?

komkhóosánáakaan láaw — Lao information service

   càw hùu tháaŋ paj kom
   khóosánáakaan láaw bɔɔ?

   Do you know the way to the
   Lao information service?

M-2

lìaw sàaj — turn left

   hùu, lìaw sàaj jūu thánǒn
   nâa.

   Yes (I know), turn left on
   the next street.

lìaw khǔa — turn right

   hùu, lìaw khǔa jūu thánǒn
   nâa

   Yes, turn right on the next
   street.

paj s̄yy s̄yy	go straight ahead
hùu, paj s̄yy s̄yy taam thánɔ̌n nìi	Yes, go straight ahead on this street.
lìaw khǔa lɛ̀ɛw paj s̄yy s̄yy	turn right then go straight
hùu, lìaw khǔa jūu thánɔ̌n làan sàaŋ lɛ̀ɛw paj s̄yy s̄yy	Yes, turn right on Lane Xang Street then go straight.
bɔɔ	no
bɔɔ, khɔ̂j bɔɔ hùu	No, I don't know.

C-1

(hàan tátphɔ̌m)

A. càw hùu tháaŋ paj hàan tátphɔ̌m bɔɔ? — Do you know the way to the barbershop?

(sàaj, thánɔ̌n nâa)

B. hùu, lìaw sàaj jūu thánɔ̌n nâa — Yes, turn left on the next street.

ຈິວພະຍາຍາມຈໍາກັດຄວາມໃຊ້ຄໍາວ່າ "ຊູ" ໄວ້ແຕ່ສະເພາະກັບ "ຊູທາງ" ເຮັ້ງກ່ອນ. ຢ່າພະຍາຍາມໃຊ້ໃຫກວາງກວ່ານັ້ນ! ໃນບົດໄປຍັງຈະມີການສອນຄໍາວ່າ "ຊູ" ໃນທາໜອງໃໝ່ອີກ. ໃນຂັ້ນນັ້ນຮຽນຂອງ ທ່ານອາດຈະສົມທະນາກັບທ່ານໄດຫລາຍເຖິແລ້ວ. ຈິວໃຫມັນຮຽນຂອງທ່ານຝຶກຫັດໃຫມາສາລາວສເມີ!

63

NOTES

1) The noun tháaŋ 'way, direction' can be followed by Verb Phrase 'modifiers', such as paj hýan láaw 'go to his house' indicating 'destination'. The whole construction tháaŋ + VP is a Noun Phrase and may serve as the NP complement of a verb, such as hùu 'to know'.

NP	+	MV	+	NP

khɔ́j	hùu	tháaŋ paj hóoŋ síinée
(I	know	way go building cinema)

'I know the way to the movies.'

2) Where English uses Verb+Adverbials or Preposition+Noun Phrase to indicate directions and locations, Lao normally has Verb+Verb or Verb+VP, as in the following examples:

(1) English: Verb + Adverbial
              Turn   left/right.

    Lao: Verb + Verb
              lìaw sàaj/khǔa

(2) English: Verb + Adverbial   + Preposition-NP
              Go   straight ahead   on   this street.

    Lao: Verb +   Verb   + Verb Phrase
              paj   sȳȳ sȳȳ   taam thánǒn nìi

3) The affirmative response to bɔ̄ɔ type (Yes-No) questions is repetition of the Verb; the negative response is bɔ̄ɔ, bɔ̄ɔ + Verb.

NP	+	MV	+	Complement	+	Question

càw	hùu	tháaŋ paj tálâat	bɔɔ

'Do you know the way to the market?'

Affirmative
Response: hùu, (lìaw sàaj jūu thánŏn nâa)
'Yes, I do. (Turn left at the next blǫçk.)'

Negative
Response: bɔ̄ɔ, (khɔ̂j) bɔ̄ɔ hùu
'No, I don't.'

The negative is normally followed by another sentence supplying
additional information.

APPLICATION

1. In the sentence láaw hùu tháaŋ paj hýan càw, paj hýan càw is
   (a) the predicate (b) VP (c) 'modifier' of thaaŋ (d) NP
   (e) verb.

2. In the above sentence tháaŋ paj hýan càw is (a) NP (b) VP
   (c) predicate (d) complement of the verb hùu (e) subject
   of the sentence.

3. In the sentence lìaw sàaj (a) both lìaw and sàaj are verbs
   (b) sàaj is an adjective (c) neither is a verb (d) only
   lìaw is a verb.

4. In the sentence paj sȳy sȳy taam thánŏn nìi, tam is (a) a
   preposition (b) NP (c) verb (d) VP (e) particle (f) it
   means 'to follow or go along'.

5. Complete the following sentences: (a) lìaw... jūu thánŏn nâa
   (b) ...sȳy sȳy (c) bɔ̄ɔ, khɔ̂j... hùu (d) ...khŭa jūu thánŏn
   làan sàaŋ (e) càw hùu thaaŋ... hýan laaw bɔɔ (f) hùu, paj
   ... ... taam... nìi.

Answers: 1b and c, 2a and d, 3a, 4c and f, 5(a)sàaj/khŭa
          (b)paj (c)bɔ̄ɔ (d)lìaw (e)paj (f)sȳy sȳy... thánŏn

CYCLE 18

M-1

phūu njíŋ phūu nìi   this woman

   càw hùucák phūu njíŋ phūu   Do you know this woman?
   nìi bɔɔ?

phūu sáaj phūu nìi   this man

   càw hùucák phūu sáaj phūu   Do you know this man?
   nìi bɔɔ?

déknɔɔj phūu nìi   this child

   càw hùucák déknɔɔj phūu   Do you know this child?
   nìi bɔɔ?

nɔɔŋ sáaj khɔ̂j   my younger brother

   càw hùucák nɔɔŋ sáaj   Do you know my younger
   khɔ̂j bɔɔ?   brother?

nɔɔŋ sǎaw khɔ̂j   my younger sister

   càw hùucák nɔɔŋ sǎaw   Do you know my younger
   khɔ̂j bɔɔ?   sister?

àaj khɔ̂j   my older brother

   càw hùucák àaj khɔ̂j bɔɔ?   Do you know my older brother?

phɔ̄ɔ mɛ̄ɛ láaw   his parents

   càw hùucák phɔ̄ɔ mɛ̄ɛ láaw   Do you know his parents?
   bɔɔ?

66

yàj khɔ̃j   my older sister

    càw hùucák yàj khɔ̃j bɔɔ?   Do you know my older sister?

lùuk khɔ̃j   my child

    càw hùucák lùuk khɔ̃j bɔɔ?   Do you know my child?

M-2

hóoŋkaan càw   your office

    hùu, khɔ̃j dàj hùucák káp   Yes, I met him at your office.
    láaw juu hóoŋkaan càw

wāt inpɛɛŋ   Inpeng temple

    hùu, khɔ̃j dàj hùucák káp   Yes, I met her at the Wat
    láaw juu wāt inpɛɛŋ   Inpeng.

sámóosɔ̌on   club

    hùu, khɔ̃j dàj hùucák káp   Yes, I met him at the club.
    láaw juu sámóosɔ̌on

náj rōtfáj   on the train

    hùu, khɔ̃j dàj hùucák káp   Yes, I met him on the train.
    láaw juu náj rōtfáj

náj ŋáan kinlìaŋ   at the party

    hùu, khɔ̃j dàj hùucák káp   Yes, I met her at the party.
    láaw juu náj ŋáan kinlìaŋ

67

M-3

phŭa   husband

    khɔ̌j sɪ dàj hùucàk kàp   I'll get to meet her husband.
    phŭa láaw

mía   wife

    khɔ̌j sɪ dàj hùucák káp   I'll get to meet his wife.
    mía láaw

phɔ̄ɔ thâw   father in law

    khɔ̌j sɪ dàj hùucák káp   I'll get to meet his father-
    phɔ̄ɔthâw láaw   in-law.

mɛ̄ɛ thâw   mother-in-law

    khɔ̌j sɪ dàj hùucák káp   I'll get to meet his
    mɛ̄ɛ thâw láaw   mother-in-law.

phɔ̄ɔ pūu   father-in-law

    khɔ̌j sɪ dàj hùucák káp   I'll get to meet her father-
    phɔ̌ɔ pūu láaw   in-law.

mɛ̄ɛ njāa   mother-in-law

    khɔ̌j sɪ dàj hùucák káp   I'll get to meet her
    mɛ̄ɛ njāa láaw   mother-in-law.

C-1

(phūu nj́íŋ)   woman

  A. càw hùucák phūu nj́íŋ   Do you know this woman?
     phūu nìi bɔɔ?

(wāt inpɛɛŋ)   Inpeng temple

  B. hùu, khɔ̌j dàj hùucák   Yes, I met her at the
     káp láaw jūu wāt inpɛɛŋ   Inpeng temple.

C-2

(làaw)   she

  A. càw dàj hùucák káp   Where did you meet her?
     láaw jūu sǎj?

(hóoŋhían)   school

  B. khɔ̌j dàj hùucák káp   I met her at school.
     láaw jūu hóoŋhían

C-3

A. càw hùucák mía láaw bɔɔ?   Do you know his wife?
B. bɔɔ, khɔ̌j bɔɔ hùucák láaw   No, I don't know her.

A. càw si dàj hùucák káp láaw bɔɔ?   Will you get to meet her?
B. mɛ̌ɛn lɛ̀ɛw, khɔ̌j si dàj hùucák   Yes, I'll get to meet her.
    káp láaw
    khácàw si máa hýan khɔ̌j   They will come to my house.

_____

ເມື່ອສ່ອນຍົຄຣຸມຍົຄມແລ້ວ ຕາມລອງຖາມນັກຣຽນກ່ຽວກັບຜົມຍອາຍຍອງຂອງວະເຈົ້າເບິ່ງຄູ! ຂ້ສຳຄັນກໍຄື
ບໍແມນວາະເຈົ້າຕອບໄດ້ແລ້ວຈະແລ້ວ. ຈົ່ງສັ່ງເກດເບິ່ງວ່າ ວິຕຕອບຂອງວະເຈົ້າພໍໃຈຕາມແລ້ວຫລືບໍ!

NOTES

1) hùucák means 'to be acquainted or familiar with (someone or something)'.

khɔ̌j hùucák láaw   'I know her.'

càw hùucák my̌aŋ wíaŋcan bɔɔ?   'Are you familiar with Vientiane?'

2) dàj + Main Verb means 'to have the opportunity (to do something as in these examples:

khɔ̌j dàj hùucák káp láaw   (I had the opportunity to become acquainted with him.

     'I got to meet him.'

khɔ̌j si dàj hùucák káp láaw   'I will get to meet her.'

3) ŋáan kinlìaŋ is a Noun Compound meaning 'a party' and is made up of ŋáan 'celebration' + kin 'to eat' + lìaŋ 'to treat s.o.'

4) In Lao when referring to the male and female offspring in a family one must indicate not only their sex but also their relative ages. Consider this hypothetical family of 5 children

Sex:	M	F	M	F	M
Age:	21	19	17	15	10
Rank:	1	2	3	4	5

Child number 3 refers to

1 as àaj (khɔ̌j)   'older brother'.

2 as yàj (khɔ̌j)   'older sister'.

4 as nɔ̀ɔŋsǎaw (khɔ̌j) 'younger sister.'

5 as nɔ̀ɔŋsáaj (khɔ̌j) 'younger brother'.

5) When referring to <u>in-laws</u>, one must indicate whether they are the husband's or the wife's.

phɔ̄ɔ pūu (1)   mɛ̄ɛ njāā (2)   phɔ̄ɔ thâw (3)   mɛ̄ɛ thâw (4)

phŭa   mía

'husband'   'wife'

(1) her father-in-law   (2) her mother-in-law

(3) his father-in-law   (4) his mother-in-law

APPLICATION

1. If you heard someone say <u>kh3̂j dàj hùucák káp láaw</u>, you would assume that the speaker (a) <u>knew</u> the person he was talking about, (b) did <u>not know</u> that person, (c) had met that person, (d) had <u>not</u> met that person.

2. If you heard someone say <u>kh3̂j hùucàk mýaŋ wíaŋcan</u>, (a) you would know that he had been to Vientiane. (b) You would know that he knew at least where Vientiane is located.

3. If a person says <u>ỳaj kh3̂j</u>, you know the person he is talking about is (a) older than he, (b) younger than he, (c) male, (d) female, (d) you can not tell whether the person is younger or older, male or female.

4. If a person says <u>àaj kh3̂j</u>, you know the person he is talking about is (a) female, (b) male (c) younger than the speaker (d) older than the speaker (e) sex and age are unclear.

5. Is the situation described in the following statement possible? <u>láaw pen nòoŋ sǎaw kh3̂j lɛ̄? kh3̂j pen nɔ̀oŋsáaj láaw</u>

6. In the situation described in the following statement possible? <u>kh3̂j pen ỳaj càw lɛ̄? càw pen nɔ̀oŋsáaj kh3̂j.</u>

Answers: 1a and c, 2b, 3a and d, 4b and d, 5no, 6yes

7. Fill in the blanks with déknɔɔj or lùuk as appropriate:
   càw hěn _____ phūu nàn bɔɔ? láaw pen _____ sǎaw khɔ̌j
           (1)   (2)

8. If a person said to someone phɔ̌ɔ pūu càw pen phɣan khɔ̌j would
   he be talking to (a) a man (b) a woman (c) either (d) neither

9. If someone said khɔ̌j dàj hùucák káp mɛ̄ɛ thâw càw, you would
   know she was talking to a man. True or false?

10. Could this be a true statement? mɛ̄ɛ njāa càw pen mɛ̄ɛ khɔ̌j

11. Could this be true? phɔ̌ɔ thâw khɔ̌j pen phɔ̌ɔ pūu càw

CYCLE 19

M-1

phàak kaaŋ	Central part
khɔ̌j máa câak phàak kaaŋ	I am from the Central part.
phàak tàj	Southern part
khɔ̌j máa câak phàak tàj	I am from the Southern part.
phàak nɣa	Northern part
khɔ̌j máa câak phàak nɣa	I am from the Northern part.
phàak táwén ɔ̀ɔk	Eastern part
khɔ̌j máa câak phàak táwén ɔ̀ɔk	I am from the Eastern part.
phàak táwén tók	Western part
khɔ̌j máa câak phàak táwén tók	I am from the Western part.

Amswers: 7(1)déknɔɔj (2)lùuk, 8b, 9true, 10yes, 11no

72

M-2

phàak kaaŋ	Central part
mýaŋ khɔ́j jūu tháaŋ phàak kaaŋ khɔ̆ɔŋ pátheet láaw	My hometown is in the Central part of Laos.

phàak táwén ɔ̀oksĭaŋtàj	Southeastern part
mýaŋ khɔ́j jūu tháaŋ phàak táwén ɔ̀oksĭaŋtàj khɔ̆ɔŋ pátheet láaw	My hometown is in the Southeastern part of Laos.

phàak táwén ɔ̀oksĭaŋn̄ya	Northeastern part
mýaŋ khɔ́j jūu tháaŋ phàak táwén ɔ̀oksĭaŋn̄ya	My hometown is in the Northeastern part of Laos.

phàak táwén tóksĭaŋn̄ya	Northwestern part
mýaŋ khɔ́j jūu tháaŋ phàak táwén tóksĭaŋn̄ya khɔ̆ɔŋ pátheet láaw	My hometown is in the Northwestern part of Laos.

phàak táwén tóksĭaŋtàj	Southwestern part
mýaŋ khɔ́j jūu tháaŋ phàak táwén tóksĭaŋtàj khɔ̆ɔŋ pátheet láaw	My hometown is in the Southwestern part of Laos.

C-1

A. náaj khúu máa câak phàak
daj khɔ̌ɔŋ páthèet láaw?

What part of Laos is the
teacher from?

B. láaw máa câak phàak...

He is from the... part.

จิวใจแผนตี้ และใຫมักธรูบอกตัดตาววตามมบเบ๊อๆ! มายตสฺตถจะมยายามใจกินอุยาย
ตาววเผื่อย่วเบ๊วตวามเຂำใจຂอวมักธรูม.

C-2

(phàak táwén ɔ̌oksĭaŋtàj)

Southeastern

A. phɣ̌an càw máa câak phàak
táwén ɔ̌oksĭaŋtàj khɔ̌ɔŋ
páthèet láaw, mɛ̌ɛn bɔɔ?

Your friend is from the
Southeastern part of Laos,
isn't he?

(phàak táwén tóksĭaŋtàj)

Southwestern

B. bɔ̌ɔ mɛ̌ɛn, láaw máa câak
phàak táwén tóksĭaŋtàj
khɔ̌ɔŋ páthèet láaw

No, he is from the South-
western part of Laos.

ทามถิวเຂำใจกิแล้ວอๆ มาก C ยู่ใນบົດธรูมเป็ນມธຣວແຕถือย่าวตลิແມอตาวแมะมຫในทาม
ผึກตัດต่ำมับ. ແລະແຕ່ລະบົດ C ยู่ใນແຕ່ລะใຈเทือย่วยມธຣວມສຳລับยทามผึກตัด.

C-3

A. càw sɣ̄ɣ̄ njǎŋ?

What's your name?

B. khɔ̌j sɣ̄ɣ̄ súksɔ̌mbuun

My name is Souksomboun.

A. càw pen khón láaw mɛ̌ɛn bɔɔ?

You are a Laotian, aren't you?

B. mɛ̌ɛn lɛ̀ɛw, khɔ̌j pen khón láaw

Yes, I am a Laotian.

74

A. càw máa câak sǎj?	Where are you from?
B. khɔj máa câak mýaŋ wíaŋcan	I am from the city of Vientiane.
A. mýaŋ wíaŋcan jɑu sǎj?	Where is Vientiane?
B. mýaŋ wíaŋcan jɑu náj pátheet láaw	Vientiane is in Laos?
A. mýaŋ wíaŋcan jɑu náj phàak daj khɔ̌ɔŋ pátheet láaw?	In what part of Laos is Vientiane?
B. mýaŋ wíaŋcan jɑu náj phàak kaan khɔ̌ɔŋ pátheet láaw	Vientiane is in the Central part of Laos.

ນາຍຄຊະຕອງເປັນຄົນທ່ຽາຄຄຄົມແຂວງຫາວຽວມມາໃຫມັກຣຽນຝຶກຫັດ. ຍ່ງຄົນໄປ ແຂວງທຈະນ້ ມາຝຶກຝົນໄດ້ຄ່ວນຢ່ຈະຕລາຍຂນ. ຕ່ວນກ່ຍວມຄຊຮ້ວານັກຣຽນເຂ້າໃຈຕຍ້ວຕລຄຄຈະບເຂ້າໃຈຕຍ້ວ.

NOTES

1) Except for <u>tâj</u> 'South' and <u>nỹa</u> 'North' all compass points are compounds:

    <u>táwén3ok</u> 'East': <u>táwén</u> 'sun' + <u>3ok</u> 'to come up'

    <u>táwéntók</u> 'West': <u>táwén</u> 'sun' + <u>tók</u> 'to fall'

Compounds such as Southeast are made with <u>sǐaŋ</u> 'direction':

    <u>táwéntók sǐaŋnỹa</u> 'Northwest': <u>táwéntók</u> 'West' + <u>sǐaŋ</u> 'direction' + <u>nỹa</u> 'North'

    <u>táwén3oksǐaŋtâj</u> 'Southeast': <u>táwén3ok</u> 'East' + <u>sǐaŋ</u> 'direction' + <u>tâj</u> 'South'. <u>táwéntóksǐaŋtâj</u> 'Southwest' and <u>táwén3oksǐaŋnỹa</u> 'Northeast' are formed in a similar fashion.

2) In longer Noun Phrases <u>khɔ̌ɔŋ</u> 'of' must be used so that the relationship between the parts of the NP are clear, as in: <u>phàak táwén3oksǐaŋtâj khɔ̌ɔŋ pátheet láaw</u> 'The Southeastern part of Laos.'

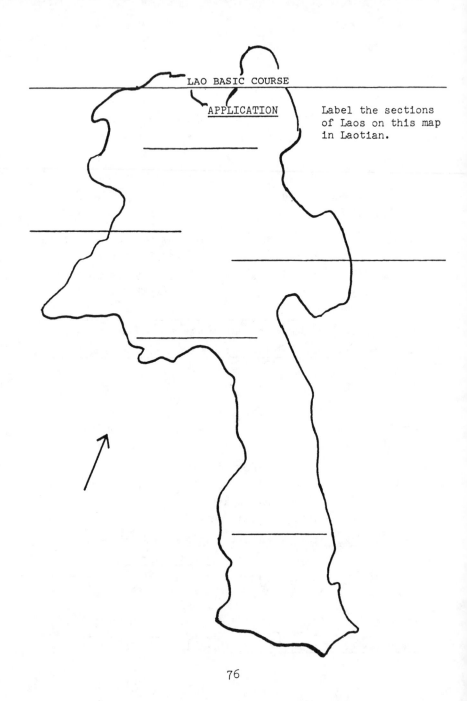

APPLICATION

Label the sections
of Laos on this map
in Laotian.

76

CYCLE 20

M-1

<u>wáaŋ wàj</u>   put

    càw si wáaŋ wàj sǎj?   Where are you going to put
    wàj phìi bɔɔ?   (it)? Over here?

thée <u>lóŋ</u>   pour out

    càw si thée lóŋ sǎj?   Where are you going to pour
    lóŋ phìi bɔɔ?   (it) out? Over here?

<u>tàŋ wàj</u>   set up

    càw si tàŋ wàj sǎj?   Where are you going to set
    wàj phìi bɔɔ?   (it) up? Over here?

<u>njíŋ sāj</u>   shoot at

    càw si njíŋ sāj sǎj?   Where are you shooting at?
    sāj phìi bɔɔ?   Over here?

<u>lɛɛn ɔ̀ok</u>   run out

    càw si lɛɛn ɔ̀ok sǎj?   What exit are you going to
    ɔ̀ok phìi bɔɔ?   run out through? (The one)
                                  here?

M-2

<u>wáaŋ wàj</u>   put down

    khɔ̀j si aw paj wáaŋ wàj   I'm going to take it over
    phùn   there and put it down.

<u>páʔ wàj</u>   leave

    khɔ̀j si aw paj páʔ wàj phùn   I'm going to take it over
                                  there and leave it.

77

<u>tít sǎj</u>   stick up

    khɔ̌j si aw paj tít sǎj phǔn   I'm going to take it over
                               there and stick it up.

<u>ɔ̌ok</u>   take out

    khɔ̌j si aw paj ɔ̌ok phǔn   I'm going to take it out
                               that exit over there.

<u>thǐm lóŋ</u>   drop

    khɔ̌j si aw paj thǐm lóŋ   I'm going to take it over
    phǔn   there and drop it.

C-1

    A. càw si wáaŋ pỳm hǔa nìi   Where are you going to put
       wáj sǎj? wàj phìi bɔɔ?   this book? Over here?

    B. bɔɔ, khɔ̌j si aw pỳm hǔa   No. I'm going to take this
       nìi paj wáaŋ wàj phǔn   book and put it over there.

C-2

    A. càw si aw pỳm hǔa nìi paj   Are you going to take this
       páʔ wàj phǔn bɔɔ?   book and leave it over there?

    B. bɔɔ, khɔ̌j si páʔ pỳm hǔa   No. I'm going to leave this
       nìi wàj nìi   book here.

ຈົງສະແດງທ່າຕິຕາວງປະກອບກັບຄວາມໝາຍຂອງປໂຍກຢູ່ໃນບົດຮຽນນີ້. ເປັນຕົ້ນວ່າ: "ເອົາໄປພຸ້ນ"
ຕາງກັນກັບ ເອົາມານີ້ ຢ່າງໃດ. ຕລັວຈາກນັ້ນແລ້ວຕານລອງບອກໃຫ້ນັກຮຽນປະຕິບັດຕາມຕາມເບິງດູ!

78

LAO BASIC COURSE

NOTES

1) In Lao Verb Compounds are used in situations where Verb +
Preposition or Verb + Adverb would be used in English: wáaŋ
wàj 'to put something in a place and leave it there': wáaŋ
'to put, place' + wàj 'to leave for future use'; thée lóŋ
'to pour, dump something out': thée 'to pour, dump' + lóŋ
'to go down'; tàŋ wàj 'to set something up and leave it
there': tàŋ 'to put something in a standing position' + wàj
'Leave for future use' njíŋ sāj 'to shoot towards': njíŋ 'to
shoot a firearm; etc.' + sāj 'to put in'; lɛɛn ɔ̀ok 'to escape
out through': lɛɛn 'to run' + ɔ̀ok 'to go out'.

2) If we analyze an English verb like 'bring', we will see that
at least two things are involved: (1) taking hold of something
and (2) moving it from one place to another in the direction of
the speaker. In Lao both of these actions are reflected in the
verb combination aw... máa (aw 'to take hold of' + máa 'to go
towards the speaker). aw... paj is used to indicate that the
action is away from the speaker.

   (a) Any object that is to be carried occurs after aw, thus
   aw pỳm paj 'take the book away', etc.

   (b) A series of other verbs may occur after aw... paj, etc.
   aw paj wáaŋ wàj phùn 'to take (it) over there and leave
   it'.

3) thîm lóŋ means literally 'to throw down' but corresponds to
English 'drop'.

4) páʔ means 'to leave something', thus páʔmía 'to divorce your
wife'; páʔwàj 'to leave something temporarily.'

APPLICATION

1. In the sentence khɔ̀j sì aw pàj wáaŋ wàj phùn, aw pàj wàaŋ wàj
is (a) a series of Nouns, (b) Verb + Preposition (c) a
series of verbs (d) none of these.

2. True or false? aw means 'to bring'.

3. wàj in the Verb Compound wáaŋ wàj indicates that (a) the
speaker has no further use for something, (b) He has further
use for it, (c) There is no reference to further use.

4. Match these Lao sentences with the English sentences:

(a) aw sɔ̌odam láaw pàj wàj phùn   (a) He didn't drop his
umbrella.

(b) láaw sì aw mûak pàj pá? wàj   (b) Is the policeman aiming
sǎj   his gun over there?

(c) láaw bɔɔ dàj thîm khán hɔ̌m   (c) Put his pencil over
láaw lóŋ   there.

(d) tamlûat sì njíŋ sǎj phùn bɔɔ   (d) Where is he going to
leave his hat?

Answers: 1c, 2false, 3b, 4a and c, b and d, c and a,
d and b.

CYCLE 21

M-1

<u>náj káp</u>	in the box
jᴆu sǎj? jᴆu náj káp nìi nìi bɔɔ?	Where? In this box here?
<u>thén lǎn tùu</u>	on top of the cabinet
jᴆu sǎj? jᴆu thén lǎn tùu nìi nìi bɔɔ?	Where? On top of this cabinet here?
<u>náj lìnsāk</u>	in the drawer
jᴆu sǎj? jᴆu náj lìnsāk nìi nìi bɔɔ?	Where? In this drawer here?
<u>náj kápɔɔn</u>	in the can
jᴆu sǎj? jᴆu náj kápɔɔn nìi nìi bɔɔ?	Where? In this can here?
<u>khâan màanān</u>	beside the bench
jᴆu sǎj? jᴆu khâan màanān nìi nìi bɔɔ?	Where? Beside this bench here?

M-2

<u>thǒn</u>	bag
jᴆu náj thǒn nàn hân	In that bag there.
<u>hɔɔ</u>	package
jᴆu náj hɔɔ nàn hân	In that package there.

81

kɛ̀ɛw, nűaj   bottle, classifier

  jűu nǎj kɛ̀ɛw nűaj nàn hân   In that bottle there.

cɔ̌ɔk, nűaj   glass, classifieŗ

  jűu nǎj cɔ̌ɔk nűaj nàn hân   In that glass there.

kátāa, nűaj   basket, classifier

  jűu nǎj kátāa nűaj nàn hân   In that basket there.

C-1

A. jűu sǎj? jűu nǎj káp   Where? In this box here?
   nìi nìi bɔɔ?
B. bɔ̌ɔ, jűu nǎj káp nàn hân   No. In that box there.

C-2

A. jűu sǎj? jűu nǎj kɛ̀ɛw   Where? In that bottle there?
   nàn hân bɔɔ?
B. bɔ̌ɔ, jűu nǎj kɛ̀ɛw nìi nìi   No. In this bottle here.

ການສະແດງໃຫ້ນັກຮຽນເຫັນດ້ວຍຕາຈະຊ່ອຍໃຫ້ນັກຮຽນຈຳໄດ້ໄວກວ່າການແປຄວາມໝາຍ. ດັ່ງນັ້ນ, ທ່ານຄວນຈະສະແດງໃຫ້ນັກຮຽນເບິ່ງໃນເວລາທີ່ຂະເຈົ້າກຳລັງລ້ວງຮຽນ. ຈະໂຕດກໍອີກກໍໄດ້ ແຕ່ຈົ່ງໃຫ້ຈຳກັດ!

82

NOTES

1) As can be seen in this grammatical exposition, nìi may function both as a **Determiner** and as an **Adverb** **of** **Place**:

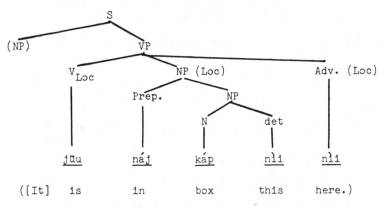

```
                          S
        ┌─────────────────┴──────────────┐
      (NP)                               VP
                    ┌──────────────┬──────────────────────────────┐
                  V_Loc         NP (Loc)                      Adv. (Loc)
                    │        ┌─────┴─────┐                         │
                    │      Prep.        NP                         │
                    │        │       ┌───┴───┐                     │
                    │        │       N      det                    │
                    │        │       │       │                     │
                   jɯu      náj     káp     nìi                   nìi

      ([It]        is       in      box     this                 here.)
```

'It's in this box here.'

A complete list of words functioning like nìi is given here:

Determiner		Adverb of Place	
nìi	'this'	nìi	'here'
		phìi	'around here'
nàn	'that'	hân	'there'
		phùn	'way over there'

APPLICATION

1. In the sentence <u>jꞟꞟ</u> náj <u>thƏŋ</u> <u>nàn</u> hân, <u>hân</u> is (a) NP
   (b) preposition   (c) determiner   (d) adverb.

2. In the sentence above <u>nàn</u> is (a) NP   (b) determiner
   (c) adverb   (d) none of these.

3. Complete the following sentences using the English translation
   as a guide:

   (a) jꞟꞟ náj kátaa nꞟaj _____ _____   'In that basket there.'

   (b) jꞟꞟ thƏŋ lǎŋ tùu _____ _____boo   'On top of this cabinet
                                               here?'

   (c) jꞟꞟ khâaŋ màanâŋ _____ _____boo   'Beside that bench way
                                               over there?'

   (d) jꞟꞟ _____?   'Where?'

   (e) jꞟꞟ _____   'Way over there.'

   (f) jꞟꞟ _____   'Near here.'

   (g) jꞟꞟ náj thƏŋ _____   'In that bag.'

   (h) jꞟꞟ náj kɛ̀ɛw _____ nàn hân   'In that bottle there.'

   (i) jꞟꞟ _____ _____ tùu nìi nìi boo 'On top of this cabinet
                                               here?'

Answers: 1d, 2b, 3(a)nàn hân (b)nìi phìi (or) nìi nìi (c) nàn
          phùn   (f) phìi (or nìi) (g)nàn (h)nꞟaj (i)thƏŋ lǎŋ

CYCLE 22

M-1

khǎj pátuu   open the door

    càw si khǎj pátuu nìi   Are you going to open this
    phìi bɔɔ?   door over here?

át pɔɔŋ-jìam   close the window

    càw si át pɔɔŋ-jìam nìi   Are you going to close this
    phìi bɔɔ?   window over here?

sǎj kácɛɛ lìnsāk   lock the drawer

    càw si sǎj kácɛɛ lìnsāk   Are you going to lock this
    nìi phìi bɔɔ?   drawer over here?

khǎj kácɛɛ hîip   unlock the trunk

    càw si khǎj kácɛɛ hîip   Are you going to unlock
    nìi phìi bɔɔ?   this trunk over here?

lóŋ khândaj   go down the stairs

    càw si lóŋ khândaj nìi   Are you going down these
    phìi bɔɔ?   stairs over here?

M-2

khǎj pátuu   open the door

    khɔ̂j si khǎj pátuu nàn phùn   I'm going to open that door
                                    over there.

pīan jaaŋ   change the tire

    khɔ̂j si pīan jaaŋ nàn phùn   I'm going to change that
                                    tire over there.

paj hǎa, phūu   go to,(classifier)

    khɔ̌j si paj hǎa phūu nàn
phùn

       I'm going to see that person over there.

sɔɔjlỹa, phūu   help,(classifier)

    khɔ̌j si sɔɔjlỹa phūu nàn
phùn

       I'm going to help that person over there.

tít-tɔɔ káp   contact, communicate with

    khɔ̌j si tít-tɔɔ káp phūu
nàn phùn

       I'm going to contact that person over there.

C-1

    A. càw si át pɔɔŋ-jìam nìi
phìi bɔɔ?

       Are you going to close this window over here?

    B. bɔɔ khɔ̌j si át pɔɔŋ-jìam
nàn phùn

       No. I'm going to close that window over there.

C-2

    A. càw si lóŋ khândaj nàn
phùn bɔɔ?

       Are you going to go down those stairs over there?

    B. bɔɔ, khɔ̌j si lóŋ khândaj
nìi phìi

       No. I'm going to go down these stairs over here.

ຊາຕາກຕາມຄຶດເຕັນວາມິດໄກໍຣິຍາຄໄໍໄດ ທີ່ຈະເປັນປໂຍດໄໍລັຍນັກຣຽນກໍໄຕບອກອະເຈົ້າຕໍມອິກກໍໄດ.
ແຕຄວາມາອະເຈົ້າຣຽນເອົາໃຫໍໄດ ບໍແມນວາເອົາໃຫໍໄປຊື່ໆ. ອອງໃຫໍນັກຣຽນປະຕິບັດຕາມດໍໄບອກບໍ່ໆຄ!

86

NOTES

1) phǐi and phùn may serve to indicate the location of the Noun Phrase they follow as in the example below:

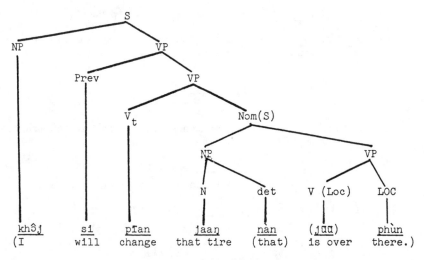

khɔ̌j	si	pɪan	jaaŋ	nan	(jŭu)	phùn
(I	will	change	that tire	(that)	is over	there.)

'I will change that tire over there.'

In this example the reference is to a particular thing which is in a particular place. If a person didn't understand the statement above, his question would be jaaŋ daj? 'Which tire?'

2) khǎj 'to open, unlock', át 'to close', and sǎj 'to put in' occur in constructions like these:

khǎj pátuu, pɔ̌ɔŋ-jlam, tùu, etc.   'to open the door, window, closet, etc.

khǎj kácɛɛ pátuu, hîip, tùu, lìnsǎk, etc.   'to unlock the door, trunk, closet, drawer, etc.'

87

át pátuu, pɔɔŋ-jìam, etc.   'to close the door, etc.'

sǎj kǎcɛɛ pátuu, hîip, tùu,   'to lock the door, etc.'
lìnsāk, etc.

3) paj hǎa + Person means 'to go to see a person'.

4) tít tɔɔ káp + Person means 'to contact someone (in person,
or by telephone, or some other way).'

APPLICATION

1. Complete the following sentences using the English translation
as a guide:

   (a) càw si khǎj _____ pátuu nìi phìi bɔɔ?
       'Are you going to unlock this door over here?'

   (b) khɔ̂j si paj _____ phɤan phɯɯ nàn phùn
       I'm going to see that friend over there.'

   (c) láaw si bɔɔ _____ tùu nìi bɔɔ?

       'Isn't he going to close this closet?'

   (d) khɔ̂j si tít tɔɔ _____ phɯu nàn phùn
       'I'm going to contact that person over there.'

   (e) khɔ̂j si _____ láaw
       'I'll help her.'

2. Read the Noun Phrase and answer the questions:

   (a) pátuu nìi phìi. ˙pátuu jɯɯ sǎj? _____

   (b) jaaŋ nàn phùn. jaaŋ jɯɯ sǎj? _____

Answers: 1(a)kácɛɛ,(b)hǎa, (c)át, (d)káp, (e)sɔɔj lỹa 2(a)jɯɯ
phìi (b)jɯɯ phùn

3. (c) phɯɯ nàn phùn. phɯɯ nàn jɯɯ sǎj?_____

   (d) pɔɔŋ jlam nìi phìi. pɔɔŋ jlam jɯɯ sǎj? _____

3. In the NP lìnsāk nìi phìi, phìi is (a) determiner   (b) adverb
   (c) verb (d) none of these.

4. In the NP above, phìi (a) indicates the location of lìnsāk,
   (b) modifies nìi, (c) has no grammatical relationship to
   lìnsāk nìi.

CYCLE 23

M-1

āan, pỳm, hŭa   to read, book, (classifier)

     càw si āan pỳm hŭa nìi   Are you going to read this
     jūu phìi bɔɔ?   book over here?

pɛɛŋ, lōt, khán.   to fix, car, (classifier)

     càw si pɛɛŋ lōt khán nìi   Are you going to fix this
     jūu phìi bɔɔ?   car over here?

sàj, khɔ̆ɔŋ, lāwnìi.   to use, thing, these

     càw si sàj khɔ̆ɔŋ lāwnìi   Are you going to use these
     jūu phìi bɔɔ?   things over here?

sāk, sỹa-nɔ̀ɔk, phỹyn.   to wash, jacket, (classifier)

     càw si sāk sỹa-nɔ̀ɔk phỹyn   Are you going to wash this
     nìi jūu phìi bɔɔ?   jacket over here?

M-2

āan, pỳm, hŭa   to read, book, (classifier)

     khɔ̂j si paj āan pỳm hŭa   I'm going to read this book
     nìi jūu phùn   over there.

phím, nǎŋsỹy   to print, type; letter

     khɔ̂j si paj phím nǎŋsỹy   I'm going to type this
     nìi jūu phùn   letter over there.

sỳy, cìa   to buy, paper

    khɔ̌j si paj sỳy cìa nìi   I'm going to buy this paper
    jūu phùn   over there.

sìicɛɛŋ, lỳaŋ   to explain; matter, about

    khɔ̌j si paj sìicɛɛŋ lỳaŋ   I'm going to explain this
    nìi jūu phùn   matter over there.

M-3

lɔ̌tdút, pɛɛŋ, khán   bulldozer; to repair, fix;
                                            (classifier)

    láaw si aw lɔ̌tdút khán   Is he going to bring that
    nàn máa pɛɛŋ jūu phìi bɔɔ?   bulldozer over here and
                                           fix it?

khȳaŋcák, nūaj, pák3op   engine, motor, machine,
                                           (classifier), to assemble

    láaw si aw khȳaŋcák nūaj   Is he going to bring that
    nàn máa pák3op jūu phìi   engine over here and
    bɔɔ?   assemble it?

mɔ̌ofáj, nūaj, sâak   battery (car), (classifier),
                                           charge (electricity)

    láaw si aw mɔ̌ofáj nūaj   Is he going to bring that
    nàn máa sâak jūu phìi bɔɔ?   battery over here and
                                           charge it?

thûaj, sáam, lāwnàn, làaŋ   bowl, plate, those, wash

    láaw si aw thûaj-sáam   Is he going to bring those
    lāwnàn máa làaŋ jūu phìi   dishes over here and wash
    bɔɔ?   them?

M-4

jaaŋ lɔ̌t, sên, tâap	tire (car),(classifier), patch
láaw sɨ aw jaaŋ lɔ̌t sên nàn paj tâap jɑ̄u phùn	He is going to take that tire over there and patch it.
tákiaŋ, nɑ̄aj, tàj	lamp,(classifier), to light
láaw sɨ aw tákiaŋ nɑ̄aj nàn paj tàj jɑ̄u phùn	He is going to take that lamp over there and light it.
phâahɔ̌m, lǎwnàn, cêɛkjaaj	blanket, those, to distribute
láaw sɨ aw phâahɔ̌m lǎwnàn paj cêɛkjaaj jɑ̄u phùn	He is going to take those blankets over there and distribute them.
tiaŋ, nɑ̄aj, tàŋ	bed,(classifier), to set up
láaw sɨ aw tiaŋ nɑ̄aj nàn paj tàŋ jɑ̄u phùn	He is going to take that bed over there and set it up.

C-1

A. càw sɨ āan pỳm hǔa nìi
jɑ̄u phǐi bɔɔ?

Are you going to read this book over there?

B. bɔɔ, khɔ̌j sɨ āan jɑ̄u
phùn

No. I'm going to read it over there.

C-2

A. láaw si aw lōtdút khán
   nàn máa pɛɛŋ jūu phìi
   bɔɔ?

Is he going to bring the
bulldozer over here and
fix it?

B. bɔ̄ɔ, láaw si aw paj pɛɛŋ
   jūu phùn

No. He is going to take it
over there and fix it.

C-3 (With reference to Cycles 20, 21 and 22)

Tutor: 'láaw si ãan pỳm hǔa
       nìi nìi.'

'He is going to read this
book here.'

A. láaw si hēt njǎŋ?   What is he going to do?

B. láaw si ãan pỳm   He is going to read a book.

A. láaw si ãan pỳm hǔa daj?   Which book is he going to
                                    read?

B. láaw si ãan pỳm hǔa nìi.   He is going to read this
                                    book.

A. pỳm hǔa nìi jūu sǎj?   Where is this book?

B. pỳm hǔa nìi jūu nìi   This book is here.

A. láaw si ãan pỳm jūu sǎj?   Where is he going to read
                                    the book?

B. khɔ̌j bɔ̄ɔ hùu   I don't know.

ຕາມລວງຕາງປໄຍກດ້າຍວງກັນກັບຢູ່ໃນຂໍ້(3)ນອນຈັກສານສີປໄຍກຂື່ວໆ ແລວຈິວພານັກຮຽນຝຶກຕັດໃນ
ຕຳນວງດຽວກັນ.

93

C-4

Tutor: 'láaw si pīaŋ jaaŋ   'He is going to change that
       sên nàn jūu phùn.'   tire over there.'

A. láaw si hēt njǎŋ?   What is he going to do?

B. láaw si pīan jaaŋ.   He is going to change a tire.

A. láaw si pīan jaaŋ sên daj?   Which tire is he going to
                                   change?

B. láaw si pīan jaaŋ sên nàn   He is going to change that
                                   tire.

A. láaw si pīan jūu sǎj?   Where is he going to change
                                   it?

B. láaw si pīan jūu phùn   He is going to change it
                                   over there.

A. jaaŋ sên nàn jūu sǎj?   Where is that tire?

B. khɔ̌j bɔ̄ɔ hùu   I don't know.

ຂໍ້(4)ນັກໃຫ້ໃຈວ່າຜຶກຫັດຄຳຫມວດຄຸວກັນກັບຂໍ້(3). ຕາມເຕີມຄວາມແຕກຕ່າງກັນໃນຄຳຖາມສຸດທ້າຍ
ຂອງຕົວສອງຂໍ້? ແລະນັກຣຽນຕານຄກກ່ຕືມຄືກັນບໍ?

NOTES

1) If instead of indicating the location of a particular object
(pátuu nìi phìi), the reference is to the location of a
particular activity, jɯ̄ɯ + LOC is attached to the main VP
as illustrated below:

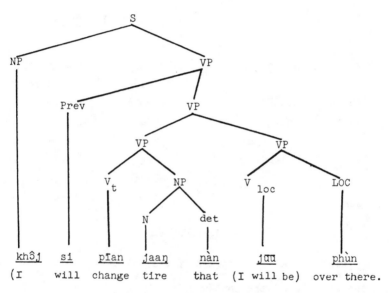

(I   will   change tire   that   (I will be) over there.

'I will change that tire (in that spot) over there.'

The emphasis here is on where the changing will take place
not on the particular tire to be changed;   hence, the question
which would elicit this response is:

càw sì pīan (jaaŋ) jɯ̄ɯ sǎj   'Where will you change the tire?'

95

2) lāw 'group, bunch' is frequently used with Count Nouns to indicate 'plurality'.

> khɔ̌oŋ lāw nǐi   'these things'
>
> phâahɔ̌m lāw nàn   'those blankets'

3) A list of unit classifiers and the nouns they are used with is given below:

Classifier		Noun Referent	
hǔa	'head'	pȳm	'book'
khán	'vehicle'	lōt	'automobile'
		lōtdút	'bulldozer'
phȳyn	'cloth'	sȳa nɔ̀ɔk	'jacket'
nūaj	'unit' (It is used for fruit,	khyáŋcák	'engine'
		tákiaŋ	'lamp'
	machines,	tiaŋ	'bed'
	furniture, equipment, etc.	mɔ̂ɔfáj	'battery'
sên	'string'	jaaŋ (lōt)	'tire'

APPLICATION

1. In each of the following sentences indicate whether the emphasis is on the location of the NP or the VP by writing NP or VP in the blank after the sentence:

   (a) khɔ̂j si paj āān pȳm hǔa nǐi jūu phùn _____

   (b) khɔ̂j si paj hǎa phūu nàn phùn _____

   (c) càw si lóŋ khândaj nǐi phǐi bɔɔ? _____

   (d) láaw si aw thûaj-sáam lāwnàn máa làaŋ jūu phǐi bɔɔ? _____

   (e) càw si sàj khɔ̌oŋ lāwnǐi jūu phǐi bɔɔ? _____

Answers: 1(a)VP (b)NP (c)NP (d)VP (e)VP

2. Complete the following sentences using the English as a guide:

(a) càw si aan pỳm _____ nìi bɔɔ?
    'Are you going to read this book?'

(b) khɔ̀j si paj _____ lỳaŋ nìi jʊʊ phùn
    'I'm going to explain this matter over there.'

(c) aw lɔ̃tdút _____ _____ máa pɛɛŋ jʊʊ phìi
    'Bring that bulldozer over here and fix it.'

(d) láaw si aw phâahŏm lāwnàn paj cêɛkjaaj _____ _____
    'He is going to take those blankets over there and
    distribute them.'

(e) khɔ̀j si sāk sŷanɔ̀ɔk _____ _____ jʊʊ phìi
    'I'm going to wash this jacket over here.'

(f) láaw si aw jaaŋ lɔ̃t _____ nàn paj _____ jʊʊ phùn
    'He's going to take that tire over there and patch it.'

Answers: 2(a)hŭa (b)sìicɛɛŋ (c)khán nàn (d)jʊʊ phùn (e)phŷyn
          nìi (f) sên /tâap

97

CYCLE 24

M-1

sǔun   zero

   sǔun káp nȳŋ pen nȳŋ   Zero and one is one.

nȳŋ   one

   nȳŋ káp nȳŋ pen sɔ̌ɔŋ   One and one is two.

sɔ̌ɔŋ   two

   sɔ̌ɔŋ káp nȳŋ pen sǎam   Two and one is three.

sǎam   three

   sǎam káp nȳŋ pen sīi   Three and one is four.

sīi   four

   sīi káp nȳŋ pen hâa   Four and one is five.

hâa   five

   hâa káp nȳŋ pen hók   Five and one is six.

hók   six

   hók káp nȳŋ pen cét   Six and one is seven.

cét   seven

   cét káp nȳŋ pen pɛ̂ɛt   Seven and one is eight.

pɛ̂ɛt   eight

   pɛ̂ɛt káp nȳŋ pen kàw   Eight and one is nine.

kàw   nine

   kàw káp nȳŋ pen síp   Nine and one is ten.

M-2

nȳŋ   one

    síp káp nȳŋ pen síp-ét   Ten and one is eleven.

nȳŋ   one

    síp-ét káp nȳŋ pen sípsɔ̌ɔŋ   Eleven and one is twelve.

pêɛt·   eight

    sípsɔ̌ɔŋ káp pêɛt pen sáaw   Twelve and eight is twenty.

nȳŋ   one

    sáaw káp nȳŋ pen sáaw-ét   Twenty and one is twenty one.

nȳŋ   one

    sáaw-ét káp nȳŋ pen sáawsɔ̌ɔŋ   Twenty-one and one is twenty two.

pêɛt   eight

    sáawsɔ̌ɔŋ káp pêɛt pen sǎamsíp   Twenty-two and eight is thirty.

nȳŋ   one

    sǎamsíp káp nȳŋ pen sǎamsíp-ét   Thirty and one is thirty-one.

nȳŋ   one

    sǎamsíp-ét káp nȳŋ pen   Thirty-one and one is thirty two.
    sǎamsípsɔ̌ɔŋ

kàw   nine

    sǎamsípsɔ̌ɔŋ káp kàw pen   Thirty-two and nine is forty one.
    sɨ̀isíp-ét

hâasíp-ét | fifty one

  sĭisíp-ét káp hâasíp-ét
pen kàwsípsɤɔŋ

Forty-one and fifty-one is ninety two.

pɛ̂ɛt | eight

  kàwsípsɤɔŋ káp pɛ̂ɛt pen
nɣ̄ŋ hɔ̀ɔj

Ninety-two and eight is one hundred.

kàw hɔ̀ɔj | nine hundred

  nɣ̄ŋ hɔ̀ɔj káp kàw hɔ̀ɔj pen
nɣ̄ŋ phán

One hundred and nine hundred is one thousand.

nɣ̄ŋ | one

  nɣ̄ŋ phán káp nɣ̄ŋ pen nɣ̄ŋ
phán káp nɣ̄ŋ

One thousand and one is one thousand and one.

kàwsípkàw | ninety nine

  nɣ̄ŋ phán káp nɣ̄ŋ káp kàwsíp
kàw pen phán-ét lɣ̆y nɣ̄ŋ
phán nɣ̄ŋ hɔ̀ɔj

One thousand and one and ninety nine is one thousand one hundred.

phán-ét | one thousand one

  phán-ét káp phán-ét pen sɤ̆ɔŋ
phán sɤ̆ɔŋ

One thousand and one and one thousand is two thousand and one.

M-3

sɔ̌oŋ, hâa	two, five
sɔ̌on kȧp hâa pen thāwdaj?	What is two and five?
sípsɪ̄i, sǎam	fourteen, three
sípsɪ̄i kȧp sǎam pen thāwdaj?	What is fourteen and three?
sáawhók, cét	twenty-six, seven
sáaw hók kȧp cét pen thāwdaj?	What is twenty six and seven?
sǎam síp sɔ̌oŋ, sɔ̌oŋ	thirty-two, two
sǎm síp sɔ̌oŋ kȧp sɔ̌oŋ pen thāwdaj?	What is thirty two and two?
hâa síp-ét, hók	fifty-one, six
hâa síp-ét kȧp hók pen thāwdaj?	What is fifty one and six?

C-1

A. ... kȧp ... pen thāwdaj?   ... and ... is how much?
B. ... kȧp ... pen .... and ... is ... .

C-2

A. ... kȧp ... pen ... mɛ̄ɛn bɔɔ?   ... and ... is ...,isn't it?
B. bɔ̄ɔ mɛ̄ɛn, ... kȧp ... pen ...   No, it isn't. .. and --- is
                                          ...

ย่าสอมมักธรมมัยตามลำดับຂອງຕົວເລກ. ຈີ່ງໃຫ້ນັກธรมตัดยอกຕົວເລກເປັນมาสาลาวย่างไว โดย
ตะเจ้ายตอวดคตຖิ่วลำดับຂອງຕົວເລກ. ตามจะสอมภามบอก, อัย, คุม, ตาม ใຫ້ຂະเจ้ากำได.

101

NOTES

1) The Lao numerical system is a decimal system and with a few exceptions complex numbers are made by multiplying by and/or adding to the numbers from 1 to 10.

   The numbers from 1 to 10 are: nɣ̄ŋ '1', sɔ̌ɔŋ '2', sǎam '3', sīī '4', hâa '5', hók '6', cét '7', pɛ̂ɛt '8', kaw '9', síp '10'.

   Multiples of ten (except for 20) are made by putting the multiplier in front of ten, thus 30 is sǎam síp (3x10), 70 is cét síp (7x10), etc. Numbers to be added to ten or multiples of ten occur afterwards, thus 13 is síp sǎam (10+3), 34 is sǎam síp sīī (3x10+4), etc. 20 is sáaw; 22 is sáaw sɔ̌ɔŋ, etc.

   The number one alone is nɣ̄ŋ, but in compounds it is -ét, thus 21 is sáaw-ét; 51, hâa síp-ét; 61, hók síp-ét, etc.

   100 is nɣ̄ŋ hɔ̀ɔj (lɔ̀ɔj) or hɔ̀ɔj (lɔ̀ɔj), but 101 is hɔ̀ɔj ét (lɔ̀ɔj ét) and 400 is sīī hɔ̀ɔj (sīī lɔ̀ɔj). hɔ̀ɔj and lɔ̀ɔj are interchangeable. phán-ét means '1100'; 1001 is phán káp nɣ̄ŋ.

2) káp means 'and' or 'plus' when used as a connective between Nouns, NP, and numbers. It indicates that something has been added.

   (1) sɔ̌ɔŋ káp sǎam pen hâa   'two plus three is five'

   (2) náaj khúu káp nākhían   'the teacher and students'

   káp is not used as a sentence connective.

3) thāwdaj 'how much, how many' is used to request a numerical or quantitative response:

   Q: sǎam síp sɔ̌ɔŋ káp sɔ̌ɔŋ pen thāwdaj
        'How much is 32 and 2?'

   A: sǎam síp sīī.   '34'.

APPLICATION

1. If the correct Lao form is written after the arabic number, write 'correct' after the Lao; if it is incorrect, write in the correct Lao form.

(a) 93 : kàw síp sǎam   _____

(b) 27 : sɔ̌oŋ síp cét   _____

(c) 71 : cét síp nʄŋ   _____

(d) 58 : pɛ̀ɛt síp hâa   _____

(e) 101 : hɔ̀ɔj ét   _____

(f) 24 : sáaw sɪ̌i   _____

(g) 605 : hók lɔ̀ɔj hâa   _____

(h) 42 : sɪ̌i sɔ̌oŋ   _____

(i) 1 : ét   _____

(j) 25 : sáaw síp hâa   _____

2. Write in the correct answers to the following problems. Use arabic numbers.

(a) pɛ̀ɛt káp hók pen   _____

(b) sǎam síp ét káp sɪ̌i síp kàw pen   _____

(c) hâa hɔ̀ɔj káp cét síp cét pen   _____

(d) sǔun káp sǔun pen   _____

(e) sáaw kàw káp pɛ̀ɛt síp cét pen   _____

Answers: 1(a)correct (b)sáaw cét (c)cét síp-ét (d)hâa síp
pɛ̀ɛt (e)correct (f)correct (g)correct (h)sɪ̌i síp
sɔ̌oŋ (i)nʄn (j)sáaw hâa   2(a)14 (b)80 (c)577
(d)0 (e)116

CYCLE 25

M-1

m̀yy n̂li	today
m̀yy n̂li mɛɛ̀n wán njǎŋ?	What day is today?
m̀yy-ȳyn	tomorrow
m̀yy-ȳyn mɛɛ̀n wán njǎŋ?	What day is tomorrow?
m̀yy-hýy	the day after tomorrow
m̀yy-hýy mɛɛ̀n wán njǎŋ?	What day is the day after tomorrow?
m̀yy-wáan n̂li	yesterday
m̀yy-wáan n̂li mɛɛ̀n wán njǎŋ?	What day was yesterday?
m̀yy-sýyn	day before yesterday
m̀yy-sýyn mɛɛ̀n wán njǎŋ?	What day was the day before yesterday?
m̀yy kɔɔ̌n	three days ago
m̀yy kɔɔ̌n mɛɛ̀n wán njǎŋ?	What day was three days ago?
sǐi m̀yy kɔɔ̌n	four days ago
sǐi m̀yy kɔɔ̌n mɛɛ̀n wán njǎŋ?	What day was four days ago?

M-2

wán-aathǐt	Sunday
m̀yy n̂li mɛɛ̀n wán-aathǐt	Today is Sunday.

104

wán-can	Monday
m̀yy nìi mɛ̌ɛn wán-can	Today is Monday.
wán-aŋkháan	Tuesday
m̀yy nìi mɛ̌ɛn wán-aŋkháan	Today is Tuesday.
wán-phūt	Wednesday
m̀yy nìi mɛ̌ɛn wán-phūt	Today is Wednesday.
wán-phāhát	Thursday
m̀yy nìi mɛ̌ɛn wán-phāhát	Today is Thursday.
wán-súk	Friday
m̀yy nìi mɛ̌ɛn wán-súk	Today is Friday.
wán-sǎw	Saturday
m̀yy nìi mɛ̌ɛn wán-sǎw	Today is Saturday.

C-1

A. m̀yy nìi mɛ̌ɛn wán njǎŋ?   What day is today?
B. m̀yy nìi mɛ̌ɛn ....   Today is ....

C-2

A. m̀yy-wáan nìi mɛ̌ɛn ...,   Yesterday was ..., right?
   mɛ̌ɛn bɔɔ?
B. bɔɔ mɛ̌ɛn, m̀yy-wáan nìi   No, yesterday was ......
   mɛ̌ɛn ......

ການສອນອ້ມກ໌ຮັດດົ່ວດຣວກັນກັບເລກ ຈົ່ງໃຫ້ນັກຣຽນຈົ່ມຕ່າງວງໂດຍຍົກອວດກຳນົ່ວຈຳວລກັນກ່ອນ.

LAO BASIC COURSE

NOTES

1) m̀yy 'day' is used in constructions indicating relative time,
thus: m̀yy nìi 'today', m̀yy ɣ̄yn 'tomorrow', etc. m̀yy is also
used when referring to a period of time, thus sɔ̌ɔŋ m̀yy 'two
days' khǝŋ m̀yy 'half a day', etc.

wán 'day' is used when giving the names of the days of the
week: wán aathɪ́t 'Sunday', wán aŋkháan 'Tuesday', etc.

2) When asking the day of the week, m̀yy nìi mɛɛn wán njǎŋ 'What
day is today?' is used.

3) kɔ̄ɔn 'before', ago' is used to refer to a specific time in
the past. sɪ̀i m̀yy kɔ̄ɔn 'four days ago', etc.

APPLICATION

1. Starting with the assumption that today is Wednesday fill in
the blanks:

(a) m̀yy hýy mɛɛn   _____

(b) sɪ̀i m̀yy kɔ̄ɔn mɛɛn   _____

(c) m̀yy wáan nìi mɛɛn   _____

(d) m̀yy nìi mɛɛn   _____

(e) m̀yy sýn mɛɛn   _____

(f) m̀yy ɣ̄yn mɛɛn   _____

Answers: 1(a)wán-súk (b)wán-sǎw (c)wán-aŋkháan (d)wán-phʊt
(e)wán-can (f)wán-phāhát

106

2) Starting with the assumption that today is <u>Sunday</u>, fill in the blanks below:

(a) _____ mɛɛn wán-aŋkháan

(b) _____ mɛɛn wán-sǎw

(c) _____ mɛɛn wán-súk

(d) _____ mɛɛn wán-aathít

(e) _____ mɛɛn wán-phǎhát

(f) _____ mɛɛn wán-can

(g) _____ mɛɛn wán-phút

Answers: 2(a)mỳy-hýy (b)mỳy-wáan nìi (c)mỳy-sỳyn (d)mỳy nìi (e) myy kɔɔn (f)mỳy ɣɣn (g)síi mỳy kɔɔn

CYCLE 26

M-1

mɔ̌kkáráa	January

mɔ̌kkáráa mɛ̄ɛn dyan thíi nɏ̄ŋ,
tɔ̄ɔ paj mɛ̄ɛn dyan njǎŋ?

January is the first month.
What's the next month?

kumpháa — February

kumpháa mɛ̄ɛn dyan thíi sɔ̌ɔŋ
tɔ̄ɔ paj mɛ̄ɛn dyan njǎŋ?

February is the second month.
What's the next?

míináa — March

míináa mɛ̄ɛn dyan thíi sǎam,
tɔ̄ɔ paj mɛ̄ɛn dyan njǎŋ?

March is the third month.
What's the next?

méesǎa — AprÍl

méesǎa mɛ̄ɛn dyan thíi sÍi,
tɔ̄ɔ paj mɛ̄ɛn dyan njǎŋ?

April is the fourth month.
What's the next?

phɏ̄tsápháa — May

phɏ̄tsápháa mɛ̄ɛn dyan thíi
hâa, tɔ̄ɔ paj mɛ̄ɛn dvan njǎŋ?

May is the fifth month.
What's the next?

mÍthúnáa — June

mÍthúnáa mɛ̄ɛn dyan thíi hók,
tɔ̄ɔ paj mɛ̄ɛn dyan njǎŋ?

June is the sixth month.
What's the next?

kɔɔrākádaa — July

kɔɔrākádaa mɛ̄ɛn dyan thíi
cét, tɔ̄ɔ paj mɛ̄ɛn dyan njǎŋ?

July is the seventh month.
What's the next month?

síŋhǎa   August

síŋhǎa mɛɛn dyan thíi pêɛt,   August is the eighth month.
tɔɔ paj mɛɛn dyan njǎŋ?   What's the next?

M-2

mǒkkáráa   January

  lǎŋcâak dyan mǒkkáráa mɛɛn   The month after January is
  dyan kumpháa   February.

kumpháa   February

  lǎŋcâak dyan kumpháa mɛɛn   The month after February is
  dyan míináa   March.

míináa   March

  lǎŋcâak dyan míináa mɛɛn   The month after March is April.
  dyan méesǎa

méesǎa   April

  lǎŋcâak dyan méesǎa mɛɛn   The month after April is May.
  dyan phɣtsápháa

phɣtsápháa   May

  lǎŋcâak dyan phɣtsápháa   The month after May is June.
  mɛɛn dyan míthúnáa

míthúnáa   June

  lǎŋcâak dyan míthúnáa mɛɛn   The month after June is July.
  dyan kɔɔrākádaa

109

M-3

mɔ̌kkáráa	January
kɔ̌on dyan mɔ̌kkáráa mɛɛn dyan thánwáa	The month before January is December.
thánwáa	December
kɔ̌on dyan thánwáa mɛɛn dyan phȳtsácíkaa	The month before December is November.
phȳtsácíkaa	November
kɔ̌on dyan phȳtsácíkaa mɛɛn dyan túláa	The month before November is October.
túláa	October
kɔ̌on dyan túláa mɛɛn dyan kannjáa	The month before October is September.
kannjáa	September
kɔ̌on dyan kannjáa mɛɛn dyan sǐŋhǎa	The month before September is August.
sǐŋhǎa	August
kɔ̌on dyan sǐŋhǎa mɛɛn dyan kɔɔrākádaa	The month before August is July.

110

C-1

A. ... mɛɛn dyan thíi ...,tɔɔ   ... is the ... month.

paj mɛɛn dyan njǎŋ?   What's the next?

B. tɔɔ paj mɛɛn dyan ....   The next is ....

C-2

A. lǎŋcâak dyan ... mɛɛn   What's the month after....?

dyan njǎŋ?

B. lǎŋcâak dyan ... mɛɛn   The month after ... is ...

dyan ......

C-3

A. kɔɔn dyan ... mɛɛn dyan   What's the month before ...?

njǎŋ?

B. kɔɔn dyan ... mɛɛn dyan ...   Before ... is ...

ໃຫມຍາຍາມໃຊ້ປະຕິບັຕິມປະກອບໃນການສອນ ແລວໃຫມັກຮຽນຕັດໃຈເປັນພາສາລາວ. ຄຳວ່າ "ຕລິວຈາກ",
"ກອນ", "ຕໍ່ໄປ" ແລະ "ຕິ" ຈະນຳໄປໃຊ້ຝຶກຫັດກັບດາຫອນວຸທຮຽນມາແລວກໍໄດ.

111

NOTES

1) The names of the months in Lao are (in order)! mōkkáráa, kumpháa, míináa, méesǎa, phȳtsápháa, mīthúnáa, kɔɔrākádaa, sǐŋhǎa, kannjáa, túláa, phȳtsácíkaa, thánwáa.

2) Ordinal numbers (first, second, etc.) are formed by placing thíi before Cardinal numbers (one, two, etc.): thíi nȳŋ 'first', thíi sǎam 'third', thíi hóksíp '60th', thíi pêɛtsípkàw '89th', etc.

3) tɔɔ paj 'next' is a Verb Phrase made up of tɔɔ 'to join, extend' + paj '(to go) forward' (in this type of construction). tɔɔ paj may be used to indicate an extension in time or space. In time expressions it normally refers to future time.

   tɔɔ paj mɛɛn dyan njǎŋ   'What month is next?'

4) lǎŋcâak 'after' is a Verb Phrase and refers to time. It may be followed by NP, VP, or S.

   With NP: lǎŋcâak dyan mōkkáráa   'After January'

   With VP: lǎŋcâak kin khâw   'After eating'

   With S: lǎŋcâak láaw paj   'After he went to the
             tálâat...   market...'

5) kɔɔn 'before, previous' is a verb. It refers only to time. It may be followed by NP, VP, or S.

   Before NP: kɔɔn dyan thánwáa   'Before December'

   Before VP: kɔɔn paj kin khâw   'Before going to eat'

   Before S: kɔɔn láaw paj ...   'Before he went...'

112

APPLICATION

1. Fill in the blanks with the name of the month:
   (a) dyan thíi hók mɛɛn dyan _____
   (b) dyan thíi síp-ét mɛɛn dyan _____
   (c) dyan thíi sɔ̌ɔŋ mɛɛn dyan _____
   (d) dyan thíi hâa mɛɛn dyan _____
   (e) dyan thíi pɛ̂ɛt mɛɛn dyan _____
   (f) dyan thíi sɪɪ mɛɛn dyan _____

2. Fill in the blanks with the number of the month:
   (a) dyan thíi _____ mɛɛn dyan míináa
   (b) dyan thíi _____ mɛɛn dyan mɔ̌kkáráa
   (c) dyan thíi _____ mɛɛn dyan túláa
   (d) dyan thíi _____ mɛɛn dyan kɔɔrãkádaa
   (e) dyan thíi _____ mɛɛn dyan kannjáa
   (f) dyan thíi _____ mɛɛn dyan thánwáa

3. Fill in the blanks with tɔ̌ɔ paj, kɔɔn, or lǎŋcâak as required:
   (a) _____ dyan phy̆tsácíkaa mɛɛn dyan túláa
   (b) _____ dyan kumpháa mɛɛn dyan míináa
   (c) kannjáa mɛɛn dyan thíi kàw. _____ mɛɛn dyan túláa

Answers: 1(a)mɪthúnáa (b)túláa (c)kumpháa (d)phy̆tsápháa
(e)sɪ̌ŋhǎa (f)méesǎa, 2(a)sǎam(b)nȳŋ (c)síp (d)cét(e)kàw
(f)síp sɔ̌ɔŋ, 3(a)kɔɔn (b)lǎŋcâak (c)tɔ̌ɔpaj

113

CYCLE 27

M-1

mỳy nìi	today
mỳy nìi mɛɛn wánthíi thāwdaj?	What's the date today?
wán-kə̂ət	birthday
wán-kə̂ət càw mɛɛn wánthíi thāwdaj?	What's your birth date?
pii-mǎj láaw	Lao New Year
pii-mǎj láaw mɛɛn wánthíi thāwdaj?	What's the date of the Lao New Year?
wán êekkáràat	Independence Day
wán êekkáràat mɛɛn wánthíi thāwdaj?	What's the date of Independence Day?
wán rāthāthámmānúun	Constitution Day
wán rāthāthámmānúun mɛɛn wánthíi thāwdaj?	What's the date of Constitution Day?
wán kammǎkɔɔn	Labor Day
wán kammǎkɔɔn mɛɛn wánthíi thāwdaj?	What's the date of Labor Day?

M-2

kə̂ət	born
càw kə̂ət wánthíi thāwdaj?	What date were you born?

114

tɛ̄ɛŋɲáan	get married
càw tɛ̄ɛŋɲáan wánthíi thāwdaj?	What date did you get married on?
míi nāt	have a date
càw míi nāt wánthíi thāwdaj?	What date do you have a date on?
ɔ̄ok dəəntháaŋ	begin a trip
càw ɔ̄ok dəəntháaŋ wánthíi thāwdaj?	What date did you begin your trip?
paj/máa hɔ̀ɔt	arrive
càw paj hɔ̀ɔt wánthíi thāwdaj?	What date did you arrive there?

C-1

A. mỳy nìi mɛ̄ɛn wánthíi thāwdaj?　　What's the date today?

B. mỳy nìi mɛ̄ɛn wánthíi síps̄ii　　Today is the 14th of May 1970.
   phȳtsápháa pii phán kàw
   hɔ̀ɔj cét-síp

C-2

A. càw kə̀ət wánthíi thāwdaj?　　What date were you born?

B. khɔ̄j kə̀ət wánthíi síp hâa　　I was born on the fifteenth
   mɔ̄kkáráa pii phán kàw　　of January nineteen forty-one.
   hɔ̀ɔj s̄iisíp-ét

115

C-3

A. càw sí ɔ̀ɔk dəəntháaŋ   You are going to begin your
   wánthíi kàw mɛ̄ɛn bɔɔ?   trip on the ninth, right?

B. bɔ̀ɔ mɛ̄ɛn, khɔ̂j sí ɔ̀ɔk   No. I'll begin my trip on
   dəəntháaŋ wánthíi síp   the tenth of March.
   míináa

ຊາມວັນເກີດຂອງບຸກຄົນຕາງໆຫລົວນທີ່ສໍາຄັນຕາງໆເບົ່ວໆ! ຕໍ່ໄປກໍໃຫນັກຮຽນຖາມກັນໂດຍມາຍຄຣູ
ເປັນຜູດອບກ່ອກກ່າມເວົ້າຂອງຂະເຈົ້າ. ຈົ່ງພຍາຍາມໃຈຄໍທີ່ຮຽມມາແລວໃຫຫລາຍໆ.

NOTES

1) wán thíi thǎwdaj (lit. the how many-eth day) 'What day?' is
   used in asking for dates. In the response the sequence of
   elements is (a) day (b) month (c) year.

   Q: càw kə̀ət wánthíi thǎwdaj   'When were you born?'

   A: khɔ̂j kə̀ət wánthíi síp hâa mɔ̌kkáráa   'I was born January
      pii phán kàw hɔ̀ɔj sɪ̄ı síp ét   15, 1941.'

   (a) day: wánthíi síp hâa   'the fifteenth'
   (b) month: mɔ̌kkáráa   'January'
   (c) year: pii phán kàw hɔ̀ɔj sɪ̄ı   (Lit. year thousand
              síp-ét   nine hundred forty
                                          one) '1941'

   pii 'year' always precedes the designation for year. The
   year is always given thusly: phán ... hɔ̀ɔj ... (one thousand
   ... hundred ...) and never: síp kaw hɔ̀ɔj ... (nineteen
   hundred ...).

116

APPLICATION

1. On a separate piece of paper write out in full the dates given below, then check your answers:

(a) May 7, 1931   (b) September 23, 1919
(c) February 1, 1947   (d) December 25, 1963
(e) August 30, 1926   (f) April 14, 1970

Answers: (a)wánthíi cét dyan phɣtsápháa phán kàw hɔ̀ɔj
sǎam síp-ét (b)wánthíi sáaw sǎam dyan kannjáa
phán kàw hɔ̀ɔj síp kàw (c)wánthíi nɣŋ dyan kumpháa
phán kàw hɔ̀ɔj sɪɪ síp cét (d)wánthíi sáaw hâa dyan
thánwáa phán kàw hɔ̀ɔj hók síp sǎam (e)wánthíi sǎam
síp dyan siŋhǎa phán kàw hɔ̀ɔj sáaw hók (f)wánthíi
síp sɪɪ dyan méesǎa phán kàw hɔ̀ɔj cét síp

117

CYCLE 28

M-1

m̀ȳy	day
càw sì paj m̀ȳy daj?	When (what day) will you go?
pii	year
càw sì paj pii daj?	When (what year) will you go?
aathɪ̀t	week
càw sì paj aathɪ̀t daj?	When (which week) will you go?
ookâat	occasion
càw sì paj ookâat daj?	When (on what occasion) will you go?
wéeláa	time
càw sì paj wéeláa daj?	When will you go?
sɑ̄amóoŋ	hour
càw sì paj sɑ̄amóoŋ daj?	Which hour will you go?
dyan	month
càw sì paj dyan daj?	What month will you go?

M-2

sɑ̄amóoŋ thíi sɤ̌oŋ	second hour
khɔ̂j sì paj sɑ̄amóoŋ thíi sɤ̌oŋ	I will go at the second hour.

118

aathīt nâa   next week

    khɔ̂j sỉ paj aathīt nâa   I will go next week.

pii nâa   next year

    khɔ̂j sỉ paj pii nâa   I will go next year.

mỳy ỹyr.   tomorrow

    khɔ̂j sỉ paj mỳy ỹyn   I will go tomorrow.

nǎj ookâat bun thàat lǔaŋ   on the occasion of That Luang
                              festival

    khɔ̂j sỉ paj nǎj ookâat bun   I will go on the occasion
    thàat lǔaŋ   of That Luang festival.

wéeláa càw máa   when you come

    khɔ̂j sỉ paj wéeláa càw máa   I will go when you come.

M-3

khâw hóoŋhían   enter school

    mỳy daj càw sỉ khâw   When will you enter
    hóoŋhían?   school?

ɔ̀ɔk lùuk   give birth

    mỳy daj càw sỉ ɔ̀ɔk lùuk ?   When will you have your baby?

cὲɛŋ tamlûat   report to the police

    mỳy daj càw sỉ cὲɛŋ   When will you report to
    tamlûat ?   the police?

aw khỹyn hâj láaw   return (it) to him

    mỳy daj càw sỉ aw khỹyn   When will you return it
    hâj láaw ?   to him?

119

hían sǎmrēt   finish study

   mỳy daj càw si hían sǎmrēt   When will you finish
                                  your studies?

M-4

   mỳy nìi càw si hēt njǎŋ?   What are you going to do today?

   aathīt nìi càw si paj sǎj?   Where are you going to go this
                                 week?

   sūamóoŋ nìi càw si hían njǎŋ?   What are you going to study
                                 this hour?

   wéeláa nìi càw phǎk jūu sǎj?   Where are you staying at the
                                 present time?

paj thīaw   to go on a pleasure trip (or walk)

   pii nìi láaw si paj thīaw   Where is he going to go on
   sǎj?   a pleasure trip this year?

sɔ̌ɔn   to teach

   mỳy wáncan nìi láaw si   Who is she going to teach
   sɔ̌ɔn phǎj?   this Monday?

M-5

týkbét   to fish

   aathīt nìi khɔ̂j si paj   This week I am going to go
   týkbét   fishing.

kinkhâw pāa   picnic

   aathīt nìi khɔ̂j si paj   This week I'm going to go
   kinkhâw pāa.   picnicking.

120

khéɛm thālée	seashore
aathīt nìi kh3j si paj khéɛm thālée	This week I'm going to go to the seashore.
làa sát	hunt
aathīt nìi kh3j si paj làa sát	This week I'm going to go hunting.
thātsánáacɔɔn	sightseeing
aathīt nìi kh3j si paj thātsánáacɔɔn	This week I'm going to go sightseeing.
tāaŋ pátheet	foreign country
aathīt nìi kh3j si paj tāaŋ pátheet	This week I'm going abroad.

C-1

(mỳy)	day
A. càw si paj mỳy daj?	{ When { What day are you going?
(mỳy nìi)	today
B. kh3j si paj mỳy nìi	I am going today.

C-2

(láaw)	she
A. láaw si paj bɔɔ?	Is she going?
B. paj	Yes, she is going.

(wéeláa)   time

A. láaw si paj wéeláa daj?   When is she going?

(phùakháw paj)   we go

B. láaw si paj wéeláa   She is going when we go.
   phùakháw paj

C-3

A. mỳy nìi càw si hēt njǎŋ?   What are you going to do
                                  today?

B. mỳy nìi khɔ̀j si paj   Today I'm going to go
   kinkhâw pāa   picnicking.

C-4

A. pii daj càw si hían   What year will you complete
   sǎmrēt   your studies?

B. khɔ̀j si hían sǎmrēt pii nâa   I'll complete my studies
                                  next year.

ບົດນຍາວແຕ່ຈັກຫມອຍ. ສະນັ້ນ ຈິ່ງເຮັດໃຫແນໃຈວ່ານັກຮຽນຂອງທ່ານເຂົ້າໃຈຢ່າງລະອຽດ. ຜູ້ຮຽນ
ປາກຂໍແນນນຫ່ອິກເຕຶ່ອນວ່າ ການສອນ"ໃຊ້ເກີລ"ນີ້ ຄົນເບຍ່ວເຜິນວແລວຄືຈະວາຍວ. ແຕ່ຖ້າຈະໃຫໄດ
ຜົນຢ່າງພໃຈແລວ ນາຍຄຣຈະຕອງຄິດປູຊເມືວ່າ ກອນຫນັກຮຽນຈະເສານມາຄວາມສາຫນຸ່ເຈຈຈ່ານຮຽນໄດ
ຢ່າວສະນາຍແລະແນນນຮມ ຂະເຈ້າຈະຕອງມີຄວາມເຊື່ອຫມັ້ນໃນຄົວເວ; ການເວ້າຢ່າວຄ່ະຖຸກຄະດຶກ
ຍອມສະແຄງໃຫເຫັນເຖິງຄວາມຫມັ້ນໃຈ ແລະຄວາມເຊື່ອມລາວໃນຄວາມຮູ້ວຫ່ອວຫຸຜູ້ເວ້າ. ເນຶ່ອ
ເຫັນອາເປັນຄ່ວນແລວ ກໍຈິ່ວພານັກຮຽນຂອງທ່ານເວ້າຫຼວຍໄບກໍນ່ລໍຮຽນເສັ່ຣກອນຈ່ວຮຽນອັນໃຫມຕໄປ.

NOTES

1) Time Expressions, such as aathīt nâa, etc. may occur in sentence initial or sentence final position with little or no difference in meaning. Their position is determined by the type of sentence they occur in. (1) When they occur in sentences with njǎŋ or sǎj as question words, they are in sentence initial position:

Q: mὺy nîi càw si hět njǎŋ   'What are you going to do today?'

A: mὺy nîi khɔ̀j si hět kaan   'Today I'm going to work.'

2) When they occur in other types of sentences, they may occur in sentence initial or sentence final position:

Q: mὺy daj càw si khâw hóoŋhían   'When will you start school?'

Q: càw si khâw hóoŋhían mὺy daj   'When will you start school?'

A: khɔ̀j si khâw hóoŋhían mὺy ɣyn   'I'm starting tomorrow.'

A: mὺy ɣyn   'Tomorrow'.

mὺy ɣyn khɔ̀j si khâw hóoŋhían might occur in a statement, but it would not occur in a response to a question.

2) daj 'which, what' may occur after time words like mὺy 'day' aathīt 'week', pii 'year', etc. with the meaning 'one particular unit of time': mὺy daj 'what day?', pii daj 'which year', etc. Or it may occur after weeláa 'time' with the meaning 'indefinite time': weeláa daj 'when (what time)'

3) weeláa 'time' is used in the following senses:

(a) a time for doing something

weeláa kin khâw 'time to eat'

123

(b) a particular moment or period of time

weeláa láaw máa   'when (the time) he came'

In this last sense it may serve as a connector between the Main Sentence and an included sentence as illustrated in the example below:

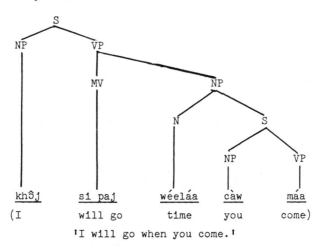

'I will go when you come.'

kɔɔn 'before' and lǎncâak 'after' can replace weeláa in the construction above.

APPLICATION

1. In the sentence khɔj sĭ paj pii nâa, pii nâa is (a) VP (b) NP (c)MV (d) time expression.

2. A possible answer to the question càw sĭ máa pii daj would be (a) aathIt nâa (b) pii daj (c) bɔɔ máa (d) pii nâa

_____

Answers: 1b and d, 2d

3. Which of the following are acceptable answers to the question
càw si paj wéeláa daj (a) mỳy ȳyn, (b) náj ookâat bun thàat
lŭaŋ (c) aathɪt nâa (d) sɑ̃a mooŋ thíɪ sɔ̌oŋ (e) all of these.

4. Give reasonable answers to the following questions: (a) càw si
máa wéeláa daj (b) dyan nâa yaj càw si paj sǎj (c) aathɪt
nâa càw si paj tát phǒm jɑ̃u hǎan tát phǒm bɔɔ (d) láaw si paj
mỳy daj (e) càw si sɔ̀okhǎa phȳan láaw wéeláa daj...

5. Using wéeláa as a connective, combine the following pairs of
sentences.

(a) khɔ̃j si paj _____ càw máa

(b) láaw si máa _____ khácàw paj

(c) láaw si paj thóorᾱsáp _____ càw máa

(d) khɔ̃j si paj kin khâw _____ càw máa

(e) déknɔ̀oj phɑ̃u nàn lîn _____ mɛɛ láaw fáŋ wɪ́thᾱnjɑ̃?

(f) láaw si sóŋ thóorᾱlèek _____ phɔɔ láaw máa

6. Repeat No.5 using kɔ̃on as a connective.

7. Repeat No.5 using lᾰŋcâak as a connective.

Answers: 3e, 4(a)khɔ̃j si máa aathɪt nâa (or) aathɪt nâa,etc.
(b)dyan nâa láaw si paj... (c)bɔɔ, bɔɔ paj (or)
si paj (d)mỳy ȳyn (or) láaw si paj mỳy ȳyn
(e)dyan nâa (or) khɔ̃j si sɔ̀okhǎa phȳan láaw dyan
nâa 5put wéeláa in the spaces between sentences
6put kɔ̃on in the spaces 7put lᾰŋcâak in the spaces.

125

CYCLE 29

M-1

pêɛt	eight
diawnìi pêɛt móoŋ	It's eight o'clock.
síp	ten
diawnìi síp móoŋ	It's ten o'clock.
pêɛt... khǝ̌ŋ	eight, half
diawnìi pêɛt móoŋ khǝ̌ŋ	It's half past eight.
kàw, síphâa	nine, fifteen
diawnìi kàw móoŋ síphâa	It's 9:15.
cét, njáŋ síp	seven, ten of
diawnìi cét móoŋ njáŋ síp	It's ten to seven (6:50).
hâa... sáaw	five, twenty
diawnìi hâa móoŋ sáaw	It's 5:20
sǎam, njáŋ síphâa	three, 15 of
diawnìi sǎam móoŋ njáŋ síphâa	It's 2:45.
sīi, síp	four, ten
diawnìi sīi móoŋ síp	It's 4:10.
hók... khǝ̌ŋ	six, half
diawnìi hók móoŋ khǝ̌ŋ	It's 6:30.

M-2

    diawnìi cák móoŋ lὲεw?   What time is it?

C-1

    A. diawnìi cák móoŋ lὲεw   What time is it?

    B. diawnìi ....   It's ....

ຈົງຖາມນັກຮຽນຂອງທ່ານກ່ຽວກັບເຮືອງໂມງແລະເວລາຕາງໆຢູ່ບັດດຸ! ດຽວນັກໂມງແລວ? ຈົງຖາມ
ເຖົ່າເວລາຂອງການປະກອບກິຈວັດປະຈຳວັນຂອງນັກຮຽນເຮົາ ແລະຈົງໃຫ້ຂະເຈົ້າຕອບຈົນຕາມພໍໃຈ.

NOTES

1) <u>móoŋ</u> 'o'clock' is used in asking and telling time.

    Asking the time:

        <u>diawnìi</u> + Number (Q) + <u>móoŋ lὲεw</u>

        <u>diawnìi   cák</u>   <u>móoŋ lὲεw</u>
        'What time is it?'

2) Telling time:

        (diawnìi) + Number + <u>móoŋ</u> + Part of hour

        <u>diawnìi   pὲ̂εt   móoŋ   síp hâa</u>

        (now   it's   8   o'clock   15)
                 'It's 8:15.'

127

If it is after the half hour, the number of minutes remaining before the hour is indicated by putting njáŋ 'yet' after the hour followed by the number of minutes remaining:

síp   móoŋ   njáŋ   síp

(ten o'clock yet   ten)

'10 minutes to ten.'

APPLICATION

1. Using the numbers as a guide, complete the following time expressions:

(a) diawnìi pɛ̂ɛt móoŋ _____ (8:15)

(b) diawnìi _____ móoŋ (9:00)

(c) diawnìi síp móoŋ _____ síp (9:50)

(d) diawnìi sǐi móoŋ _____ (4:30)

(e) diawnìi _____ móoŋ lɛ̂ɛw? (What time is it?)

(f) diawnìi hâa móoŋ _____ (5:10)

(g) diawnìi sɔ̌ɔŋ móoŋ njáŋ _____ (1:35)

(h) diawnìi cét móoŋ _____ (7:20)

2. Look at your watch and write out in full the correct time on this line. _____

Answers: 1(a)síphâa (b)kàw (c)njáŋ (d)khǝ̀ŋ (e)cák (f)síp
(g)sáaw hâa (h)sáaw 2you'll have to decide what
the correct answer to this is yourself.

128

CYCLE 30

M-1

pêɛt, sàw

    khɔ̌j paj sỳy khɔ̌oŋ pêɛt
    móoŋ sàw

8, morning

    I go shopping at eight in
    the morning.

sípsɔ̌oŋ, thīaŋ

    khɔ̌j paj sỳy khɔ̌oŋ síp
    sɔ̌oŋ móoŋ thīaŋ

12, noon

    I go shopping at 12 noon.

sɔ̌oŋ, bāaj

    khɔ̌j paj sỳy khɔ̌oŋ bāaj
    sɔ̌oŋ móoŋ

2, afternoon

    I go shopping at 2 in the
    afternoon.

hâa, lέɛŋ

    khɔ̌j paj sỳy khɔ̌oŋ hâa
    móoŋ lέɛŋ

5, evening

    I go shopping at 5 in the
    evening.

kàw, kaaŋkhýyn

    khɔ̌j paj sỳy khɔ̌oŋ kàw
    móoŋ kaaŋkhýyn

9, night

    I go shopping at 9 in the
    evening.

síp ét, khǝ̄ŋ

    khɔ̌j paj sỳy khɔ̌oŋ síp-
    ét móoŋ khǝ̄ŋ

11, half

    I go shopping at 11:30.

129

M-2

hóoŋhían	school
càw paj hóoŋhían cák móoŋ?	What time do you go to school?
h̄ētkaan	work
càw paj h̄ētkaan cák móoŋ?	What time do you go to work?
sỳy khɔ̌oŋ	shop
càw paj sỳy khɔ̌oŋ cák móoŋ?	What time did you go shop?
kin kaafée	have coffee
cáw paj kin kaafée cák móoŋ?	What time do you go to drink coffee?
dȳm nàmsáa	drink tea
càw paj dȳm nàmsáa cák móoŋ?	What time do you go to drink tea?
nɔ́ɔn	sleep
càw paj nɔ́ɔn cák móoŋ?	What time do you go to bed?
lɔ́ɔj nàm	swim
càw paj lɔ́ɔj nàm cák móoŋ?	What time do you go to swim?

M-3

hóoŋhían, kàw móoŋ sàw	school, 9:00 a.m.
khɔ̌j paj hóoŋhían kàw móoŋ sàw	I go to school at 9:00 a.m.

hḗtkaan, pɛ̂ɛt móoŋ khǝ̌ŋ tɔ̀ɔn   work, 8:30 a.m.
sàw

   khɔ̂j paj hḗt kaan pɛ̂ɛt   I go to work at 8:30 a.m.
   móoŋ khǝ̌ŋ tɔɔn sàw

sɣ̀y khɔ̌ɔŋ, síp-ét móoŋ sàw   shopping, 11 a.m.

   khɔ̂j paj sɣ̀y khɔ̌ɔŋ síp-ét   I went shopping at 11 a.m.
   móoŋ sàw

kin kaafée, bāāj sǎam móoŋ   drink coffee, 3 p.m.

   khɔ̂j paj kin kaafée bāāj   I went to drink coffee at
   sǎam móoŋ   3:00 p.m.

dɣ̄m nàmsáa, bāāj sīī móoŋ khǝ̌ŋ   drink tea, 4:30 p.m.

   khɔ̂j paj dɣ̄m nàmsáa bāāj   I went to drink tea at 4:30
   sīī móoŋ khǝ̌ŋ   p.m.

nɔ̀ɔn, síp móoŋ kaaŋkhɣ́yn   (go) to bed, 10:00 p.m.

   khɔ̂j paj nɔ̀ɔn síp móoŋ   T go to bed at 10:00 p.m.
   kaaŋkhɣ́yn

bǝ̄ŋ siinée, cét móoŋ lɛ́ɛŋ   go to the movies, 7:00 p.m.

   khɔ̂j paj bǝ̄ŋ siinée cét   I went to the movies at
   móoŋ lɛ́ɛŋ   7:00 p.m.

lɔ́ɔj nàm, síp sɔ̌ɔŋ móoŋ thꞮaŋ   go swimming, 12. noon

   khɔ̂j paj lɔ́ɔj nàm síp   I go·swimming at twelve noon.
   sɔ̌ɔŋ móoŋ thꞮaŋ

C-1

(lóoj nàm)

A. càw si paj lóoj nàm cák   What time will you go to
   móoŋ?   swimming?_

(9, njáŋ 15)

B. khôj si paj kàw móoŋ njáŋ   I will go at a quarter
   síp hâa   to 9.

C-2

(sǎj)

A. láaw paj sǎj?   Where did he go?

(kin kaafée)

B. láaw paj kin kaafée   He went to have coffee.

(cák móoŋ)

A. láaw paj cák móoŋ?   What time did he go?

(pêɛt, síp)

B. láaw paj pêɛt móoŋ síp.   He went at ten past eight.

_____

ຈຸດຈຸງໃຫມັກຮຽນເອົາໃຈຄືວກາານໃຊ້ຫລົບອກເວລາຕ່າງໆ ຈົນຮຽນເຂົ້າບອກເວລາໄດຢ່າງວ່ອງດາຍ.
ອັນໃດເລັມເວລາໃດ? ໃຫຈະເຮັດຫຍັງຕລົມຫຍັງເຄິດຂຶນເວລາໃດ? ຄວນເປັນຕົນ.

132

NOTES

1 Words designating the part of the day like sàw 'a.m.' are
   usually placed after móoŋ in time expressions, thus

   cét móoŋ sàw '7 a.m.' síp sǒoŋ móoŋ thiaŋ '12 noon'

   hâa móoŋ lέεŋ '5 p.m.' síp-ét móoŋ kaaŋkhýyn '11 p.m.'

   The approximate period of time referred to by such terms as
   sàw, etc. is indicated on the clock faces below

Noon   Midnight

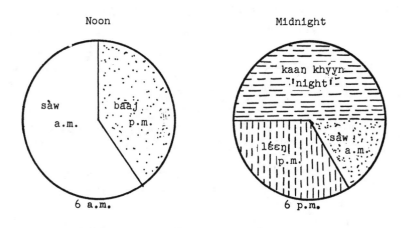

APPLICATION

1. Complete the following examples:

    (a) 9:00 a.m. kàw móoŋ _____

    (b) 1:30 p.m. _____ móoŋ khǝŋ

    (c) 5:00 p.m. hâa móoŋ _____

    (d) 12:00 síp sɔ̌ɔŋ móoŋ _____

    (e) 4:00 p.m. bāaj sīī _____

    (f) 11:00 a.m. síp-ét móoŋ _____

    (g) 10:00 p.m. síp móoŋ _____

    (h) 8:00 p.m. pɛ̂ɛt móoŋ _____

    (i) 6:50 cét móoŋ _____ síp

    (j) 3:20 p.m. bāaj sǎam móoŋ _____

    (k) 10:30 a.m. síp móoŋ _____ tɔɔn sàw

    (l) 12:15 p.m. síp sɔ̌ɔŋ móoŋ _____ tɔɔn thīaŋ

2. Complete the blanks with the time that you normally do the
    things indicated:

    (a) khɔ̂j paj hóoŋhían _____

    (b) khɔ̂j paj kin kaafée _____

    (c) khɔ̂j paj sỳy khɔ̌ɔŋ _____

    (d) khɔ̂j paj nɔ́ɔn _____

Answers: 1(a)sàw (b)bāaj (c)lɛ́ɛŋ (d)thīaŋ (e)móoŋ (f)sàw
           (g)kaaŋ khýyn, lɛ́ɛŋ (h)lɛ́ɛŋ (i)njáŋ (j)sáaw
           (k)khǝŋ (l)síphâa   2you will have to check own
           answers here.

CYCLE 31

M-1

sáwmy̆aj, náathíi, síp	rest, minute, ten
láaw sáwmy̆aj síp náathíi	He rested ten minutes.
phӑkphɔ̌on, aathɪ̌t, sӑam	take vacation, week, three
láaw phӑkphɔ̌on sӑam aathɪ̌t	He took three weeks vacation.
bɔ̌ɔ sábaaj, my̆y, sɪ̌i	sick, day, four
láaw bɔ̌ɔ sábaaj sɪ̌i my̆y	He was sick for three days.
tiisèk, dyan, sɔ̌ɔŋ	fight the war, month, two
láaw tiisèk sɔ̌ɔŋ dyan	He fought (in a war) for two months.
jɯ̄ɯ my̆aŋnɔ̀ɔk, pii, hók	be abroad, year, six
láaw jɯ̄ɯ my̆aŋnɔ̀ɔk hók pii	He spent six years abroad.
kàncaj, wɪnáathíi, sӑamsíphâa	hold one's breath, second, thirty-five
láaw kàncaj sӑamsíphâa wɪnáathíi	He held his breath for 35 seconds.
thâa càw, sɯ̄amóoŋ, khɜ̌ŋ	wait for you, hour, half
láaw thâa càw khɜ̌ŋ sɯ̄amóoŋ	He waited for you for half an hour.
khâw thɛ̌ɛw	form a line
láaw khâw thɛ̌ɛw sɯ̄amóoŋ khɜ̌ŋ	He was in line for one and a half hours.

135

M-2

jɯɯ mýaŋ láaw, pii	be in Laos, year
láaw jɯɯ mýaŋ láaw cák pii?	How many years was he in Laos?
lɤ̆ŋtháaŋ, sɯamóoŋ	lose one's way, hour
láaw lɤ̆ŋtháaŋ cák sɯamóoŋ?	How many hours was he lost?
ãan, bóthían, náathíi	read, lesson, minute
láaw ãan bóthían cák náathíi?	How many minutes did he read the lessons?
dəəntháaŋ, aathɪt	travel, week
láaw dəəntháaŋ cák aathɪt?	How many weeks did he travel?
tiisək, mỳy	fight the war, day
láaw tiisək cák mỳy?	How many days was he in battle?

M-3

phãkphɔɔn	rest, take vacation
càw si phãkphɔɔn don paandaj?	How long will you take for vacation?
fýk-hát	practice
càw si fýk-hát don paandaj?	How long will you practice?
páʔ wàj, lõt	leave, car
càw si páʔ lõt càw wàj nìi don paandaj?	How long will you leave your car here?

136

sǎksàa   delay, be delayed

   càw sî sǎksàa don paandaj?   How long will you be delayed?

khǎŋ, lâaw   imprison, he

   càw sî khǎŋ lâaw don   How long will you imprison
   paandaj?   him?

khùapkhúm   control

   càw sî khùapkhúm lâaw don   How long will you keep him
   paandaj?   under control?

C-1

  A. lâaw sî hět njǎŋ?   What is he going to do?

  B. lâaw sî (sáwmỹaj)   He is going to (take a rest.)

  A: lâaw sî (sáwmỹaj) cák   How many (minutes) will he
    (náathíi)?   (rest)?

  B. (sáaw náathíi).   (Twenty minutes).

C-2

  A. khácàw sî hět njǎŋ?   What are they going tc do?

  B. khácàw sî (paj phǎkphɔ̃ɔn).   They are going to (take a
                                   vacation.)

  A. khácàw sî (paj phǎkphɔ̃ɔn)   How long will they be going?
    don paandaj?

  B. (sɔ̌ɔŋ aathīt).   (Two weeks).

ໃຕ້ນັກຮຽນຕັດໄຊໄລຍະເວລາ ຕົ້ງສັນແລະຍາວ. ຖາມນັກຮຽນກ່ຽວກັບເຮັດວຽກໃນຕົນອອກຕໜ່ອໄປກວ່າ
ທີ່ຢູ່ໃນບົດຮຽນນີ້ບ່ວງໆ! ແຕກວ່າພະຍາຍາມໃຫ້ຜູ້ພາຍໃນຂອບເຂດຕໍ່ນັກຮຽນໄດຮຽນຮູ້ມາແລວຕໍ່ານນັ້ນ.

137

NOTES

1) The following words are used for various periods of time: pii
'year', dyan 'month', aathīt 'week', myy 'day', sūamóoŋ 'hour',
náathíi 'minute', and wīnaathíi 'second.' If one wishes to find
out precisely how many units of time (hour, minute, etc.) were
used in a particular activity cák + Time Unit is used: cák
aathīt 'how many weeks', etc. The question can be put in a
more general and less precise way by saying don paandaj (lit.
long to what extent) 'How long?'. don paandaj is always used
in situations in which the speaker has no idea how long a time
was involved (hence no knowledge of what time units the response
might be given in).

2) khə̄ŋ 'half' may occur before or after a Time Unit. When it
occurs before the unit it means 'half of the unit': khə̄ŋ myy
'half a day', khə̄ŋ pii 'half a year', etc.

When khə̄ŋ occurs after a time unit, it means 'one and one half
units': sūamóoŋ khə̄ŋ 'one and a half hours', náathíi khə̄ŋ 'one
and a half minutes', etc.

If numbers precede a time unit and khə̄ŋ follows it, khə̄ŋ means
'one half is added to the other number':

sǎam myy khə̄ŋ '3 1/2 days', hók pii khə̄ŋ '6 1/2 years.' etc.

APPLICATION

1. Fill in the blanks below with the correct information:

   (a) _____ nyŋ míi síp-sɔ̌ɔŋ dyan.

   (b) náathíi nyŋ míi 60 _____

   (c) _____ nyŋ míi 24 sūamóoŋ

Answers: 1(a)pii (b)wīnáathíi (c)myy

(d) dyan nȳŋ míi 30 _____

(e) 60 wīnáathíi mɛɛn 1 _____

(f) 4 sūamóoŋ mɛɛn 240 _____

(g) 12 dyan mɛɛn 1 _____

(h) 7 mỳy mɛɛn 1 _____

(i) mỳy nȳŋ míi 86,000 _____

(j) _____ sūamóoŋ (how many hours?).

(k) _____ paandaj (how long?).

(l) _____ sūamóoŋ (half an hour).

(m) kàw mỳy _____ (9 1/2 days).

(n) pii _____ (1 1/2 years).

Answers: (d)mỳy (e)náathíi (f)náathíi (g)pii (h)aathīt
(i)wīnáathíi (j)cák (k)don (l)khāŋ
(m)khāŋ (n)khāŋ

CYCLE 32

M-1

míi wéeláa, phɔ́ɔ, sǎmlāp	have time, enough, for
càw bɔ̃ɔ míi wéeláa phɔ́ɔ sǎmlāp njǎŋ?	What don't you have enough time for?
sàj	use
càw sàj wéeláa nìi hēt njǎŋ?	What did you use this time for?
phɛ́ɛŋ wàj	save
càw phɛ́ɛŋ wéeláa wàj hēt njǎŋ?	What did you save the time for?
sɪ̌a wéeláa, njɔ̀ɔn	lose time, because of
càw sɪ̌awéeláa njɔ̀ɔn njǎŋ?	What caused you to lose time?

M-2

khúakin	cook
khɔ̃j bɔ̃ɔ míi wéeláa phɔ́ɔ sǎmlāp khúakin.	I don't have enough time to cook.
pɛɛŋ, lōtcák	fix, motor bike
khɔ̃j sàj wéeláa nìi pɛɛŋ lōtcák.	I used this time to fix the motorbike.
sáwmȳaj	rest
khɔ̃j phɛ́ɛŋ wéeláa nìi wàj sáwmȳaj	I saved this time for resting.

sɔ̀ɔkhǎa, phỹan | look for, friend

khɔ̌j sɪ̌a wéeláa njɔ̀ɔn
sɔ̀ɔkhǎa phỹan khɔ̌j | I lost the time in looking for my friend.

M-3

hían nǎŋsỹy, aathɪt | study, week

càw míi wéeláa hían nǎŋsỹy
cák aathɪt? | How many weeks do you have for studying?

khúakin, sǔamóoŋ | cook, hour

càw míi wéeláa khúakin
cák sǔamóoŋ? | How many hours do you have for cooking?

sɔ̀ɔkhǎa, mỳy | look for, day

càw sàj wéeláa sɔ̀ɔkhǎa
phỹan càw cák mỳy? | How many days did you use in looking for your friend?

pɛɛŋ lɔ̌t, sǔamóoŋ | fix the car, hour

càw sàj wéeláa pɛɛŋ lɔ̌t
cák sǔamóoŋ? | How many hours did you use for fixing your car?

sɪ̌a wéeláa, khón sàj | lose time, servant

càw sɪ̌a wéeláa sɔ̀ɔkhǎa
khónsàj càw cák mỳy? | How many days did you want for looking for your servant?

pɛɛŋ, thóorāthāt | fix, television

càw sàj wéeláa pɛɛŋ
thóorāthāt cák sǔamóoŋ? | How many hours did it take you to fix the television set?

M-4

míi, dyan, pɛ̂ɛt	have, month, eight
càw míi wéeláa hían pháasǎa láaw pɛ̂ɛt dyan	You have eight months to study Lao.
sáwmɣaj, náathíi, síphâa	rest, minute, fifteen
càw míi wéeláa sáwmɣaj síphâa náathíi	You have fifteen minutes to rest.
sàj, kinkhâw, sǎamsíp	use, eat, thirty
càw sàj wéeláa kinkhâw sǎamsíp náathíi.	You took thirty minutes to eat.
slicɛɛŋ, lɣaŋ, sáaw	explain, matter, twenty
càw sàj wéeláa slicɛɛŋ lɣaŋ nìi sáaw náathíi	You took twenty minutes to explain this matter.
síphâa	fifteen
càw sǐa wéeláa khúakin síphâa náathíi	You wasted fifteen minutes cooking.
thâa, hâa	wait for, five
càw sǐa wéeláa thâa phɣan càw hâa sɔ̄amóoŋ	You wasted five hours waiting for your friend.

142

C-1

A. càw bɔ̄ɔ míi wéeláa phɔ́ɔ
sǎmlāp njǎŋ?

You don't have enough time
for what?

B. khɔ̌j bɔ̄ɔ míi wéeláa phɔ́ɔ
sǎmlāp khúakin

I don't have enough time
to cook.

C-2

A. càw sǐa wéeláa sɔ̀ɔkhǎa
láaw cák náathíi?

How much time did you waste
looking for him?

B. khɔ̌j sǐa wéeláa sīisíphâa
náathíi

I wasted forty five minutes.

C-3

A. càw míi wéeláa phɔ́ɔ bɔɔ?

Do you have enough time?

B. wéeláa sǎmlāp njǎŋ?

Enough time for what?

A. sǎmlāp (khúakin).

For (cooking).

B. phɔ́ɔ, khɔ̌j míi wéeláa
lǎaj síp náathíi

Oh yes, I have tens of
minutes.

ນັກຮຽນອອງຕາມໃຈຄຳວ່າ "ໄມງ" ແລະ "ຈ້ອໄມງ" ໄດຢ່າງຖືກຕ້ອງແລ້ວບໍ? ຈິງຖາມນັກຮຽນຕໍໄຕນັກ
ຮຽນຖາມກັນເບິງດູວ່າ ຂະເຈົ້ານີ, ເສັ້ງ, ໃຂ... ເວລາສາໄລຍຕຍ້ວຕະຄຳປານໃດ?

143

NOTES

1) As was indicated in Cycle 28 wéeláa 'time' may be followed
   by VP indicating some kind of activity: wéeláa kin khâw
   'time to eat/for eating'. When wéeláa is followed by phɔ́ɔ
   'enough, sufficient', sǎmlǎp 'for the purpose of' occurs
   before the VP of Purpose:

   mɨ́i wéeláa phɔ́ɔ sǎmlǎp khúakin   (have time enough for (to)
                                        cook)

                                        'have enough time to cook'

   In questions the VP of Purpose is replaced by njǎŋ: mɨ́i
   wéeláa phɔ́ɔ sǎmlǎp njǎŋ? 'You have sufficient time for what?'

2) njɔ̀ɔn 'because of, due to' + VP of Activity is used to provide
   an explanation for some action:

   khɔ̌j sǐa wéeláa njɔ̀ɔn sɔ̀ɔkhǎa   (I lost time due to looking
   phɣan khɔ̌j   for my friend.)

                                        'I spent time (in vain)
                                        looking for my friend.'

APPLICATION

1) Complete the following sentences:

   (a) khɔ̌j mɨ́i wéeláa _____ (fix motorbike)

   (b) càw bɔ̄ɔ mɨ́i wéeláa _____ (to rest)

   (c) láaw sǐa wéeláa _____ thâa phɣan láaw (due to)

Answers: 1(a)pɛɛŋ lōtcák (b)sáwmɣaj (c) njɔ̀ɔn

(d) khɔ̃j bʊʊ míi wéeláa _____ sǎmlǎp khúakin (enough time
                                                time...)

(e) càw sàj wéeláa kin khâw cák _____? (how many minutes)

(f) càw míi wéeláa _____ hók dyan (study Lao)

(g) wéeláa _____ njǎŋ (for what?)

(h) càw sĭa wéeláa sɔ̀ɔkhǎa khónsàj càw _____ (how long?)

2. Answer the following questions:

(a) mỳy wáan nìi càw sàj wéeláa hían pháasǎa láaw don paandaj?

(b) mỳy ȳȳn càw si míi wéeláa nɔ́ɔn cák sūamóoŋ?

(c) wán sǎw lɛ̀ɛw nìi (last Saturday) càw jyyn thâa mía càw
     don paandaj?

(d) mỳy ȳyn càw si míi wéeláa phɔ́ɔ sǎmlǎp hían pháasǎa láaw bɔɔ?

(e) càw sĭa wéeláa njɔ̀ɔn njǎŋ?

Answers: 1(d)phóc (e)náathíɪ (f)hían pháasǎa láaw
          (g)sǎmlǎp (h)don paandaj 2You can work
          out the answers yourself.

145

CYCLE 33

M-1

lŏt mée	bus
kh3j si paj nám lŏt mée	I will go by bus.
hýa	boat
kh3j si paj nám hýa	I will go by boat.
hýa bin	airplane
kh3j si paj nám hýa bin	I will go by air plane.
lŏt	car
kh3j si paj nám lŏt	I will go by car.
lŏt thîip	bicycle
kh3p si paj nám lŏt thîip	I will go by bicycle.
lŏt fáj	train
kh3j si paj nám lŏt fáj	I will go by train.
sǎam lɔ̀ɔ	tricycle
kh3j si paj nám sǎam lɔ̀ɔ	I will go by tricycle.

M-2

nám	with, by
càw si paj nám njǎŋ?	How will you go?
nɛ́ɛw daj	how
càw si paj nɛ́ɛw daj?	How will you go?

C-1

(nám)   with, by

   A. càw si paj nám njǎŋ?   How will you go?

(lǒt)   car

   B. khɔ̆j si paj nám (lǒt)   I will go by (car).

C-2

(nɛ́ɛwdaj)   how

   A. càw si paj nɛ́ɛwdaj?   How will you go?

(hýa)   boat

   B. khɔ̆j si paj nám (hýa).   I will go by (boat).

_____

ເມື່ອນັກຮຽນເວົ້າແລະເອົາໃຈບິດຮຽນນີ້ໄດ້ດີແລ້ວ ຄານຈະສອນການໃຊຍານພາຫະນະຢ່າງອື່ນອິກຫໄດ້.
ຈົງໃຈແຕສ່ວນນັກຮຽນຊຸດຕັນ ແລະຕາມຄວາມຄິດວ່າຈະເປັນປໄຍກ; ບດົງນນ ຈະຄ່ສົຄວລາຈລາງ.

_____

NOTES

1) Mode of Transportation may be indicated by <u>nám</u> '(to go) along
   with' + Type of Vehicle following a verb of motion.

        NP   +   MV   +   VP (Mode of Transportation)

        <u>khɔ̆j</u>   <u>si paj</u>   <u>nám lǒt mée</u>

        (I   will go   go along with bus)

          'I will go by bus.'

147

2) The Verb Phrase nám + Vehicle may be questioned in either of two ways:

Statement:	khɔ̂j si paj nám lōt	'I'll go by car'.
Question 1:	càw si paj nám njǎŋ	'How will you go?'
Question 2:	càw si paj nɛ́ɛw daj	'How will you go?'

APPLICATION

1. In the sentence khɔ̂j si paj nám lōt fáj, nám lōt fáj is (a) NP (b) VP (c) preposition plus noun (d) MV (e) predicate.

2. In the question càw si paj nám njǎŋ, njǎŋ probably refers to (a) a person (b) a vehicle (c) a motion (d) a place.

3. In the question càw si paj nɛ́ɛwdaj, nɛ́ɛw means something like (a) how? (b) manner, way (c) by what means? (d) what? (e) none of these.

4. Complete the following sentences:

   (a) _____ si paj nám hỹa   (b) càw si paj nɛ́ɛw _____?

   (c) láaw si paj _____ hỹa bin (d) khɔ̂j si paj nám _____ mée

   (e) càw si paj _____ njǎŋ?

5. Translate the following sentences into English:

   (a) láaw si paj nám lōtfáj   (b) càw máa hóoŋhían nám njǎŋ?

   (c) wéeláa càw si paj hàanaahǎan, càw si paj nám njǎŋ?

   (d) phỹan càw paj nɛ́ɛwdaj?

Answers: 1b, 2b, 3b, 4(a)càw, khɔ̂j, etc. (b)daj (c)nám (d)lōt (e)nám 5(a)He'll go by train. (b)How did you come to school? (c)When you go to the restaurant, how will you go? (d)How did your friend go?

148

CYCLE 34

M-1

náaj tháaŋ	a guide
láaw si paj nám náaj tháaŋ	He will go with the guide.
káp paj	return
láaw si káp paj nám náaj tháaŋ	He will return with the guide.
lùuk láaw	his children
láaw si káp paj nám lùuk láaw	He will return with his children.
pýksǎa	consult
láaw si pýksǎa nám lùuk láaw	He will consult with his children.
phǔu hǔam ŋáan	colleagues
láaw si pýksǎa nám phǔu hǔam ŋáan láaw	He will consult with his colleagues.
aasǎj jǔu	live
láaw si aasǎj jǔu nám phǔu hǔam ŋáan láaw	He will live with his colleagues.
phīīnɔ̀ɔŋ	relatives
..láaw si aasǎj jǔu nám phīīnɔ̀ɔŋ láaw	He will live with his relatives.

M-2

khɔ̌ɔ anŭnjàat	ask permission
láaw si khɔ̌ɔ anŭnjàat nám phǎj?	From whom will he ask permission?
fýkhát	practice
láaw si paj fýkhát nám phǎj?	With whom is he going to practice?
hŭam ɲáan	cooperate
láaw si paj hŭam ɲáan nám phǎj?	With whom is he going to cooperate?
sámák hɛ̄tkaan	apply for the job
láaw si paj sámák hɛ̄tkaan nám phǎj?	To whom is he going to apply for the job?

C-1

(pýksǎa)	consult
A. càw si paj pýksǎa nám phǎj?	Who are you going to consult with?
(náaj tháaŋ)	guide
B. khɔ̀j si paj pýksǎa nám náaj tháaŋ	I am going to consult with the guide.

C-2

(aasǎj jɯɯ)   to live

  A. phǎj si máa aasǎj jɯɯ   Who will come to live with
    nám càw?   you?

(phɯɯ hɯam ŋáan)   colleague

  B. phɯɯ hɯam ŋáan khɔ̃j si   My colleague is going to
    máa aasǎj jɯɯ nám khɔ̃j   come to live with me.

C-3

(lùuk)   children

  A. càw si paj hēt njǎŋ   What are you going to do
    nám lùukcàw?   with your children?

(fýkhát)   practice

  B. khɔ̃j si paj fýkhát nám   I am going to practice
    khácàw   with them.

ລອງປະຕິດເຮືອງຍນປະກອບອິກເບິ່ງຄຸ! ຈົ່ງພຍາຍາມແຕ່ງເຮືອງງ່າຍໆແລະແປກປລາດ ຕລະເຮືອງທີເປັນ
ຫມາຍາກທີວ ຊົ່ງຈະພາໃຫ້ບັນຍາກາດຢູ່ໃນຫ້ອງຮຽນມີຊີວິດຊີວາຍິ່ງອນ.

151

LAO BASIC COURSE

NOTES

1) When nám is followed by NP in which the N is human, the
relationship between the persons involved may be any one
of the following:

(a) Accompaniment:

láaw si káp paj nám lùuk láaw
'He will return with his child.'

(b) Joint effort (with participants having equal status).

láaw si pýksǎa nám phǔu hǔam ŋáan láaw
'He will consult with his colleagues.'

(c) Joint effort (with participants have unequal status).

láaw si paj sámák hětkaan nám phǎj?
'Who is he going to apply to for a job?'

APPLICATION

1. Translate the following sentences into English: (a) láaw si
njāaŋ paj nám nǎkhían (b) láaw si khīī lōt nám khǒj (c) láaw
si hían nám náaj khúu (d) láaw si khǒothòot nám khácaw (e)
láaw si paj hǎa paa nám khácaw (f) láaw si wáw nám náaj khúu
(g) láaw jūu myaŋ láaw nám phǒo láaw (h) láaw bǒo mǎk hětwíak
nám hǔa nǎa láaw (i) láaw khǒo paj naj myaŋ nám khácaw. (j) láaw
si bǒo pýksǎa nám phěn.

Answers: 1(a)He will walk with the students. (b)He will ride
with me. (c)He will study with the teacher (or under
the teacher) (d)He will ask their pardon. (e)He will
go fishing with them. (f)He will talk with (or to)
the teacher. (g)He lives in Laos with his father.
(h)He doesn't like to work with his boss. (i)He asked
(to be allowed) to go into town with them. (j)He won't
consult with him.

152

CYCLE 35

M-1

njāāŋ — to walk

khɔ̌j si njāāŋ { paj / máa } — I will walk.

kháp lɔ̌t — to drive

khɔ̌j si kháp lɔ̌t { paj / máa } — I will drive (there).

lɛɛn — to run

khɔ̌j si lɛɛn { paj / máa } — I will run.

khɪɪ hýa — to ride in a boat

khɔ̌j si khɪɪ hýa { paj / máa } — I will go by boat.

tèn khâam — to jump over

khɔ̌j si tèn khâam { paj / máa } — I will jump over it.

lɔ́ɔj nàam — to swim

khɔ̌j si lɔ́ɔj nàam { paj / máa } — I will swim (there).

M-2

<u>nám</u>   with, by

    càw sì paj nám njǎŋ   How will you go?

<u>nέεw daj</u>   how

    càw sì paj nέεw daj   How will you go?

M-3

<u>njāāŋ</u>   walk

    láaw njāāŋ $\begin{cases} \text{paj} \\ \text{máa} \end{cases}$ He walked to the country
    bàannòok   side.

<u>khīī màa</u>   ride a horse

    láaw khīī $\begin{cases} \text{máa} \\ \text{paj} \end{cases}$ He rode a horse to the
    bàannòok   country side.

<u>khīī kian</u>   ride in an ox car

    láaw khīī kian $\begin{cases} \text{paj} \\ \text{máa} \end{cases}$ He rode in an ox cart to
    bàannòok   the country side.

<u>dəəntháaŋ</u>   travel

    láaw dəəntháaŋ $\begin{cases} \text{máa} \\ \text{paj} \end{cases}$ He travels to the country
    bàannòok   side.

<u>ɔ̀ɔk</u>   exit

    láaw ɔ̀ɔk $\begin{cases} \text{paj} \\ \text{máa} \end{cases}$ He went (came) out to the
    bàannòok   country.

M-4

njāaŋ, kinkhâw, hàan aahǎan	walk, eat, restaurant
khɔ̌j si njāaŋ paj kin khâw jʉ̄ʉ hàan aahǎan	I'll walk over to the restaurant and eat.
kháplɔ̌t, āan nǎŋsʉ̌y, hɔ̌oŋsámút	drive, read, library
khɔ̌j si kháplɔ̌t paj āan nǎŋsʉ̌y jʉ̄ʉ hɔ̌oŋsámút	I'll drive over to library and read.
khīi lɔ̌tmée, jaam, hýan	ride on a bus, visit, house
láaw si khīi lɔ̌tmée máa jaam khɔ̌j jʉ̄ʉ hýan khɔ̌j	He will ride on a bus over to my house to visit me.
lɛ̌ɛn, cɛ̀ɛŋ tamlûat, komtamlûat	run, report to the police, police station
láaw si lɛ̌ɛn paj cɛ̀ɛŋ tamlûat jʉ̄ʉ komtamlûat	He will run over to report to the police at the police station.

M-5

kháp lɔ̌t	drive
láaw si kháp lɔ̌t paj sǎj?	Where is he driving to?
lɛ̌ɛn	run
láaw si lɛ̌ɛn paj sǎj?	Where is he running to?

155

C-1

(nám)

    A. càw si paj nám njǎŋ?   How are you going?

(lŏt mée)

    B. khɔ̀j si paj nám lŏt mée   I'm going by bus.

C-2

(nɛ́ɛwdaj)

    A. láaw si paj nɛ́ɛwdaj?   How will she go?

(njāāŋ)

    B. láaw si njāāŋ paj   She will walk.

C-3

(sǎj)

    A. càw si dəəntháaŋ paj sǎj?   Where are you travelling to?

(bàannɔ̀ɔk)

    B. khɔ̀j si dəəntháaŋ paj   I'm travelling to the country
       bàannɔ̀ɔk   side.

ທານແມ່ໃຈແລວວ່ຽວ່ານັກຮຽນຂອງທ່ານເຂົ້າໃຈແລະຮູ້ຈັກຄວາມແຕກຕາງລະຫວ່າງຄຳວ່າ "ໄປນຳທ່ຽ່ງ"
ແລະ "ໄປນຳໃຜ". ແລະຄຳວ່າ "ຂີ່ບຶກໄປ" ແລະ "ໄປຂີ່ບຶກ" ຄຊ? ທ່ານລອງທຶດສອບຢະເຈົ້າເບິ່ງຄຸ!

156

NOTES

1) paj and máa may occur as the Main Verb in the sentence indicating motion in a particular direction (máa 'toward the speaker; paj, 'away from the speaker'):

máa hàanaahǎan   'to come to the restaurant'

paj kin khâw   'to go eat'

paj and máa also occur as secondary verbs indicating direction of motion after VP indicating type of locomotion (njāaŋ 'to walk', kháp lōt 'to drive', etc.); in fact, if any actual travel is indicated either paj or máa must follow VP of this kind:

kháp lōt paj   'to drive (some place)'

khīi hýa máa   'to come (some place) by boat'

njāaŋ paj kin khâw   'to walk (some place) to eat'

kháp lōt paj kin khâw jūu   'to drive to the restaurant to
hàanaahǎan   eat'

2) Although paj nám njǎŋ and paj nέεw daj both mean 'How are (you) going?', there is a little difference in meaning between them. paj nám njǎŋ suggests that you are going on some sort of vehicle; whereas, paj nέεw daj is simply a request as to how you are going from one place to another. The following exchange will illustrate this difference:

Q: càw paj nám njǎŋ?   'How are you going?'

A: khɔ̀j si bɔɔ paj nám njǎŋ   'I'm not going in any kind of
   khɔ̀j si njāaŋ paj   vehicle. I'm going to walk.'

APPLICATION

1. Add <u>paj</u> or <u>máa</u> and rearrange the following sentence parts into sentences:

(a) khīī hýa, hɔ́oŋ sámút, āān nǎŋsўy

(b) hàan aahǎan, njāāŋ, kin khâw

(c) páthèet cīīn, dəəntháaŋ

(d) sǎj, khīī kian

(e) jaam phȳan, kháp lŏt, hýan

(f) bàannɔ̀ok, ɔ̀ok

(g) hóoŋhían, lɛ̄ɛn

(h) jūū náj mýaŋ, lîn, njāāŋ

(i) pásúm, khīī lŏtmée, jūū hóoŋhían

(j) jūū sǎj, sɔ̄ŋ thóorālèek

(k) si, njāāŋ, phùn

(l) mýaŋ wíaŋcan, dəəntháaŋ

Answers: Either <u>paj</u> or <u>máa</u> may be used. <u>khɔ̌j</u>, <u>càw</u>, <u>láaw</u>, etc. may be used as the subject. (a)khɔ̌j khīī hýa paj āān nǎŋsўy jūū hɔ́oŋsámút (b)láaw njāāŋ máa kin khâw jūū hàan aahǎan (c)càw si dəəntháaŋ paj páthèet cīīn bɔɔ (d)láaw si khīī kian paj sǎj (e)khɔ̌j si kháp lŏt máa jaam phȳan khɔ̌j jūū hýan láaw (f)khɔ̌j si ɔ̀ok paj bàannɔ̀ok (g)láaw lɛ̄ɛn paj hóoŋhían (h)láaw njāāŋ paj lîn jūū náj mýaŋ (i)láaw khīī lŏtmée paj pásúm jūū hóoŋhían (j)càw si paj sɔ̄ŋ thóorālèek jūū sǎj (k)láaw si njāāŋ paj phùn (l)khɔ̌j si dəəntháaŋ paj mýaŋ wíaŋcan

CYCLE 36

M-1

hɛ̄twlȧk   to work

   càw sǐ hɛ̄twlȧk dȧj bɔɔ?   Will you be able to work?

njāāŋ paj   walk

   càw sǐ njāāŋ paj dȧj bɔɔ?   Will you be able to walk?

sỳy   buy

   càw sǐ sỳy dȧj bɔɔ?   Will you be able to buy (it)?

nɔ́ɔn   sleep

   càw sǐ nɔ́ɔn dȧj bɔɔ?   Will you be able to sleep?

thǎam   ask, question

   càw sǐ thǎam dȧj bɔɔ?   Will you be able to ask?

njíŋ   shoot

   càw sǐ njíŋ dȧj bɔɔ?   Will you be able to shoot?

tɔ̄ɔp   answer

   càw sǐ tɔ̄ɔp dȧj bɔɔ?   Will you be able to answer?

M-2

dȧj   can, be able

   dȧj   Yes, (I will be able to...)

bɔɔ   no

   bɔɔ dȧj   No, (I will not be able to...)

C-1

(hɛ̄twlak)

    A. càw si hɛ̄twlak dàj bɔɔ?   Will you be able to work?

(dàj)

    B. dàj   Yes.

C-2

(njíŋ)

    A. càw si njíŋ dàj bɔɔ?   Will you be able to shoot?

(bɔɔ)

    B. bɔɔ dàj   No.

ຈົ້ງຖາມນັກຮຽນຈຸກໍອີກຄືວຄວາມສາມາດຂອງຂະເຈົ້າໃນຄານຕ່າງໆເບິ່ງຄູ! ຂະເຈົ້າຕອບຫານໄດ້
ຢ່າງເປັນທີ່ພໍໃຈແລ້ວບໍ? ລົມຄົນໃຈຄໍສັຍເກົ່າອີກແດ່ ຍ້ວມິຕລາຍຄໍອີກທີ່ຈະໃຊ້ກັບ"ໄດ້"ໄດ້.

160

NOTES

1) dàj means 'to be able, possible', and it normally occurs as VP (Predicate) with a Sentence as NP (Subject).

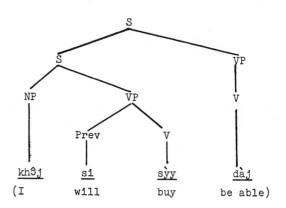

```
                            S
                  _____/ _____
                 S                    VP
              __/ \__                  |
           NP        VP                V
            |      _/ \_               |
            |   Prev    V              |
            |    |      |              |
          khƆj   si     sýy           dàj
          (I    will   buy         be able)
```

'I will be able to buy it.'

2) Negation of this type of sentence is Sentence + bɔɔ dàj: khƆj paj bɔɔ dàj 'I can't go.'

The question form is Sentence + dàj + bɔɔ? 'Can you...?'

The affirmative response is: dàj 'Yes, I can.'

The negative response is: bɔɔ dàj 'No, I can't.'

APPLICATION

1. Change the following questions into 'possibility' situations:

    (a) càw si khǎj pátuu nìi phìi bɔɔ?
    (b) càw si át pɔɔŋ-jìam nìi phìi bɔɔ?
    (c) càw si sǎj kácɛɛ lìnsǎk nìi phìi bɔɔ?
    (d) càw si khǎj kácɛɛ hîip nìi phìi bɔɔ?
    (e) càw si lóŋ khândaj nìi phìi bɔɔ?

2. Change the following statements into statements indicating one's inability to do something.

    (a) khɔ̂j si khǎj pátuu nàn phùn
    (b) khɔ̂j si pîan jaaŋ nàn phùn
    (c) khɔ̂j si paj hǎa phùu nàn phùn
    (d) khɔ̂j si sɔɔjlŷa phùu nàn phùn
    (e) khɔ̂j si tít-tɔɔ káp phùu nàn phùn

3. Respond affirmatively to the questions in 1 above.

4. Give negative responses to the questions in 1 above.

Answers: 1change bɔɔ to dàj bɔ̌ɔ 2Add bɔ̌ɔ dàj to the sentence. 3the response to all questions is dàj 4the response to all questions is bɔɔ dàj.

CYCLE 37

M-1

kháp lōt   drive

    càw kháp lōt pen bɔɔ?   Do you know how to drive?

njín pyyn   shoot a gun

    càw njín pyyn pen bɔɔ?   Do you know how to shoot
                                    a gun?

pɛɛŋ lōt   fix a car

    càw pɛɛŋ lōt pen bɔɔ?   Do you know how to fix a car?

wàw pháasǎa aŋkít   speak English

    càw wàw pháasǎa aŋkít   Do you know how to speak
    pen bɔɔ?   English?

thāaj hùup   take picture

    càw thāaj hùup pen bɔɔ?   Do you know how to take
                                    pictures?

M-2

pen   be

    pen   Yes, (I know how to...)

bɔɔ   no

    bɔɔ pen   No, (I don't know how to...)

C-1

(kháp lõt)   drive

    A. càw kháp lõt pen bɔɔ?   Do you know how to drive?

(pen)

    B. pen   Yes, I do.

C-2

(pɛɛŋ lõt)

    A. càw pɛɛŋ lõt pen bɔɔ?   Do you know how to fix a car?

(bɔ̄ɔ̄)

    B. bɔ̄ɔ̄ pen   No, I don't.

ຖາມນັກຮຽນຄົນບ່ວງດູວ່າຂະເຈົ້າເຮັດຫຍັງເປັນແດ່! ໃຫ້ຂະເຈົ້າຫັດຕອບຫ້ວອກສັນແລະວິທຍາວ. ຈົງເຮັດ
ໃຫ້ແນ່ໃຈວ່າຂະເຈົ້າເຂົ້າໃຈຄວາມໝາຍຂອງຄຳວ່າ " ເປັນ " ຢູ່ໃນທີນ.

NOTES

1) Compare S + dàj constructions with S + pen constructions

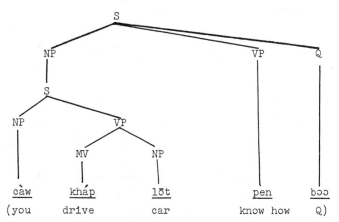

'Do you know how to drive?'

The S + dàj and S + pen structure   identical; the difference
arises from the difference in meaning between pen 'to know how
to perform some activity' and dàj 'to be able to do something'.

2) The affirmative response to S + pen bɔɔ is pen. The negative
response is bɔɔ pen. S + pen constructions are negated by
putting bɔɔ before pen.

3) dàj and pen may be combined with questions as in these examples:

láaw hēt njǎŋ pen   'What does he know how to do?'

càw sỳy njǎŋ dàj   'What' can you buy?'

APPLICATION

1. láaw pɛɛŋ lŏt bɔɔ pen. This sentence indicates that (a) he doesn't have any tools (b) he doesn't know how to fix cars (c) he doesn't want to fix the car (d) he doesn't have a car.

2. If someone said, khɔj kháp lŏt bɔɔ dàj, this might indicate that (a) he doesn't feel like driving (b) he has his right leg in a cast (c) he forgot his driver's license (d) he is ill.

3. In the sentence láaw thāaj hùup bɔɔ pen, the subject of the sentence is (a) láaw (b) thāaj hùup (c) láaw thāaj hùup (d) láaw thāaj.

4. Which of the sentences below means 'I don't know how to shoot a gun'? (a) khɔj njíŋ pyyn pen (b) khɔj bɔɔ njíŋ pyyn pen (c) khɔj njíŋ pyyn bɔɔ pen (d) khɔj njíŋ pyyn pen bɔɔ.

5. Change the following sentences to the negative: (a) càw pɛɛŋ lŏt pen bɔɔ? (b) khɔj wàw pháasǎa aŋkít pen.

6. Answer this question affirmatively: càw pɛɛŋ lŏt pen bɔɔ? ____

7. Answer this question negatively: càw thāaj hùup pen bɔɔ? ____

Answers: 1b, 2b, c, or d, 3c, 4c, 5(a)càw pɛɛŋ lŏt bɔɔ pen bɔɔ? (b)khɔj wàw pháasǎa aŋkít bɔɔ pen 6pen 7bɔɔ pen.

166

CYCLE 38

M-1

tiicák	to type
láaw tiicák dàj bɔɔ?	Can she type?
sāk hùup	to take pictures
láaw sāk hùup dàj bɔɔ?	Can she take pictures?
sỳy khɔ̌ɔŋ	to shop
láaw sỳy khɔ̌ɔŋ dàj bɔɔ?	Can he shop?
tát phɔ̌m	to cut hair
láaw tát phɔ̌m dàj bɔɔ?	Can she cut hair?
púk hỹan	to build a house
láaw púk hỹan dàj bɔɔ?	Can she build a house?
khúakin	to cook
láaw khúakin dàj bɔɔ?	Can she cook?

M-2

khúakin

bɔɔ dàj, phɔ̄wāa láaw khúakin bɔɔ pen
No, because she doesn't know how to cook.

púk hỹan
build a house

bɔɔ dàj, phɔ̄wāa láaw púk hỹan bɔɔ pen
No, because he doesn't know how to build a house.

167

tát phǒm   cut the hair

   bɔɔ dàj, phɔwǎa láaw tát   No, because he doesn't know
   phǒm bɔɔ pen   how to cut hair.

sỳy khǒɔŋ   to shop

   bɔɔ dàj, phɔwǎa láaw sỳy   No, because he doesn't know
   khǒɔŋ bɔɔ pen   how to shop.

sǎk hùup   take a picture

   bɔɔ dàj, phɔwǎa láaw sǎk   No, because he doesn't know
   hùup bɔɔ pen   how to take a picture.

tiicák   type

   bɔɔ dàj, phɔwǎa láaw tii   No, because he doesn't know
   cák bɔɔ pen   how to type.

C-1

(khúakin)
   A. láaw khúakin dàj bɔɔ?   Can he cook?
(bɔɔ)
   B. bɔɔ dàj, phɔwǎa láaw khúa-   No, because he doesn't know
     kin bɔɔ pen   how to cook.

LAO BASIC COURSE

C-2
(njǎŋ)
  A. láaw hɛt njǎŋ pen?   What does he know how to do?
(púk hýan)
  B. láaw púk hýan pen   He knows how to build the
                           house.

บົດນຕານລອງຈອມຄວາມເຂົ້າໃຈຂອງນັກຮຽນໂດຍການປຽບທຽບຄຳວ່າ"ເປັນ"ແລະ"ໄດ້"ເບຶ່ງຄ!
ຂະເຈົ້າຄົນຄວາມແຕກຕ່າງກັນແລວບໍ? "ຂອຍແປວຮົດເປັນ ແຄວາມນນຂອຍແປວຮົດບໍໄດ້".

NOTES

1) **phɔ̌wáa** 'because' is a sentence connective. The sentence
that follows **phɔ̌wáa** stands in causal relatiohship to the
one that precedes it.

Sentence 1: láaw khúakin bɔɔ dàj
Sentence 2: láaw khúakin·bɔɔ pen
S 1 + S 2: láaw khúakin bɔɔ dàj phɔ̌wáa (láaw khúakin) bɔɔ pen
          'She can't cook because she doesn't know how
          (to cook).'

2) The difference in meaning between S + dàj 'to be in a position
or situation to do something' and S + pen 'to know how to do
something' may be illustrated in sentences like this one:
(láaw sāk hùup) bɔɔ dàj phɔ̌wáa láaw sāk hùup bɔɔ pen
'He is unable to (take a picture) because he doesn't know how
to take a picture'.

However, there are situations in which pen and dàj may be
interchanged, as follows:
càw wàw pháasǎa aŋkít bɔɔ pen / dàj 'You can't speak English.'

169

APPLICATION

1. Complete the following sentences:

   (a) bɔɔ dàj, phɔwāā láaw tát phɤm _____

   (b) bɔɔ _____, phɔwāā láaw sāk hùup bɔɔ pen.

2. Fill in the blanks in the following sentences:

   (a) khɔ̃j si paj nám lɤ̃t thîip _____ khɔ̃j bɔɔ míi lɤ̃t

   (b) khɔ̃j si njāāŋ paj _____ khɔ̃j kháp lɤ̃t bɔɔ pen

   (c) khɔ̃j si khīī hýa paj _____ khɔ̃j njāāŋ paj bɔɔ dà.

3. Fill in the blanks with <u>pen</u> or <u>dàj</u> as indicated. If either is possible, put in both.

   (a) khɔ̃j paj nám hýa bɔɔ _____

   (b) láaw njāāŋ paj _____

   (c) láaw hēt njăŋ _____

   (d) càw sāk hùup _____ bɔɔ?

   (e) láaw tii cák bɔɔ_____

Answers: 1(a)bɔɔ pen (b)dàj 2a, b and c: phɔwāā
3(a)dàj (b)dàj (c)dàj/pen (d)dàj/pen (e)dàj/pen

CYCLE 39

M-1

<u>sỳy</u>   buy

   càw sỳy màa cák too?   How many horses did you buy?

<u>hěn</u>   see

   càw hěn màa cák too?   How many horses did you see?

<u>míi</u>   have

   càw míi màa cák too?   How many horses do you have?

<u>khǎaj</u>   sell

   càw khǎaj màa cák too?   How many horses did you sell?

<u>dàj</u>   get

   càw dàj màa cák too?   How many horses did you get?

<u>lìaŋ</u>   raise

   càw lìaŋ màa cák too?   How many horses did you raise?

M-2

<u>pỳm</u>   book

   khɔ̀j hěn pỳm sɔ̌ɔŋ hǔa   I see two books.

<u>sāaŋmàj</u>   carpenter

   khɔ̀j hěn sāaŋmàj sɔ̌ɔŋ khón   I see two carpenters.

<u>·mǎa</u>   dog

   khɔ̀j hěn mǎa sɔ̌ɔŋ too.   I see two dogs.

mâak k̀laŋ   orange

      khɔ̂j hěn mâak k̀laŋ sɔ̌ɔŋ nʉaj   I see two oranges.

paa   fish

      khɔ̂j hěn paa sɔ̌ɔŋ too   I see two fish.

hùup   picture

      khɔ̂j hěn hùup sɔ̌ɔŋ phɛɛn   I see two pictures.

ŋə́n, k̀ip   money, kip

      khɔ̂j hěn ŋə́n sɔ̌ɔŋ k̀ip   I see two kips.

C-1
(paa, too)
    A. càw sỳy paa cák too   How many fish did you buy?
(sǎam)
    B. sǎam too.   Three.

C-2
(hěn)
    A. càw hěn njǎŋ?   What do you see?
(mǎa)
    B. khɔ̂j hěn mǎa.   I see some dogs.
(cák too)
    A. càw hěn mǎa cák too?   How many dogs do you see?
(sīī)
    B. sīī too   Four.

NOTES

1) When d̀àj is the Main Verb in a Sentence and is followed by NP (object), it has the meaning 'to get, earn, procure'.

 khɔ̌j d̀àj pỳm 2 hǔa   'I procured 2 books.'

2) lìaŋ means 'to look after, raise'. It may occur only with animate NP as objects.

 lìaŋ lùuk   'to raise' or 'to take care of children'

 lìaŋ màa   'to raise horses'

 lìaŋ sát   'to raise animals'

3) sǎaŋ means 'artisan, skilled craftsman'. màj means 'wood'. sǎaŋ màj is used to refer to a 'person who is skilled in working with wood', hence it includes carpenters, cabinet makers, coffin makers, etc.

NO APPLICATION PHASE

173

CYCLE 40

M-1

tóʔ	table
tóʔ nūaj nìi	This table
sát	animal
sát too nìi	This animal
pỳm	book
pỳm hǔa nìi	This book
hýan	house
hýan lǎŋ nìi	This house
lōt	car
lōt khán nìi	This car
náaj pháasǎa	interpreter
náaj pháasǎa phūu nìi	This interpreter
màa	horse
màa too nìi	This horse

M-2

tóʔnūaj nìi láakháa hâa hòɔj kîip	This table costs 500 kips.
kòɔŋ thāaj hùup nūaj nìi láakháa hâa hòɔj kîip	This camera costs 500 kips.

174

fáj sǎaj an nìi láakháa hâa hɔ̀ɔj kîip	This flashlight costs 500 kips.
móoŋ nûaj nìi láakháa hâa hɔ̀ɔj kîip	This watch costs 500 kips.
pyyn káb3ɔk nìi láakháa hâa hɔ̀ɔj kîip	This gun costs 500 kips.
sŷa phỹyn nìi láakháa hâa hɔ̀ɔj kîip	This shirt costs 500 kips.
mûak baj nìi láakháa hâa hɔ̀ɔj kîip	This hat costs 500 kips.

M-3

wɛɛntaa khǔu nìi	this pair of glasses
wɛɛntaa khǔu nìi láakháa thǎwdaj?	How much does this pair of glasses cost?
thɤ̌nthàw khǔu nìi	this pair of socks
thɤ̌nthàw khǔu nìi láakháa thǎwdaj?	How much does this pair of socks cost?
jaasûup sɔ́ɔŋ nìi	this pack of cigarettes
jaasûup sɔ́ɔŋ nìi láakháa thǎwdaj?	How much does this pack of cigarettes cost?
káp fáj káp nìi	this box of matches
káp fáj káp nìi láakháa thǎwdaj?	How much does this box of matches cost?

mĺit duaŋ nĺi	this knife
mĺit duaŋ nĺi láakháa thǎwdaj?	How much does this knife cost?
kápaw nũaj nĺi	this briefcase
kápaw nũaj nĺi láakháa thǎwdaj?	How much does this briefcase cost?

M-4

pỳm, hǔa	book (classifier)
pỳm nĺi càw khǎaj hǔa lǎ? cák kĩip	How many kips do these books cost apiece?
sĺin, kiilóo	meat, kilo
sĺin nĺi càw khǎaj kiilóo lǎ? cák kĩip	How many kips does this meat cost per kilo?
kápuu, too	crab (classifier)
kápuu nĺi càw khǎaj too lǎ? cák kĩip?	How many kips do these crabs cost each?
mâaklēn, nũaj	tomato (classifier)
mâaklēn nĺi càw khǎaj nũaj lǎ? cák kĩip	How many kips do these tomatoes cost apiece?
móoŋ, nũaj	watch, clock (classifier)
móoŋ nĺi càw khǎaj nũaj lǎ? cák kĩip?	How many kips do these watches cost apiece?'

M-5

hâasíp kîip	fifty kips
hŭa lã? hâasíp kîip	Fifty kips each.
sǎam l̀ɔj sáaw kîip	320 kips
kiilóo lã? sǎam l̀ɔj sáaw kîip	320 kips per kilo.
sípcét sén	seventeen cents
too lã? sípcét sén	Seventeen cents each.
sáawpêɛt kîip	twenty_eight kips
nūaj lã? sáawpêɛt kîip	Twenty_eight kips apiece.

M-6

aw	take
əə, aw sǎa!	O.K., take it!
əə, paj sǎa!	O.K., go ahead!
aw hâj	give
əə, aw hâj láaw sǎa	O.K. give it to him!
əə, kin sǎa!	O.K. eat it!

C-1

(pyyn káb̀ɔk nìi)

A. pyyn káb̀ɔk nìi láakháa thãwdaj?   How much is this gun?

(síps̀ɔŋ phán kîip)

B. síps̀ɔŋ phán kîip   Twelve thousand kips.

177

C-2

A. an nìi mɛɛn njǎŋ?   What's this?
(mḷit)

B. an nìi mɛɛn mḷit   It's a knife.
(mḷit duaŋ nìi)

A. mḷit duaŋ nìi láakháa   How much is this knife?
thǎwdaj?
(sḭḭ síp hâa kîip)

B. sḭḭ síp hâa kîip   Forty-five kips.

C-3

A. kǎj nìi láakháa too lǎ?   How much do these chickens
thǎwdaj?   cost apiece?

B. too lǎ? hâa hɔ̀ɔj sǎamsíp   They are 530 kips each.
kîip

C-4

A. sìin nìi càw khǎaj kiilóo   How many kips does this
lǎ? cák kîip?   meat cost per kilo?

B. kiilóo lǎ? sɤ̌ɔŋ lɔ̀ɔj pɛ̀ɛt   It's 280 kips per kilo.
síp kîip

A. sɤ̌ɔn lɔ̀ɔjcétsíp dàj bɔɔ?   Can you make it 270 kips?

B. bɤɤ, bɤɤ dàj. aw sɤ̌ɔŋ lɔ̀ɔj   No, I can't. Take it for
cétsíp hâa kîip sǎa   275 kips.

A. əə, aw hâj khɔ̌j sɔ̌ɔŋ   O.K., please give me two
   kiilóo dɛɛ   kilos.

ໃຫ້ນັກຮຽນຕິດໃຈສ່ວຂອງຄຳວ່າກັບຈ່ຳນວນເບິ່ງກຸ! ຂະເຈົ້າຮຸ້ຈັກໃຊ້ຄຳປະກອບນາມຸຂະນົດຄຳວ່າດີແລ້ວບໍ?
ຂະເຈົ້າຖາມລາຄາ ເວລາ ແລະກ່ອງກັບຄົມຄຳວ່າໄດຢ່າງຖືກຕ້ອງແລ້ວຫລືຍັງ? ຝຶກຕັດຕລາຍວຽມັນຈຸ່ງລ່ງ!

1) The following NP contains a CP (classifier phrase):

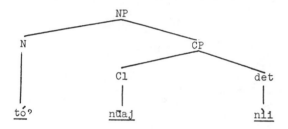

The classifier phrase marks the count noun as definite singular:

    tó? nɯ̄aj nìi   'this table'
    tó? nìi   'these tables'

Some additional unit classifiers and their noun co-occurrents
are given:

Unit Classifier		Noun	
too	'body'	sát	'animal'
		kāj	'chicken'
an	'object' (It can be used for most objects.)	fáj sǎaj	'flashlight'
baj	'sheet like'	mûak	'hat'

179

duaŋ	'something round'	mìit	'knife'
káb3ok	'barrel'	pyyn	'gun'
khūū	'objects in pairs'	wēēntaa	'eye glasses'
		thɤ̌ŋthàw	'socks'
lǎŋ		hɤ́an	'house'

With mass nouns (slin 'meat', nàam 'water, etc.) metric rather than unit classifiers are used:

Metric Classifier		Noun	
kiilóo	(either 1000 meters or 1000 grams)	slin	'meat'
káp	'small box'	káp fáj	'matches'
sɔ́ɔŋ	'small package'	jaasûup	'cigarettes'
kîip	'kip (Laotian unit of currency)		

2) When asking or giving the price of something láakháa is used in a verbless sentence:

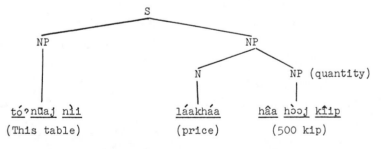

tó?nūaj nìi		láakháa	hâa hɔ̀ɔj kîip
(This table)		(price)	(500 kip)

'This table costs 500 kips.'

In the question NP (quantity) is replaced by thāwdaj. mìit duaŋ nìi láakháa thāwdaj 'How much is this knife?'

180

APPLICATION

1) Fill in the blanks using English as a guide:

(a) kápuu _____ 'these crabs'
(b) sìin _____ 'this meat'
(c) wēēntaa _____ 'this pair of glasses'
(d) màa _____ 'this horse'
(e) kɔ̀ɔŋ thāāj hùup _____ 'this camera'
(f) móoŋ _____ 'these watches'
(g) _____ nūaj nìi 'this briefcase, bag'
(h) mâaklēn _____ 'these tomatoes'
(i) mâaklēn _____ 'this tomato'
(j) kiilóo _____ 320 kîip '320 kips per kilo'
(k) _____ lā? 4000 kîip '4000 kip each (watches)'
(l) _____ lā? 15 kîip '15 kip apiece (books)'
(m) kāj nìi _____ cák kîip 'how much apiece?'
(n) baj lā? 30 _____ '30 kip apiece'
(o) mìit duaŋ nìi _____ 'What's the price of this knife?'

Answers: 1(a)nìi (b)nìi (c)khūu nìi (d)too nìi (e)nūaj nìi
(f)nìi (g)kápaw (h)nìi (i)nūaj nìi (j)lā? (k)nūaj
(l)hǔa (m)too lā? (n)kîip (o)láakháa thāwdaj?

CYCLE 41

M-1

s̀ỳy njǎŋ bɔɔ?	buy anything
láaw s̀ỳy njǎŋ bɔɔ?	Did he buy anything?
paj sǎj bɔɔ?	go anywhere
láaw paj sǎj bɔɔ?	Did he go anywhere?
paj nám phǎj bɔɔ?	going with anybody
láaw si paj nám phǎj bɔɔ?	Is he going with anybody?
phǎk jɯɯ hóoŋhéɛm daj bɔɔ?	to stay in any hotel
láaw si phǎk jɯɯ hóoŋhéɛm daj bɔɔ?	Is he going to stay in any hotel at all?

M-2

s̀ỳy, láaw si s̀ỳy kǎj too· nŷŋ	Yes, he will buy one chicken.
paj, láaw si paj hǎa mɔ̌ɔ	Yes, he is going to see the doctor.
paj, láaw si paj nám àaj láaw	Yes, he is going with his older brother.
phǎk, láaw si phǎk jɯɯ hóoŋhéɛm mǎj	Yes, he will stay in a new hotel at all?

182

M-3

m̂aak mɯ̄aŋ, nɯ̄aj	mango (classifier)
càw si sỳy m̂aak mɯ̄aŋ cák nɯ̄aj bɔɔ?	Are you going to buy any mangoes?
m̂aak kùaj, nɯ̄aj	banana (classifier)
càw si sỳy m̂aak kùaj cák nɯ̄aj bɔɔ?	Are you going to buy any bananas?
phák, m̄at	vegetable, bunch
càw si sỳy phák cák m̄at bɔɔ?	Are you going to buy any bunches of vegetables?
m̂aak phét, hɔ̄ɔ	hot pepper, pack
càw si sỳy m̂aak phét cák hɔ̄ɔ bɔɔ?	Are you going to buy any packages of hot pepper ?
nàm paa, kɛ̀ɛw	fish sauce, bottle
càw si sỳy nàm paa cák kɛ̀ɛw bɔɔ?	Are you going to buy any bottles of fish sauce?

M-4

khɔ̂j si bɔ̄ɔ sỳy pỳm cák hŭa	I'm not going to buy any books.
khɔ̂j si bɔ̄ɔ sỳy kāj cák too	I'm not going to buy any chickens.
khɔ̂j si bɔ̄ɔ sỳy m̂aak kùaj cák nɯ̄aj	I'm not going to buy any bananas.
khɔ̂j si bɔ̄ɔ sɔ̆ɔn cák khón	I'm not going to teach anybody.

183

M-5

khɔ̃j bɜɜ paj sǎj	I didn't go anywhere.
s<u>ỳy</u>	buy
khɔ̃j bɜɜ sỳy njǎŋ	I didn't buy anything.
<u>nám</u>	with
khɔ̃j bɜɜ paj nám phǎj	I didn't go with anybody.
<u>míi</u>, <u>ŋə́n</u>	have, money
khɔ̃j bɜɜ míi ŋə́n cák kîip	I have no kips. (I don't have any kips.)
<u>hùucák</u>	know
khɔ̃j bɜɜ hùucák cák khón	I do not know anybody. (in that group).
khɔ̃j bɜɜ hùucák phɯɯ daj	I don't know anybody at all.

C-1

A. càw si sỳy njǎŋ bɔɔ?　　　Will you buy anything?
B. sỳy, khɔ̃j si sỳy pỳm sɔ̌ɔŋ　Yes, I will buy two books.
　　hǔa

C-2

A. càw si sỳy paa cák too bɔɔ?　Are you going to buy any fish?
B. bɜɜ, khɔ̃j si bɜɜ sỳy paa　　No, I'm not going to buy any
　　cák too.　　　　　　　　　　fish.

C-3

A. càw sì paj nám phǎj bɔɔ?   Are you going with anybody?

B. bɔɔ, khɔ̀j sì bɔɔ paj nám   No, I'm not going with
   phǎj?   anybody.

ລອງໃຫ້ນັກຮຽນສົມມຸດຕາງກັນໄປຈຸ່ຂອງກິນ ຕລິໃຫ້ລະເຈົ້າຖາມກັນເບີ່ງດູວ່າ ຜູ້ໃດຈະໄປໃສບໍ?
ເຮັດຫຍັງບໍ? ຕລິວ່າຈະເອົາຈັກໂຕບໍ? ຈັກແຜນບໍ? ແລະຕໍ່ໄປ. ສໍາຄັນກໍຄືໃຫ້ນັກຮຽນເວົ້າຈິນລຸ່ສົມ.

NOTES

1) mâak means 'fruit of a tree or plant' and is the first element
   in many Noun Compounds referring to fruits and vegetables,
   mâak mûaŋ 'mango', mâak kwàaj 'banana', mâak klaŋ 'orange',
   mâak phét 'hot peppers'. The general word for fruit is mâakmàj;
   however, mâak does occur with this meaning in

   tônmàaj nìi bɔɔ pen mâak   'This tree has no fruit on it'.

2) mât means literally 'to tie up'. It is used to mean 'bunch,
   or bundle' of vegetables, etc.

3) hɔɔ 'to wrap up' is used to refer to 'packages, packets, etc.'
   or things that are wrapped in paper. It does not refer to
   boxes.

4) kɛ̀ɛw means 'glass as a material'. It is also used to refer to
   'glass bottles'. The word for a 'glass to drink out of' is
   cɔ̀ɔk . cɔ̀ɔk kɛ̀ɛw is a 'glass drinking glass'.

5) njǎŋ, sǎj, and phǎj usually function as question words in
   sentences:

   càw paj sǎj?   'Where are you going?'

   láaw sì khǎaj njǎŋ?   'What is he going to sell?'

   càw sì dəəntháaŋ nám phǎj?   'Who are you going to travel
                                 with?'

185

But in negative sentences or in questions with bɔɔ, they function as indefinite nouns:

láaw sẏy njǎŋ bɔɔ?   'Did he buy anything?'

láaw.. paj sǎj bɔɔ?   'Did he go anywhere?'

càw bɔɔ paj nám phǎj bɔɔ?   'You didn't go with anybody?'

cák 'How many?' functions as a question word in

càw míi pẏm cák hǔa ?   'How many books do you have?'

but in the negative sentence khɔj bɔɔ mii cák hǔa 'I don't
have a single one (book)', cák means 'any' or 'a single one'.
daj 'any' has a similar meaning in the affirmative question.

láaw si phāk jūu hóoŋhéεm   'Is he going to stay in any
daj bɔɔ ?   hotel at all?'

bɔɔ, láaw si bɔɔ phāk jūu   'No, he isn't going to stay
hóoŋhéεm daj   in any hotel.'

cák and daj are both used in the negative for emphasis. In
cases where either cák and/or daj can be used daj is usually
more general in meaning. Compare:

khɔj bɔɔ hùucák cák khón   'I don't know anybody in this
                              group.'

khɔj bɔɔ hùucák phūu daj   'I don't know anybody in this
                              town.'

186

APPLICATION

1. Translate the following sentence into Lao: (Write the answers
   on a separate piece of paper or say them aloud and check your
   answers).

   (a) What do you see? I don't see anything.
   (b) Where did your friend go? He didn't go anywhere.
   (c) Do you have any money? No, I don't have a single kip.
   (d) Do you know anybody in Vientiane? No, I don't know a
        soul there.

Answers: ı́(a)càw hɛ̌n ɲjǎŋ? khɔ̂j bɔɔ hɛ̌n ɲjǎŋ (b)phɣan càw
          paj sǎj? láaw bɔɔ paj sǎj (c)càw míi ŋén bɔɔ?
          bɔɔ, khɔ̂j bɔɔ míi ŋén cák kîip (d)càw hùucák phaŋ
          daj juu wíaŋcan bɔɔ? bɔɔ, khɔ̂j bɔɔ hùucák phaŋ
          daj juu hân cák khón

187

CYCLE 42

M-1

hùucák káp láaw	to know her
phǎj phǎj kɔɔ jâak hùucák káp láaw	Everybody wants to know her.
paj bɜŋ	to go see
phǎj phǎj kɔɔ jâak paj bɜŋ	Everybody wants to go see.
síim	to taste
phǎj phǎj kɔɔ jâak síim	Everybody wants to taste.
sỳy	to buy
phǎj phǎj kɔɔ jâak sỳy	Everybody wants to buy.
khīī	to ride
phǎj phǎj kɔɔ jâak khīī	Everybody wants to ride.
āān	to read
phǎj phǎj kɔɔ jâak āān	Everybody wants to read.

M-2

láaw, ŋáam	she, pretty
láaw ŋáaṁ lǎaj	She is very pretty.
síinée, mɯan	the film, good
síinée mɯan lǎaj	The film is very good. (enjoyable)
aahǎan, sɛɛp	the food, delicious
aahǎan sɛɛp lǎaj	The food is very delicious.

188

M-2

khɔ̌oŋ‚thŷyk   things, cheap
    khɔ̌oŋ thŷyk lǎaj   Things are very cheap.
lŏt, mā̄j   the car, new
    lŏt mā̄j lǎaj   The car is very new.
pỳm nĭi nâa sɔ̌ncaj   this book, interesting
    pỳm nĭi nâa sɔ̌ncaj lǎaj   This book is very interesting.

C-1

(ŋáam)   (pretty)
    A. láaw ŋáam bɔɔ?   Is she pretty?
(hùucák káp láaw)   (to know her)
    B. oo, láaw ŋáam lǎaj   Oh yes, she is very pretty.
       phǎj phǎj kɔɔ jâak   Everybody wants to know her.
       hùucák káp láaw

C-2

(hùucák káp láaw)   (to know her)
    A. pen njǎŋ phǎj phǎj kɔɔ   Why does everybody want to
       cȳŋ jâak hùucák káp   know her?
       láaw.
(hùucák káp láaw, ŋáam)   (to know her, pretty)
    B. phǎj phǎj kɔɔ jâak   Everybody wants to know her
       hùucák káp láaw phɔɔʔwā̄a because she is very pretty.
       láaw ŋáam lǎaj

NOTES

1) Doubling of phǎj 'who, anyone' gives it the general and all inclusive meaning 'everybody'. It is normally followed by kɔɔ, which in this case can not be translated.

2) jâak 'want, would like' is normally followed by VP: láaw jâak paj bəŋ síinée 'He wants to go to a movie.' jâak should not be confused with māk 'like to': láaw māk paj bəŋ síinée 'He likes to go to movies.'

3) lǎaj 'very' is an intensifier when it occurs after stative verbs like ɲáam 'pretty', etc.

4) mûan 'to be enjoyable, to be fun' may have only inanimate NP or VP as Subject:

   pen thāhǎan mûan bɔɔ?   'Is it fun being a soldier?'

   síinée mûan bɔɔ?   'Did you enjoy the movie?'

5) The construction pen njǎŋ... cʊ̃ŋ 'Why (how is it that...)' occurs initially in the sentence:

   pen njǎŋ láaw cʊ̃ŋ jâak paj   'Why (how is it that...) does
   pácam jūū páthèet láaw?   he want to be stationed in
                                      Laos?'

6) nâasǒncaj 'interesting' functions like a stative verb, but it is a compound made up of nâa 'to be able' or 'ing' + sóncaj 'to be interested in'. nâa may occur before other verbs with a similar function: nâakin 'look good to eat', nâajūū 'nice to live in', etc.

APPLICATION

1. Complete the following sentences using the English as a guide:

(a) _____ kɔɔ hùu lɛ̀ɛw
    (Everybody already knows that.)

(b) _____ láaw _____ bɔ̄ɔ paj bāŋ síinée
    (Why didn't he go to the movies?)

(c) míia láaw _____ ŋáam _____
    (His wife isn't very pretty.)

(d) híian pháasǎa _____ bɔɔ?
    (Is studying a language fun?)

(e) lōt càw _____ bɔɔ?
    (Is your car new?)

(f) aahǎan láaw _____ bɔɔ?
    (Is Lao food delicious?)

(g) láaw _____ lǎaj bɔɔ?
    (Is she very short in height?)

(h) khɔ̌j bɔ̄ɔ jâak _____
    (I don't want to be fat.)

(i) khɔ̌j bɔ̄ɔ _____ khón cɔ̄ɔj
    (I don't like skinny people.)

(j) jūu bàan nɔ̀ɔk _____
    (It's no fun living out in the provinces.)

191

(k) _____ càw _____ hían pháasǎa láaw ?
(How do you happen to be studying Lao?)

(l) _____ mūan lǎaj
(Flying (going by plane) is a lot of fun.)

(m) _____ bʊʊ mǎk kháp lot
(Nobody likes to drive a car.)

(n) pỳm hǔa nàn _____
(That book isn't very interesting.)

CYCLE 43

M-1

hěn nâa láaw   to see her face

    phǎj phǎj kɔɔ bɔɔ jâak   No one wants to see her face.
    hěn nâa láaw

pen phȳan láaw   to be his friend

    phǎj phǎj kɔɔ bɔɔ jâak   No one wants to be his friend.
    pen phȳan láaw

njûŋkīaw   to be concerned

    phǎj phǎj kɔɔ bɔɔ jâak   No one wants to be concerned.
    njûŋkīaw

jūū   to live (in it)

    phǎj phǎj kɔɔ bɔɔ jâak jūū   No one wants to live (in it)

thíaw tháaŋ sên nìi   to take this road

    phǎj phǎj kɔɔ bɔɔ jâak   No one wants to take this
    thíaw tháaŋ sên nìi   road.

sàj hɔ̂ɔŋ nìi   to use this room

    phǎj phǎj kɔɔ bɔɔ jâak   No one wants to use this
    sàj hɔ̂ɔŋ nìi   room.

193

M-2

boo súphàap   impolite

    láaw boo súphàap lǎaj   He is very impolite.

khón khîi thʉʉ   stingy person

    láaw pen khón khîi thʉʉ   He is a very stingy person.
    lǎaj

boo sǎmkhán paandaj   not so important

    lỳaŋ nìi boo sǎmkhán   This matter is not so importan
    paandaj

nòoj   small

    hỳan lǎŋ nìi nòoj lǎaj   This house is very small.

kandaan   dangerous

    tháaŋ sên nìi kandaan   This road is very dangerous.
    lǎaj

C-1

(boo súphàap)   (impolite)

    A. láaw boo súphàap, mɛɛn   He is impolite, isn't he?
       boo?

(hěn nâa láaw)   (to see his face)

    B. mɛɛn lɛɛw, láaw boo   Yes, he is very impolite.
       súphàap lǎaj phǎj   No one wants to see his
       phǎj koo boo jâak   face.
       hěn nâa láaw.

C-2

(jâak hĕn nâa láaw)   (want to see his face)

    A. pen njǎŋ phǎj phǎj kɔɔ   Why doesn't anybody want
       cŷŋ bɔɔ jâak hĕn nâa   to see his face?
       láaw?

(bɔɔ súphàap) láaw, bɔɔ   (impolite)
súphàap)

    B. phǎj phǎj kɔɔ bɔɔ jâak   No one wants to see his face
       hĕn nâa láaw phɔwàa   because he is so impolite.
       láaw bɔɔ súphàap lǎaj.

ມາໃນຕອນມ່ອາດຈະເປັນໂອກາດທີ່ສໍຫ້ລັຍແຕ່ງເຄື່ອງປະກອບ. ຈິ່ງຢ່າລົ້ມວ່າທຸກເຄື່ອງທີ່ແຕ່ງ ຢ່ນໃຕມ
ຈະຕ້ອງມີຄ່າຄ່ວ່າທີ່ເລິກເຊິ່ງ ຈຸ່ວມສ່ນີ ແລະຄ່ອຍໆຍາ ຈອກກາມຄວາມສາມາກ ຂອງນັກຣຽນ. ວິທີສອນ
ເຄື່ອງປະກອບທີ່ໄດ້ຜ່ນຍ່າງມ່ວ່ງກໍດີ ບໍ່ໃຫ້ນັກຣຽນ ອານເຄື່ອງທີ່ເຮັດແຕ່ງວ່ນ ແຕ່ໃຫ້ເຮັດດ່ວນ:

1. ຖາມເຄື່ອງອານໃຫ້ນັກຣຽນ ຟັງຕ່ອລະ ນ່ອຍ ແລະຖາມນັກຣຽນຢ່ສເມ່ວ່າ ຂະເຈົ້າ ເຂົ້າໃຈ ຫລ້ຍ.
ຖາຂະເຈົ້າບ ເຈົ້າ ໃຈ ກໍໃຫ້ຢຸ່ດອານ ແລ້ວ ອະ ທິບາຍ ຈ້ນ ຂະ ເຈົ້າ ເຂົ້າ ໃຈ.

2. ໃຫ້ຂະ ເຈົ້າ ເວົ້າແຕ່ລະ ປໂຍກ ຕາມ ຕ່ານ ຈ້ນລະ ຈນ.

3. ຖາມຄໍຖາມກ່ວນ ຣ່ອກັຍ ເຄື່ອງ ແລະ ໃຫ້ນັກຣຽນ ຕອບຄ່ວຍ ຄວາມ ແນ່ ໃຈ.

4. ໃຫ້ນັກຣຽນ ສຣຸບ ເຄື່ອງ ສຸ ຕ່ານ ປ໌ ງ.

CYCLE 44

M-1

<u>ŋáam kwāa</u>   prettier than

  hýan lăŋ nìi ŋáam kwāa   This house is prettier than
  lăŋ nàn   that one.

<u>kwàaŋ kwāa</u>   more spacious than

  hýan lăŋ nìi kwàaŋ kwāa   This house is more spacious
  lăŋ nàn   than that one.

<u>khèɛp kwāa</u>   less space than

  hýan lăŋ nìi khèɛp kwāa   This house has less space
  lăŋ nàn   than that one.

<u>thŷyk kwāa</u>   cheaper than

  hýan lăŋ nìi thŷyk kwāa   This house is cheaper than
  lăŋ nàn   that one.

<u>phéɛŋ kwāa</u>   more expensive than

  hýan lăŋ nìi phéɛŋ kwāa   This house is more expensive
  lăŋ nàn   than that one.

<u>sŭuŋ kwāa</u>   higher than

  hýan lăŋ nìi sŭuŋ kwāa   This house is higher than
  lăŋ nàn   that one.

M-2

lɛɛn wáj

   lŏt khán nìi lɛɛn wáj
thāw kan káp khán nàn

láakháa

   lŏt kán nìi láakháa thāw
kan káp khán nàn

njāj thɔɔ

   lŏt khán nìi njāj thɔɔ
kan káp khán nàn

māj thāw

   lŏt khán nìi māj thāw
kan káp khán nàn

run fast

   This car runs as fast as
that one.

price

   This car has the same price
as that one.

as big as

   This car is as big as that
one.

as new as

   This car is as new as that
one.

C-1

(njāj kwāā)

   A. hýan lăŋ nìi njāj kwāā
lăŋ nàn mɛɛn bɔɔ?

(njāj thɔɔ)

   B. bɔɔ mɛɛn, hýan lăŋ nìi
njāj thɔɔ kan káp lăŋ
nàn

(bigger than)

   This house is bigger than
that one, isn't it?

(as big as)

   No, this house is as (big)
as that one.

C-2

(lɛɛn wáj)   (run fast)

   A. lŏt khán nìi lɛɛn wáj   This car runs as fast as
      thāw kan káp khán nàn,   that one, doesn't it?
      mɛɛn bɔɔ?

(<u>lɛɛn wáj kwāā</u>)   (run faster than)

   B. bɔɔ mɛɛn, lŏt khán nìi   No, this one runs faster
      lɛɛn wáj kwāā khán nàn   than that one.

ຈົ້ງທ່ອຍອນາດ ຄຸນພາຍ ແລະຄຸນຄ່າຂອງສ່ວຍຂອງທຸກກົມເຕັນປູ່ໃນຕອວນເບິ່ງໆ! (ໂທຍ ນ້ອຍ ດີ ຄືກ)
ບົດນີ້ ຕັນໄປທ່ອຍການພະທາຄ້າງໆເບິ່ງໆ! (ເຣັດວຽກ ແລນ ອ້ຍຄື...). ໃຊ້ຄາກິຄາໃຕ້ຕົມິດ.

NOTES

1) Two things may be <u>equal</u> or <u>unequal</u> as far as some quality
    (goodness, etc.) is concerned; consequently, there are in
    language, constructions that may be labeled !Comparison of
    Equality! and 'Comparison of Inequality'.

    (a) The Comparison of Inequality construction in Lao is:

$$NP^1 \quad + \quad V_s \quad + \quad \underline{kwāā} \quad + \quad NP^2$$

     <u>hýan lǎŋ nìi</u>   <u>ŋáam</u>   <u>kwāā</u>   <u>lǎŋ nàn</u>
     (this house   pretty   more   that one)

       !This house is prettier than that one.!

(b) The Comparison of Equality construction is:

$$NP^1 + V_s + \underline{th\bar{a}w} \ \underline{kan} \ \underline{k\acute{a}p} + NP^2$$

lǒt khán nìi	kāw	thāw kan káp	khán nàn
(This car	old	equal to	that one.)

'This car is as old as that one'.

When the stative verb refers to 'size', thɔɔ may replace thāw in construction like the one above:

lǒt khán nìi njāj thɔɔ kan   'This car is as big as
káp khán nàn   that one.'

The stative verb may be replaced by V + Adverb (lɛɛn wáj) in either of the constructions above:

lǒt khán nìi lɛɛn wáj kwāā   'This car runs faster than
khán nàn   that one.'

lǒt khán nìi lɛɛn wáj thāwkan   'This car runs as fast as
káp khán nàn   that one.'

APPLICATION

1. Complete the following sentences using the English as a guide:

   (a) láaw _____ càw bɔɔ?
       (Is she taller than you?)

   (b) mía càw _____ mía láaw
       (Your wife's as pretty as his.)

   (c) láaw njāāŋ _____ càw
       (He walks faster than you do.)

199

(d) lỳaŋ nìi _____ lỳaŋ nàn
(This story is more interesting than that one.)

(e) láaw pen khón _____ càw
(He's as intelligent a person as you are.)

(f) láaw kháp lɔ̃t _____ phȳan càw
(He drives faster than your friend.)

(g) khɔ̃j míi ŋə́n _____ càw
(I have more money than you.)

(h) phǎj phǎj kɔɔ bɔɔ _____ láaw
(Nobody is as evil (bad as he is.)

(i) pỳm hǔa nìi _____ hǔa nàn
(This book is as cheap as that one.)

(j) mâak mɯaŋ nɯaj nìi ¨_____ nɯaj nàn
(This mango is as big as that one.)

(k) móoŋ nɯaj nìi _____ nɯaj nàn
(This watch is more expensive than that one.)

(l) hâasíp kîip! _____
(50 kip. That's very expensive.)

(m) mỳy nìi làaw khǎaj _____ mỳy wáan nìi
(He is selling it cheaper today than yesterday.)

(n) _____ nàn
(It's much more delicious than that.)

Answers: (a)sǔuŋ kwāa (b)ŋáam thāw kan káp (c)wáj kwāa (d)nâa sǒncaj kwāa (e)salâat thāw kan káp (f)wáj kwāa (g)lǎaj kwāa (h)sɯa thāw kan káp (i)láakhǎa thāw kan káp (or) thỹyk thāw kan káp (j)njǎj thɔɔ kan káp (k)phéɛŋ kwāa (l)phéɛŋ lǎaj (m)thỹyk kwāa (n)sèɛp lǎaj kwāa

CYCLE 45

M-1

ŋáam kwāā mūū   the prettiest

    náj sǎam khón nìi càw khɨt   Which of these three women do
    wāā njíŋ phūūdaj ŋáam kwāā   you think is the prettiest?
    mūū?

nâahǎk kwāā mūū   the loveliest

    náj sǎam khón nìi càw khɨt   Which of these three women do
    wāā njíŋ phūūdaj nâahǎk   you think is the loveliest?
    kwāā mūū?

khîihàaj kwāā mūū   the ugliest

    náj sǎam khón nìi càw khɨt   Which of these three women do
    wāā njíŋ phūūdaj khîihàaj   you think is the ugliest?
    kwāā mūū?

hìaphɔɔj kwāā mūū   the best-mannered

    náj sǎam khón nìi càw khɨt   Which of these three women do
    wāā njíŋ phūūdaj hìaphɔɔj   you think is the best-mannered?
    kwāā mūū?

khîi aaj kwāā mūū   the most bashful

    náj sǎam khón nìi càw khɨt   Which of these three women do
    wāā njíŋ phūūdaj khîi aaj   you think is the most bashful?
    kwāā mūū?

M-2

ŋáam thāw kan	equally pretty
njíŋ sǎam khón nìi ŋáam thāw kan	These three women are equally pretty.
kēŋ thāw kan	equally smart
njíŋ sǎam khón nìi kēŋ thāw kan	These three women are equally smart.
dii thāw kan	equally nice
njíŋ sǎam khón nìi dii thāw kan	These three women are equally nice.
dàjhǎp kaan sýksǎa thāw kan	equally educated
njíŋ sǎam khón nìi dàjhǎp kaan sýksǎa thāw kan	These three women have equal education.
míi aanjū?thāw kan	the same age
njíŋ sǎam khón nìi míi aanjū? thāw kan	These three women are the same age.
míi wìak lǎaj thāw kan	have equal amount of work
njíŋ sǎam khón nìi míi wìak lǎaj thāw kan	These three women have equal amount of work.
míi ŋéndyan thāw kan	have equal salary
njíŋ sǎam khón nìi míi ŋéndyan thāw kan	These three women have equal salaries.

C-1

(ŋáam kwāā mūu)   (the prettiest)

    A. náj sǎam khón nìi càw   Of these three women who
       khɨt wāā njíŋ phūudaj   do you think is the
       ŋáam kwāā mūu   prettiest?

(ŋáam thāw kan)   (equally pretty)

    B. khɔ̂j khɨt wāā njíŋ sǎam   I think these three women
       khón nìi ŋáam thāw kan   are equally pretty.

C-2

(ŋáam kwāā mūu)   (the prettiest)

    A. náj sǎam khón nàn míi   Of these three women there's
       njíŋ phūu nɣ̄ŋ ŋáam   one who is the prettiest,
       kwāā mūu, mɛɛn bɔɔ?   don't you think?

    B. bɔɔ mɛɛn, khɔ̂j khɨt wāā   No, I think they are
       khácàw ŋáam thāw kan   equally pretty.

NOTES

1) The construction for Comparison of Inequality when more than
   two objects are being compared is:

NP (Number of Objects) + NP (Subject) + V_s <u>kwāā</u> + <u>mūu</u>

   <u>náj sǎam khón nìi</u>   <u>njíŋ phūudaj</u> <u>ŋáam</u> <u>kwāā</u> <u>mūu</u>
   (of these 3 persons   which woman pretty more group)

   'Which of these three women is the prettiest?'

mūū 'group' always occurs in this construction. The classifier phūū is used before daj because it is the classifier for njíŋ. Observe the following construction with a different classifier:

náj sǎam nūaj nìi mâak kùaj nūaj daj sὲεp kwāā mūū

'Which of these three bananas is the most delicious?'

2) The construction of Comparison of Equality when three or more objects are being compared is:

NP (Subject)   +   V$_s$ +   thāw kan

njíŋ sǎam khóon nìi   sǔuŋ   thāw kan

'These three women are equally tall.'

thāw kan 'equal, equally' may also occur after NP:

njíŋ sǎam khón nìi míi aanjū? thāw kan

(These three women have age equal)
'These three women are the same age.'

APPLICATION

1) Complete the following sentences:

(a) náj sῑῑ khón nìi lùuk phūūdaj nâahǎk _____

(Which of the four children is the most loveable?)

(b) náj sǎam khón nìi càw khῑt wāā njíŋ phūūdaj _____

(Which of these three women do you think is the most bashful?)

(c) pỳm hók hǔa nìi _____

(These six books are priced the same.)

204

LAO BASIC COURSE

(d) phūūsáaj hâa khón nìi míi ŋə́n _____

(These five boys have equal amounts of money.)

(e) sāāŋ màj sɔ̌ɔŋ khón nìi hɛ̄t wîak _____

(These two carpenters work equally skillfully.)

(f) nǎj 3 khón nîi thāhǎan phūūdaj kháp lɔ̌t _____

(Which of these three soldiers drives the fastest?)

(g) nǎj 3 khón nìi nākhían phūūdaj _____

(Which of these three students is the most studious?)

(h) nǎj 3 too nìi kǎj toodaj _____

(Which is the biggest of these three chickens?)

(i) kɛ̀ɛw sǎam nūaj nàn míi _____

(Those three bottles have equal amounts of water in them.)

(j) nǎj 3 khón nàn sāāŋ phūūdaj pīan jaaŋ dàj _____

(Of those three artisans which can change a tire the fastest?)

Answers: (a)kwāā mūū (b)khîiaaj kwāā mūū (c)láakháa thāw kan
(d)lǎaj thāw kan (e)kēŋ thāw kan (f)wáj kwāā mūū
(g)dúʔmān kwāā mūū (h)njǎj kwāā mūū (i)nàm thāw kan
(j)wáj kwāā mūū

205

CYCLE 46

M-1

pỳm, hǔa   book, (classifier)

    diawnìi khɔ̃j njáŋ lỹa pỳm   Now I have two books left.
    jūū sɤ̃ɔŋ hǔa

ŋə̄n, kɪ̂ip   money, kip

    diawnìi khɔ̃j njáŋ lỹa ŋə̄n   Now I have two kips left.
    jūū sɤ̃ɔŋ kɪ̂ip

khâw, thɤ̌ŋ   rice, bag

    diawnìi khɔ̃j njáŋ lỹa khâw   Now I have two bags of rice
    jūū sɤ̃ɔŋ thɤ̌ŋ   left.

paa, too   fish, (classifier)

    diawnìi khɔ̃j njáŋ lỹa paa   Now I have two fish left.
    jūū sɤ̃ɔŋ too

lùukpyyn, lùuk   bullet, (classifier)

    diawnìi khɔ̃j njáŋ lỹa   Now I have two bullets left.
    lùukpyyn jūū sɤ̃ɔŋ lùuk

lābə̄ət mýy, lùuk   hand grenade, (classifier)

    diawnìi khɔ̃j njáŋ lỹa   Now I have two hand grenades
    lābə̄ət mýy jūū sɤ̃ɔŋ lùuk   left.

lâw biạ, kɛ̀ɛw   beer, bottle

    diawnìi khɔ̃j njáŋ lỹa lâw   Now I have two bottles of
    biạ jūū sɤ̃ɔŋ kɛ̀ɛw   beer left.

pàaj, khámkhŭan, phɛɛn

sign, slogan, sheet (classifier)

diawnìi khɔ̌j njáŋ lŷa pàaj
khámkhŭan jʉʉ sɔ̌oŋ phɛɛn

Now I have two slogan signs
left.

M-2

ŋə́n, dooláa

money, dollar

càw njáŋ lŷa ŋə́n jʉʉ cák
dooláa?

How many dollars do you have
left?

thɔ̌ŋ, nʉaj

sack,(classifier)

càw njáŋ lŷa thɔ̌ŋ jʉʉ cák
nʉaj?

How many sacks do you have
left?

mâak kùaj, nʉaj

banana,(classifier)

càw njáŋ lŷa mâak kùaj
jʉʉ cák nʉaj?

How many bananas do you have
left?

bótkhwáam, lỳaŋ

article, story

càw njáŋ lŷa bótkhwáam
jʉʉ cák lỳaŋɣ

How many articles (in a
newspaper) do you have left?

sámáasɪ́k, khón

member, person

càw njáŋ lŷa sámáasɪ́k
jʉʉ cák khón?

How many members do you have
left?

khón, khɔ̀ɔpkhúa

people, family

càw njáŋ lŷa khón jʉʉ cák
khɔ̀ɔpkhúa?

How many families do you
have left?

207

phâa <u>sēt</u> <u>nâa</u>, <u>phy̆y̆n</u>

   càw njáŋ ly̆a phâa sēt
   nâa jūū cák phy̆yn

towel (classifier)

   How many towels do you have
   left?

pɛɛŋ, <u>thŭu</u> <u>khêɛw</u>, <u>an</u>

   càw njáŋ ly̆a pɛɛŋ thŭu
   khêɛw jūū cák an

brush, brush teeth (classifier)

   How many tooth brushes do
   you have left?

C-1

(khâw) (sŏɔŋ thŏŋ)

  A. diawnìi khácàw njáŋ ly̆a
     khâw jūū sŏɔŋ thŏŋ,
     mɛ̄ɛn bɔɔ?

(rice, two sacks)

   Now they have two sacks of
   rice left, isn't that right?

(khâw)

  B. mɛ̄ɛn lɛ̀ɛw, diawnìi
     khácàw njáŋ ly̆a jūū
     sŏɔŋ thŏŋ

(rice)

   Yes, that's right, now they
   have two sacks (of rice) left.

C-2

(mâak kùaj)

  A. càw njáŋ ly̆a mâak kùaj
     jūū cák nūaj?

(bananas)

   How many bananas do you
   have left?

(hâa)

  B. khɔ̂j njáŋ ly̆a mâak
     kùaj jūū hâa nūaj

(five)

   I have five bananas left.

C-3

(sɔ̆ɔŋ phy̆yn)	(two objects of cloth)
A. càw njáŋ ly̆a njăŋ jūu sɔ̆ɔŋ phy̆yn?	Of what objects of cloth do you have two left?
(phâasētnâa)	(towels)
A. khɔ̂j njáŋ ly̆a phâasētnâa jūu sɔ̆ɔŋ phy̆yn?	I have two towels left.

ທ່ານລອງພານັກຮຽນຂອງທ່ານໄລເລກກັນເບິ່ງດູ! ຈົ່ງຕັ້ງເລກໂຈດກ່ອນ ແລ້ວໃຫ້ນັກຮຽນເປັນຜູ້ໄລແລ້ວໃຫ້ຄຳຕອບແກ່ທ່ານເບິ່ງດູ! ເປັນຕົ້ນວ່າ: "ມື້ວານນີ້ຂ້ອຍໄດ້ຊື້ໝາກກ້ວຍ 25 ໜ່ວຍໆລະ 5 ກີບ. ຂ້ອຍໄດ້ກິນໝາກກ້ວຍຈັກໜ່ວຍຂ້ອຍກໍບໍ່ຈື່; ຂ້ອຍຈື່ໄດ້ວ່າກ່ອນຊື້ໝາກກ້ວຍຂ້ອຍມີເງິນຢູ່ 260 ກີບ. ມື້ແລງວານນີ້ຂ້ອຍຍັງເຫຼືອໝາກກ້ວຍຢູ່ 21 ໜ່ວຍ. ຖາມວ່າ 1. ມື້ວານນີ້ຂ້ອຍກິນໝາກກ້ວຍຈັກໜ່ວຍ? 2. ດຽວນີ້ຂ້ອຍຍັງເຫຼືອເງິນຢູ່ຈັກກີບ? 3. ຂ້ອຍສິຊື້ໝາກກ້ວຍໄດ້ອີກຈັກໜ່ວຍ?"

ໝາຍເຫດ: ສິ່ງທີ່ຈະກ່າວຕໍ່ໄປນີ້ ແມ່ນວຽກທີ່ທ່ານຈະຕ້ອງພະຍາຍາມເຮັດໃຫ້ບັນລຸຜົນ:

1. ການອອກສຽງ. ນັກຮຽນຈະຕ້ອງເວົ້າພາສາລາວໃຫ້ໃກ້ສຳນຽງລາວທີ່ສຸດເທົ່າທີ່ຈະເວົ້າໄດ້.
2. ຫຼັກການເວົ້າ. ແມ່ນການເວົ້າໃຫ້ຖືກຕາມຫຼັກ ບໍ່ແມ່ນຈັບໜ້າໃສ່ຫຼັງ ຈັບຫຼັງໃສ່ໜ້າ.
3. ຄຳສັບ. ນັກຮຽນຈະຕ້ອງໃຊ້ຄຳໃຫ້ຖືກຕ້ອງແລະແມ່ນຢຳ; ໃຊ້ຄຳທີ່ກົງກັບຄວາມໝາຍ.
4. ຄວາມຄ່ອງໄວ. ນັກຮຽນຈະຕ້ອງສາມາດເວົ້າໄດ້ດ້ວຍຄວາມໄວທັມມະດາ ແລະສມ່ຳສເມີ.
5. ຄວາມເຂົ້າໃຈ. ນີ້ໝາຍເຖິງຄວາມສາມາດເຂົ້າໃຈເມື່ອເວລາຟັງຄົນອື່ນເວົ້າ.

LAO BASIC COURSE

CYCLE 47

M-1

khâw rice

    khâw háw mót lɛ̀ɛw — Our rice is all gone.

mâak phét pepper

    mâak phét háw mót lɛ̀ɛw — Our (green, red) pepper is all gone.

nàm paa fish sauce

    nàm paa háw mót lɛ̀ɛw — Our fish sauce is all gone.

kya salt

    kya háw mót lɛ̀ɛw — Our salt is all gone.

nàmtaan sugar

    nàmtaan háw mót lɛ̀ɛw — Our sugar is all gone.

phĭkthá j black pepper

    phĭkthá j háw mót lɛ̀ɛw — Our black pepper is all gone.

khâwcĭi bread

    khâwcĭi háw mót lɛ̀ɛw — Our bread is all gone.

sìin meat

    sìin háw mót lɛ̀ɛw — Our meat is all gone.

210

M-2

<u>khâw</u>   rice

   khâw háw kàj si mót lɛ̀ɛw   Our rice is almost gone.

<u>nàmmán</u> <u>bəə</u>   butter

   nàmmán bəə háw kàj si mót   Our butter is almost gone.
   lɛ̀ɛw

<u>nàmmán</u> <u>mūū</u>   lard

   nàmmán mūū háw kàj si mót   Our lard is almost gone.
   lɛ̀ɛw

<u>nàmmán</u> <u>sálát</u>   salad dressing

   nàmmán sálát háw kàj si   Our salad dressing is almost
   mót lɛ̀ɛw   gone.

<u>phákbūa</u>   onion

   phákbūa háw kàj si mót   Our onions are almost gone.
   lɛ̀ɛw

<u>phákthíam</u>   garlic

   phákthíam háw kàj si mót   Our garlic is almost gone.
   lɛ̀ɛw

<u>mâak</u> <u>tɛɛŋ</u>   cucumbers

   mâak tɛɛŋ háw kàj si mót   Our cucumbers are almost
   lɛ̀ɛw   gone.

<u>mâak</u> <u>thūa</u>   beans

   mâak thūa háw kàj si mót   Our beans are almost gone.
   lɛ̀ɛw

M-3

mót lɛ̀ɛw	All gone.
kàj si mót lɛ̀ɛw	Almost all gone.

M-4

nàmpaa	fish sauce
nàmpaa háw njáŋ jʉʉ	We still have fish sauce.
kya	salt
kya háw njáŋ jʉʉ	We still have salt.
phǐkthái	black pepper
phǐkthái háw njáŋ jʉʉ	We still have black pepper.
phákbʉa	onions
phákbʉa háw njáŋ jʉʉ	We still have onions.
khâwcǐi	bread
khâwcǐi háw njáŋ jʉʉ	We still have bread.
sìin ŋúa	beef
sìin ŋúa háw njáŋ jʉʉ	We still have beef.
mâakmàj	fruit
mâakmàj háw njáŋ jʉʉ	We still have fruit.

C-1

(màakphét)   (pepper)

  A. màakphét háw mót lɛ̀ɛw   Are we out of pepper?
     bɔɔ?

  B. əə, mót lɛ̀ɛw   Yes, we are out of it.

C-2

(nàmmán sálát)   (salad dressing)

  A. nàmmán sálát háw kàj si   Are we nearly out of salad
     mót lɛ̀ɛw bɔɔ?   dressing ?

  B. əə, kàj si mót lɛ̀ɛw   Yes, we are almost out of it.

C-3

(mâakphét)   (pepper)

  A. mâakphét háw mót lɛ̀ɛw   Are we out of pepper?
     bɔɔ?

  B. bɔ̄ɔ, mâakphét háw njáŋ   No, we still have some.
     jūū

ฑานຕາສ່ວຂອງຕາງວທີ່ແຕລະຄົນມີຢູ່ເບ້ງຖຸ! ຂະເຈົ້າຍ້ວມີຢູ່ຕລິໃຈຕມົດແລວ? ຢ້ງບຕມົດ, ຢ້ງແຕລິອ
ຢູ່ບ ຕລິ ຕມົດແລວ. ໃກ້ສົຕມົດແລວບ ຕລິວ່າຍ້ງຕລາຍຢຸ?

213

NOTES

1) m<u>ót</u> means 'to be used up'. It is used to indicate that the
   supply of something is exhausted: n<u>àmpaa</u> m<u>ót</u> l<u>ɛ̀ɛw</u> 'The fish
   sauce is all gone.'

   When k<u>àj</u> s<u>i</u> precedes m<u>ót</u>, it indicates that the supply is
   nearly used up.

   The manner in which something was consumed can be indicated
   by puting a verb before m<u>ót</u> : k<u>in</u> m<u>ót</u> 'eaten up', etc.

2) l<u>y̆a</u> is used to indicate that something remains from an amount
   which was originally set aside for some special purpose.
   Observe the use of l<u>y̆a</u> in **sentences**:

   kh<u>ɔ̌j</u> nj<u>án</u> l<u>y̆a</u> p<u>ỳm</u> j<u>ūu</u> s<u>ɔ̌ɔn</u> h<u>ŭa</u>   'I have two books left.'
   (to me still remains book 2)   (of the ones I brought
                                                 back from Germany.)

   The classifier phrase indicating the amount is not immediately
   next to its NP but follows j<u>ūu</u>.

3) nj<u>án</u> ... j<u>ūu</u> is used to indicate that a certain situation
   still continues to exist. It may be used without l<u>y̆a</u> but
   with some difference in meaning. Compare:

   m<u>âak</u> kw<u>ùaj</u> nj<u>án</u> j<u>ūu</u>   'We still have bananas.'
                                      (There's no need to buy any more).

   m<u>âak</u> kw<u>ùaj</u> nj<u>án</u> l<u>y̆a</u> j<u>ūu</u>   'We still have bananas (left over
                                      from making a banana cake).'

APPLICATION

1. Fill in the blanks:

    (a) càw njáŋ _____ sámásĭk _____ cǎk khón
        (How many members do you have left?)

    (b) nàmmán bəə háw _____ mót lὲεw
        (Our butter is almost gone.)

    (c) _____ háw mót lὲεw
        (Our garlic is all gone.)

    (d) kya háw _____
        (We still have salt.)

    (e) mâakphét háw mót lὲεw _____
        (Are we out of pepper?)

    (f) _____ háw njáŋ jūū
        (We still have beef.)

    (g) əə, _____
        (We're out of it.)

    (h) khɔ̌j njáŋ ly̌a paa jūū _____
        (I have two fish left.)

    (i) khácàw _____ aahǎan _____ lὲεw
        (They ate up the food.)

(j) diawnìi khɔ̌j nján lўa _____ __ jɯ̄ɯ _____
(Now I have two kips left.)

(k) _____ lɛ̀ɛw
(Time's up!)

(l) càw nján lўa _____ jɯ̄ɯ cák _____?
(How many bananas do you have left?)

Answers: (a)lўa... jɯ̄ɯ (b)kàj si (c)phákthíam (d)nján jɯ̄ɯ
(e)bɔɔ (f)slìin ŋúa (g)mòt lɛ̀ɛw (h)sɔ̌ɔŋ too (i)kin...
mót (j)ŋén... sɔ̌ɔŋ kîip (k)mót wéeláa (l)mâak kùaj
... nūaj.

216

CYCLE 48

M-1

ŋə́n	money
khácàw mót ŋə́n lɛ̀ɛw	They are already broke.
khwáam khĭt	idea, thought
khácàw mót khwáam khĭt lɛ̀ɛw	They are already out of ideas.
kamláŋcaj	will power, encouragement
khácàw mót kamláŋcaj lɛ̀ɛw	They are already discouraged.
khwáam penhŭaŋ	worry, concern
khácàw mót khwáam penhŭaŋ lɛ̀ɛw	They are already free of concern
thòot	punishment, penalty
khácàw mót thòot lɛ̀ɛw	They have already paid their debt to society.
wéeláa	time
khácàw mót wéeláa lɛ̀ɛw	Their time is up already.
sănnjáa	contract, agreement
khácàw mót sănnjáa lɛ̀ɛw	Their contract is already over.
wăŋ	hope
khácàw mót wăŋ lɛ̀ɛw	They have no more hope.

217

M-2

khácàw nján míi kamláncaj jūū	They are still of a mind (to...)
khwáam ótthón	patience
khácàw nján míi khwáam ótthón jūū	They still have patience.
khámthǎam	question
khácàw nján míi khámthǎam jūū	They still have questions.
panhǎa	problem
khácàw nján míi panhǎa jūū	They still have problems.
khwáam sǎmphán, kan	relations, one another
khácàw nján míi khwáam sǎmphán kan jūū	They still have relations with one another.
kîatsán	dislike
khácàw nján kîatsán kan jūū	They still dislike one another
hākphéɛn kan	love one another
khácàw nján hākphéɛn kan jūū	They still love one another.

C-1

(mót ŋə́n)   (to be broke)

    A. càw mót ŋə́n lɛ̀ɛw bɔɔ?   Are you broke?

    B. əə, khɔ̀j mót ŋə́n lɛ̀ɛw   Yes, I'm broke.

C-2

(míi kamláŋcaj)   (of a mind)

    A. khácàw njáŋ míi   Are they still of a mind
       kamláŋcaj jūū bɔɔ?   (to...)?

    B. əə, khácàw njáŋ míi   Yes, they are.
       kamláŋcaj jūū

C-3

(mót khwáam penhūaŋ)   (free of concern)

    A. càw mót khwáam penhūaŋ   Are you already free of
       lɛ̀ɛw bɔɔ?   concern?

    B. bɔ̄ɔ̄, khɔ̀j njáŋ míi   No, I am still { concerned
       khwáam penhūaŋ jūū   { worried.

219

CYCLE 49

M-1

aasǎj, hýan	live, dwell; house
láaw nján aasǎj jūu hýan càw jūu bɔɔ?	Is he still living in your house?
pen thāhǎan	to be in the military service
láaw nján pen thāhǎan jūu bɔɔ?	Is he still in the service
wāaŋŋáan	to be out of work
láaw nján wāaŋŋáan jūu bɔɔ?	Is he still out of work?
kháa, wìak	to be attached to, work
láaw nján kháa wìak jūu bɔɔ?	Is he still tied up with his work?
penni	to be indebted (to)
láaw nján penni càw jūu bɔɔ?	Is he still indebted to you?
ɔ̀ɔk paj, pátíbát ŋáan	go out, carry out a mission or dut
láaw nján ɔ̀ɔk paj pátíbát ŋáan jūu bɔɔ?	Is he still going out on the mission?

thŷyk khǎŋ	to be locked up
láaw njáŋ thŷyk khǎŋ jɯ̄ɯ bɔɔ?	Is he still locked up?
lǒŋtháaŋ	to lose one's way
láaw njáŋ lǒŋtháaɪ jɯ̄ɯ bɔɔ?	Is he still lost?

M-2

ɔ̀ɔk thāhǎan	leave the military service
láaw ɔ̀ɔk thāhǎan tɛ̄ɛ don lɛ̀ɛw	He left the service a long time ago.
míi wìak hɛ̄t	to have work to do
láaw míi wìak hɛ̄t tɛ̄ɛ don lɛ̀ɛw	He got a job a long time ago.
wǎaŋwìak	to be free of work
láaw wǎaŋwìak tɛ̄ɛ don lɛ̀ɛw	He has had spare time for a long time.
sàjnîi, mót	pay off one's debt, entirely
láaw sàjnîi mót tɛ̄ɛ don lɛ̀ɛw	He paid off his debts a long time ago.
thŷyk pɔ̄ɔj	to be released, to be let free
láaw thŷyk pɔ̄ɔj tɛ̄ɛ don lɛ̀ɛw	He was released a long time ago.

221

nǐi, câak   go away, escape; from

    láaw nǐi câak khɔ̌j   He left me a long time
    tɛɛ don lɛ̀ɛw   ago.

sáw   stop

    láaw sáw ɔ̀ɔk paj patíbát   He stopped going out on the
    ŋáan tɛɛ don lɛ̀ɛw   mission a long time ago.

C-1

(aasǎj jūu hýan càw)   (live in your house)

    A. láaw njáŋ aasǎj jūu   Is he still living in your
       hýan càw jūu bɔɔ?   house?

    B. əə, láaw njáŋ aasǎj jūu   Yes, he is still living in
       hýan khɔ̌j jūu   my house.

C-2

(ɔ̀ɔk thāhǎan)   (leave the military service)

    A. láaw ɔ̀ɔk thāhǎan lɛ̀ɛw   Has he already left the
       bɔɔ?   service?

    B. əə, láaw ɔ̀ɔk thāhǎan tɛ̄ɛ Yes, he left the service
       don lɛ̀ɛw   a long time ago.

C-3

(kháa wìak)   (tied up with the work)

    A. láaw njáŋ kháa wìaḱ   Is he still tied up with the
       jūu bɔɔ?   work?

    B. bɔɔ, láaw wǎaŋ wìak tɛ̄ɛ No, he was free (of work) a
       don lɛ̀ɛw   long time ago.

CYCLE 50

M-1

lɛɛn, dii	run; good, well
lõt láaw njáŋ lɛɛn dii jɯɯ bɔɔ?	Is his car still running well?
míi, sáphàap	have; condition, state
lõt láaw njáŋ míi sáphàap dii jɯɯ bɔɔ?	Is his car still in good condition?
kák, thŷyk kák	detain; to be detained
lõt láaw njáŋ thŷyk kák jɯɯ bɔɔ?	Is his car still being detained?
phée	break down
lõt láaw njáŋ phée jɯɯ bɔɔ?	Is his car still broken down?
jaaŋ	rubber, tire
lõt láaw njáŋ bɔɔ míi jaaŋ jɯɯ bɔɔ?	Is his car still without tires?
kháa, tom	to be stuck (to), mud
lõt láaw njáŋ kháa tom jɯɯ bɔɔ?	Is his car still stuck in the mud?
pɛɛŋ	fix, repair
lõt láaw njáŋ pɛɛŋ jɯɯ bɔɔ?	Is his car still being fixed?

223

sỳy, phǔu sỳy   buy, buyer

   lŏt láaw njáŋ bɔ̄ɔ míi   Is he still unable to find
   phǔu sỳy jǔu bɔɔ?   a buyer for his car?

M-2

taaj   die

   lŏt láaw taaj lέεw   His car is already broken down.

kāw, lǎaj   old; much, many, very

   lŏt láaw kāw lǎaj lὲεw   His car is already very old.

pεεŋ, lὲεw   repair, fix; complete, finish

   lŏt láaw pεεŋ lὲεw lὲεw   His car has already been fixed.

lεεn, lεεn dàj   run, able to run

   lŏt láaw lεεn dàj lὲεw   His car is already running.

khǎaj   sell

   lŏt láaw khǎaj lὲεw   His car has already been sold.

lāk, khǎw   steal, they

   lŏt láaw thŷyk khǎw lāk   His car has already been
   lὲεw   stolen.

fáj, mâj   fire, catch fire

   lŏt láaw thŷyk fáj mâj   His car was already burned up.

dàj khýyn   gain back, get back

   lŏt láaw dàj khýyn lὲεw   He's already gotten his car
                                        back.

224

C-1

(lɛ̄ɛn dii)   (running well)

  A. lŏt càw njáŋ lɛ̄ɛn dii   Is your car still running
    jūū bɔɔ?   well?

  B. əə, lŏt khɔ̄j njáŋ lɛ̄ɛn   Yes, my car is still running
    dii jūū   well.

C-2

(thŷyk khǎw lāk   (be stolen)

  A. lŏt láaw thŷyk khǎw lāk   His car has already been
    lɛ̀ɛw, mɛ̄ɛn bɔɔ?   stolen, isn't that right?

  B. əə, lŏt láaw thŷyk khǎw   That's right, his car has
    lāk lɛ̀ɛw   already been stolen.

C-3

(lɛ̄ɛn dii)   (running well)

  A. lŏt láaw njáŋ lɛ̄ɛn dii   Is his car still running well?
    jūū bɔɔ?

  B. bɔ̄ɔ, lŏt láaw phée lɛ̀ɛw   No, his car is broken down.

"ຍ້ວງໄປ" "ຍ້ວມີວົງຢູ່" "ຍ້ວງຕຖລ້ອຢູ່" "ສັບໄມວຍ້ວຕາມາຕິ" ຕາມຈິວພານັກຣຽນຂອຍາຍການໃຈ
ຄຳວ່າ "ຍ້ວ" ອອກໄຕກາວ່າງເບິ່ງໆ! ພວມກັນນນກໍຈຶໃຕນັກຣຽນເຂົ້າໃຈເຕົ້ວຕລະສະພາຍການ.

NOTES

(For Cycles 48, 49, 50)

1) When mót is used with abstract Nouns like kamláncaj 'will, spirit', it refers to an absence or lack of something. mót kamláncaj 'to be discouraged', mót wǎŋ 'to have no hope' mót thoot 'to be no longer under punishment'.

2) khwáam is a nominalizer, i.e. when it is placed before VP, the VP is changed into NP:

khwáam	+	VP	=	NP
khwáam		pen hǔaŋ		khwáampenhǔaŋ
....		'to be concerned'		'worry, concern'

The nouns formed in this manner are all Abstract Nouns.

3) míi kamláncaj jūu means 'to still have one's mind on (doing something) or 'not to have given up the idea of (doing something)'. láaw njáŋ míi kamláncaj pen sáaw náa jūu 'He hasn't given up the idea of being a farmer yet.'

4) kan after VP indicates 'mutuality' or 'reciprocity' in an action; it functions somewhat like a reflexive pronoun (myself, himself, etc.) in English:

khácaw njáŋ kîatsáŋ kan jūu   'They still dislike each othe:

5) When thŷyk occurs before certain VP, it functions somewhat like be in the Passive in English:

láaw njáŋ thŷyk khǎŋ jūu   'He is still locked up.'

lót láaw thŷyk khǎw lâk lɛ̂ɛw   'His car has already been stolen.'

thŷyk only occurs before verbs having a bad meaning, such as khǎŋ 'to lock up', fáj mâj 'to burn up', etc. Most verbs such as khǎaj, etc. may occur with either 'active' or 'passive' meaning, thus khǎaj 'to sell' or 'to be sold', etc.

226

6) tɛɛ don lɛ̀ɛw (lit. 'since ᴸ long time already') 'a long time ago' is used to indicate that a situation has been in effect for some time.

láaw ɔ̀ɔk thāhǎan tɛɛ don lɛ̀ɛw   'He left the military service a long time ago'.

7) hɛ̄t wìak means 'to do any kind of work'. míi wìak hɛ̄t means 'to have work to do, to have a job.' wǎaŋ wìak means 'to be free of work'. It has nothing to do with employment. kháa wìak means 'to be tied up in, or very much involved in your job or work.' wāaŋ ŋáan means 'to be out of a job, unemployed'.

8) nîi means 'debt'. pen nîi Person means 'to be indebted to a person'. sàj nîi means 'to pay off debts'.

APPLICATION

1. Complete the following sentences using the English as a guide:

   (a) láaw _____ khwáam ɔ́tthón.
   (He's out of patience.)

   (b) mót _____ lɛ̀ɛw
   (The contract has already expired.)

   (c) njáŋ lǐa _____ _ jūu 2 khɔ̌ɔ
   (two questions still remain.)

   (d) càw pen _____ bɔɔ?
   (Are you concerned, worried?)

   (e) páthèet ciin dɛɛŋ njáŋ míi _____ káp páthèet phámàa jūu
   (Red China still has relations with Burma.)

Answers: 1(a)mót (b) sǎnnjáa (c)khámthǎam (d)hūaŋ (e)khwáam sǎmphán

227

(f) càw njáŋ míi _____ pen náaj khúu jūū bɔɔ?
    (Haven't you given up the idea of being a teacher yet?)

(g) khacàw njáŋ kîatsáŋ _____ jūū
    (They still dislike each other.)

(h) càw míi _____ bɔɔ?
    (Do you have work to do?)

(i) lŏt jūū hân _____ thŷyk
    (Cars are sold cheap there.)

(j) khɔ̂j njáŋ lŷa wéeláa jūū _____
    (I still have ten minutes left.)

(k) hýan láaw _____ lὲɛw
    (His house has already burned down.)

(l) láaw thŷyk khǎŋ _____
    (How long was he locked up?)

(m) phŷan càw thŷyk pɔɔj _____
    (Your friend was released a long time ago.)

(n) càw njáŋ _____ láaw jūū cák kîip
    (How many kip do you still owe him?)

(o) láaw njáŋ _____ jūū hýan khɔ̂j
    (He's still living at my house.)

(p) khɔ̂j bɔɔ pen nîi càw _____
    (I don't owe you a single kip!)

Answers: (f)kamláŋcaj (g)kan (h)wîak hēt (i)khǎaj (j)síp
náathíi (k)thŷyk fáj mâj (l)don paandaj (m)tēɛ
don lὲɛw (n)pen nîi (o)aasǎj(p)cák kîip

228

(q) khɔ̌j _____ mót tɛɛ don lɛ̀ɛw

    (I paid off my debts a long time ago.)

(r) lŏt láaw pɛɛŋ _____ _____

    (His car has already been fixed.)

(s) càw _____ thǎaj hùup _____ _____ bɔɔ?

    (Do you still know how to take pictures?)

(t) hýan láaw _____ _____ lɛ̀ɛw bɔɔ?

    (Has his house been built yet?)

(u) pátuu njáŋ _____ jūu

    (The door is still open.)

(v) khácàw njáŋ _____ jūu

    (They still love each other.)

(w) láaw _____ jūu sǎj?

    (Where did he get lost?)

(x) láaw thŷyk pɔ̌ɔj lɛ̀ɛw phɔ̌ wǎa (láaw) _____ lɛ̀ɛw

    (He has been released already because he has already
    paid his debt to society.)

(y) khɔ̌j bɔ̌ɔ dàj wàw njǎŋ phɔ̌ɔwǎa _____ lɛ̀ɛw

    (I didn't say anything because I was already out of ideas.)

Answers: (q)sàj nîi (r)lɛ̀ɛw lɛ̀ɛw (s)njáŋ... pen jūu (t)púk
lɛ̀ɛw (u)khǎj (v)hākphéɛŋ kan (w)lǒŋ tháaŋ (x)mót
thòot (y)mót khwáamkhīt

229

CYCLE 51

M-1

dɛɛŋ	red
sŷa khɔ̂j sɪ̌i dɛɛŋ	My shirt is red.
khǎaw	white
sŷa khɔ̂j sɪ̌i khǎaw	My shirt is white.
lŷaŋ	yellow
sŷa khɔ̂j sɪ̌i lŷaŋ	My shirt is yellow.
fàa	sky
sŷa khɔ̂j sɪ̌i fàa	My shirt is blue.
dam	black
sŷa khɔ̂j sɪ̌i dam	My shirt is black.
khɪ̌aw	green
sŷa khɔ̂j sɪ̌i khɪ̌aw	My shirt is green.

M-2

nàmtaan	sugar
sŷa càw sɪ̌i njǎŋ, sɪ̌i nàmtaan mɛɛn bɔɔ?	What color is your shirt, it's brown, isn't it?
tháw	grey
sŷa càw sɪ̌i njǎŋ, sɪ̌i tháw mɛɛn bɔɔ?	What color is your shirt, it's grey, isn't it?

khĭaw ɔ̄ɔn
   sŷa càw sĭi njăŋ, sĭi khĭaw
   ɔ̄ɔn,mɛ̄ɛn bɔɔ?

light green
   What color is your shirt,
   it's light green, isn't it?

l̆ŷaŋ kɛ̄ɛ
   sŷa càw sĭi njăŋ, sĭi l̆ŷaŋ
   kɛ̄ɛ,mɛ̄ɛn bɔɔ?

dark yellow
   What color is your shirt,
   it's dark yellow, isn't it?

dam dɛɛŋ
   sŷa càw sĭi njăŋ, sĭ dam
   dɛɛŋ,mɛ̄ɛn bɔɔ?

blackish red
   What color is your shirt,
   it's blackish red, isn't it?

M-3

sôoŋ
   sôoŋ láaw sĭi njăŋ?

pants
   What color are his pants?

káravát
   káravát láaw sĭi njăŋ?

neck tie
   What color is his necktie?

kə̄əp
   kə̄əp láaw sĭi njăŋ?

shoes
   What color are his shoes?

sîn
   sîn láaw sĭi njăŋ?

Lao skirt
   What color is her Lao skirt?

thŏŋthàw
   thŏŋthàw láaw sĭi njăŋ?

socks
   What color are his socks?

kápaw
   kápaw láaw sĭi njăŋ?

brief-case
   What color is his brief-case?

C-1

(kárāvát)   (necktie)

   A. kárāvát càw sǐi njǎŋ?   What color is your tie?

(dɛɛŋ)   (red)

   B. kárāvát khɔ̂j sǐi dɛɛŋ.   My tie is red.

C-2

(kə̂əp)   (shoes)

   A. kə̂əp càw sǐi njǎŋ, sǐi   What color are your shoes?
      nàmtaan mɛɛn bɔɔ?   They are brown, aren't they?

   B. mɛɛn lɛɛw, kə̂əp khɔ̂j sǐi   Yes, my shoes are brown.
      nàmtaan.

NOTES

1) sǐi 'color' normally proceeds the word for colors, i.e., sǐi
    dɛɛŋ '(color) red', sǐi khǐaw '(color) green', etc.

2) Sentences with sǐi in the predicate are normally verbless.

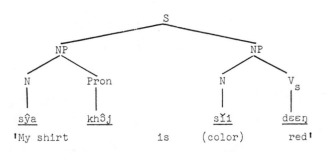

232

3) Verbs of color usually occur as modifiers of sĭi and are questionned with njǎŋ 'What (kind)?'

Q: sŷa càw sĭi njǎŋ?   'What color's your shirt?'

A: sĭi khĭaw   '(It's) green.'

4) Color verbs may be modified by the addition of kɛɛ 'dark (in shade) and ɔɔn 'light (in shade)', thus sĭi khĭaw ɔɔn means 'light green' and sĭi dɛɛŋ kɛɛ, 'dark red.' Mixtures are sometimes indicated by using two color verbs such as sĭi dam dɛɛŋ 'reddish black', or sĭi khǎaw lŷǎŋ 'yellowish white'.

APPLICATION

1. Complete the following sentences using the English as a guide:

   (a) hŷa lám nĭi _____   (What color is this boat?)

   (b) sŷa phŷyn nàn _____   (That shirt is red.)

   (c) mǎak klàŋ nŭaj njāj _____,   (That large orange is green, isn't it?)
   mɛɛn bɔɔ?

   (d) láaw míi cɔ̂ok _____ bɔɔ?   (Does he have a blue glass?)

   (e) kāj too nàn sĭi _____   (That chicken's brown.)

   (f) sŷa fǒn láaw _____   (Her raincoat is light green.)

   (g) _____ càw sĭi dam   (Your shoes are black.)

   (h) _____ láaw sĭi njǎŋ?   (What color is her Lao skirt?)

   (i) kápaw khɔ̂j _____   (My briefcase is dark brown.)

   (j) káravát càw sĭi _____   (Your tie is yellow.)

Answers: (a)sĭi njǎŋ (b)sĭi dɛɛŋ (c)sĭi khĭaw (d)sĭi fàa
(e)nàmtaan (f)sĭi khĭaw ɔɔn (g)kə̀əp (h)sîn (i)sĭi
nàmtaan kɛɛ (j)lŷaŋ

233

CYCLE 52

M-1

njāāŋ, wáj   walk; fast, quick

   láaw njāāŋ wáj phòot   He walks too fast.

sàa, hētwìak   slow, work

   láaw hētwìak sàa phòot   He works too slow.

khɔɔj, wàw   gentle; speak, say

   láaw wàw khɔɔj phòot   He speaks too softly.

dyŋ, héɛŋ, sỳak   pull, strong, rope

   láaw dyŋ sỳak héɛŋ phòot   He pulls too hard on the rope.

daŋ, wàw   loud, speak

   láaw wàw daŋ phòot   He speaks too loud.

don, jūū, hân   long time, stay, there

   láaw jūū hân don phòot   He stayed there too long.

njàak, māk   difficult, like

   láaw māk njàak phòot   He likes to make things harder
                                                      than they are.

lǎaj, kin   much, many; eat

   láaw kin lǎaj phòot   He eats too much.

M-2

láaw njāaŋ wáj paandaj?	How fast does she walk? .
ŋáam, fɔ̀ɔn	pretty, beautiful, dance
láaw fɔ̀ɔn ŋáam paandaj?	How well does she dance?
hían, kēŋ	learn, study; good, smart, clever
láaw hían kēŋ paandaj?	How is he doing in his studies?
hɔ̀ɔŋ phéeŋ, mūan	sings songs; melodious
láaw hɔ̀ɔŋ phéeŋ mūan paandaj?	How well does she sing?
dàj pháasǎa, dii	able to speak a language; well, good
láaw dàj pháasǎa láaw dii paandaj?	How well can he speak Lao?
njōk, nàmnák	lift, weight
láaw njōk nàmnák dàj lǎaj paandaj?	How much weight can he lift?

M-3

njāaŋ, wáj	walk, fast
láaw njāaŋ bɔ̄ɔ wáj paandaj	He doesn't walk very fast.
sǔuŋ, khɣ̀n, mán	high, ascend, it
mán khɣ̀n bɔ̄ɔ sǔuŋ paandaj	It doesn't go up very high.
láaw hían bɔ̄ɔ wáj paandaj	He doesn't learn very fast.

235

hέεn, lŏt   strong, powerful; car

   lŏt láaw lɛɛn bɔɔ hέεŋ   His car doesn't have much
   paandaj   power.

khĭan, ŋáam   write; pretty, beautiful

   láaw khĭan bɔɔ ŋáam paandaj   His handwriting is not very
                                    pretty.

hían, waj   learn, fast

   láaw hian bɔɔ wáj paandaj;   He doesn't learn very fast.

M-4

kháplŏt, wáj   drive, fast

   láaw bɔɔ kháplŏt wáj   He didn't drive very fast.
   paandaj

ɔɔk kamláŋ, kaaj, lyaj lyaj   exercise, physical, often

   láaw bɔɔ ɔɔk kamláŋ kaaj   He doesn't do much physical
   lyaj lyaj paandaj   exercise.

aw hâj, lăaj   give, much

   láaw bɔɔ aw hâj lăaj paandaj He didn't give very much.

aw paj, mót   take; all, completely

   láaw bɔɔ aw pym paj mót   He didn't take all the books.

kin, mót   eat, all entirely

   láaw si bɔɔ kin mót   He's not going eat all of it.

236

M-5

njāaŋ wáj wáj dɛɛ	Walk faster, please.
wàw khɔɔj khɔɔj dɛɛ	Speak softly, please.
kháplɤt sàa sàa dɛɛ	Drive slowly, please.
āan daŋ daŋ dɛɛ	Read loudly, please.
kin lǎaj lǎaj dɛɛ	Eat a lot, please.

C-1

(wàw wáj)

A. càw wàw wáj phòot. wàw
   sàa sàa dɛɛ.

You speak too fast. Speak
slowly, please.

(wàw sàa sàa)

B. khɔɔthòot. khɔ̃j si wàw
   sàa sàa.

I'm sorry. I'll speak
slowly.

C-2

(fɔɔn ŋáam)

A. láaw fɔɔn ŋáam paandaj?

How well does she dance?

(fɔɔn bɤɤ ŋáam)

B. láaw fɔɔn bɤɤ ŋáam **paandaj**

She doesn't dance very well.

C-3

(kháplɤt wáj)

A. láaw si kháplɤt wáj bɔɔ?

Is he going to drive fast?

(kháplɤt wáj)

B. bɤɤ, láaw si bɤɤ kháplɤt
   wáj

No. He's not going to drive
fast.

237

C-4

(khĬan ŋáam)

A. láaw khĬan ŋáam bɔɔ?   Is his handwriting pretty?

(khĬan bɔ̄ɔ ŋáam)

láaw khĬan bɔ̄ɔ ŋáam paandaj   His handwriting is not very
                                      pretty.

ຈິ່ງສ້ວງຄກຄເບິ່ງຈຸດປະສິ່ວຂອງແຕ່ລະພາກຂອງບົດຮຽນນີ້ ແລ້ວຕົ້ຍຕວນຄວາມເຂົ້າໃຈຂອງນັກຮຽນຄັກງເບິ່ງ
ດຸ! ຈິ່ງຂຍາຍການຝຶກຫັດໃນພາກ C ອອກອີກ ແລະແຕ່ງວເຮື່ອງປະກອບອນ! ອະຕິບາຍຮຸບພາບຄ່າງງເບິ່ງດຸ!

NOTES

1) <u>phòot</u> 'to be in excess' normally occurs after stative verbs:
   <u>láaw njáaŋ wáj phòot</u> 'He walks too fast'. The negative form
   of <u>phòot</u> is <u>bɔ̄ɔ</u> ... <u>paandaj</u> 'Not very'. The position of <u>bɔ̄ɔ</u>
   in the sentence is important: Compare <u>láaw bɔ̄ɔ njáaŋ wáj</u>
   <u>paandaj</u> 'He doesn't walk very fast' or 'He isn't walking very
   fast' (because he doesn't want to) with <u>láaw njáaŋ bɔ̄ɔ (dàj)</u>
   <u>wáj paandaj</u> 'He doesn't walk very fast' (because he is unable
   to walk faster).

2) The form <u>paandaj</u> is used after the stative verb in questions
   to find out the manner in which an activity is being carried
   out: <u>láaw hɔ̀ɔŋ phéeŋ mûan paandaj</u> 'How well does she sing?'

APPLICATION

1) Write out a reasonable answer to the following questions:

(a) láaw wàw daŋ paandaj? láaw wàw _____

(b) mía càw njāāŋ wáj paandaj? láaw njāāŋ _____

(c) láaw jūū hân don paandaj? _____

Complete the following sentences using the English as a guide:

(d) láaw át pátuu _____
     (He closed the door too quickly.)

(e) láaw _____ hían _____ dii paandaj
     (He's not learning very fast (because he doesn't want to).

(f) láaw hɔɔŋ phéeŋ _____ mūaj paandaj
     (She doesn't sing very melodiously (because she has a
      very poor voice.)

(g) càw āān wáj _____
     (You read very fast.)

(h) láaw wàw pháasǎa láaw _____
     (He speaks Lao too slowly.)

Answers: (a)daŋ phɔ̀ot (or) bɔ̃ɔ̃ daŋ paandaj (b)wáj phɔ̀ot (or) bɔ̃ɔ̃
          wáj paandaj (c)hók aathit (or) don phɔ̀ot (or) bɔ̃ɔ̃ don
          paandaj (d)wáj phɔ̀ot (e)bɔ̃ɔ̃ (f)bɔ̃ɔ̃ (g)lǎaj
          (h) sàa phɔ̀ot

CYCLE 53

M-1

āan wáj

 read fast

 láaw āan wáj bɔɔ?

  Does he read fast?

wàw cɛ̀ɛŋ

 speak clearly

 láaw wàw cɛ̀ɛŋ bɔɔ?

  Did he speak clearly?

athĪbaaj lā-Īat

 explain thoroughly

 láaw athĪbaaj lā-Īat bɔɔ?

  Did he explain it thoroughly?

hían dii

 be a good student

 láaw hían dii bɔɔ?

  Is he a good student?

hían kɛ̄ŋ

 to be a good learner

 láaw hían kɛ̄ŋ bɔɔ?

  Is he a good student?

njāaŋ njàak

 have trouble walking

 láaw njāaŋ njàak bɔɔ?

  Does he have trouble walking?

M-2

kɛ̄ŋ

 smart

 kɛ̄ŋ sǒmkhúan

  Pretty smart.

cɛ̀ɛŋ

 clear

 cɛ̀ɛŋ sǒmkhúan·

  Pretty clear.

hàaj hɛ́ɛŋ

 serious

 hàaj hɛ́ɛŋ sǒmkhúan

  Pretty serious.

240

máw   to be drunk

 máw sŏmkhúan   Pretty drunk.

mûan   enjoyable

 mûan sŏmkhúan   Pretty enjoyable.

C-1

 A. láaw āan wáj bɔɔ?   Does he read fast?

 B. wáj sŏmkhúan   Pretty fast.

C-2

 A. láaw āan wáj paandaj?   How fast does he read?

 B. wáj sŏmkhúan   Pretty fast.

C-3

 A. láaw hían kēŋ sŏmkhúan bɔɔ? Is he a pretty good student?

 B. kēŋ sŏmkhúan jɑ̄ɑ   Pretty good (smart).

NOTES

1) sŏmkhúan 'suitably, properly' is used after stative verbs to indicate a degree which is neither too much in one direction nor the other.

 láaw āan wáj sŏmkhúan 'He reads fairly fast.'

2) When njàak 'to be difficult' occurs after an action verb, it indicates that the action is taken with difficulty:

 athíbaaj njáak   'It's difficult to explain.'

241

APPLICATION

1) Answer the following questions with an indication that the
   action referred to is done fairly well:

   (a) láaw wàw pháasǎa láaw dii bɔɔ? _____

   (b) láaw lón khândaj wáj paandaj? _____

   (c) láaw lɔɔj nàm kɛ̄ŋ paandaj? _____

   (d) kàncaj sɪɪ náathíi njàak paandaj? _____

   Fill in the blanks using the English as a guide:

   (e) láaw lāw lỳaŋ nàn _____ dii
       (He told the story in detail.)

   (f) láaw kin lâw bia lǎaj kɛ̀ɛw. láaw _____
       (He drank several bottles of beer. He's pretty drunk.)

   (g) láaw kháp lōt _____
       (He drives pretty fast.)

   (h) paj bɜ̀ŋ síinée_____
       (Going to the movies is pretty good fun .)

   (i) át pɔɔŋ-jìam nàn phùn _____ bɔɔ?
       (Is it difficult to close that window over there?)

   (j) láaw áthɪbaaj _____
       (His explanations are not very thorough.)

Answers: (a)dii sǒmkhúan (b)wáj sǒmkhúan (c)kɛ̄ŋ sǒmkhúan
          (d)njàak sǒmkhúan (e)lā-ɪ̂at (f)máw sǒmkhúan (g)wáj
          sǒmkhúan (h)mūan sǒmkhúan (i)njàak (j)bɔɔ lā-ɪ̂at
          paandaj

(k) tít-tɔɔ káp phuu nàn _____
(It's not very difficult to contact that person.)

(l) pĭan jaaŋ njâak _____
(Changing a tire is fairly difficult.)

(m) láaw phím năŋsўy _____
(She types fairly well.)

(n) aakaan khɔ̆ŋ láaw _____ sŏmkhúan
(He is rather seriously ill.)

Answers: (k)bɔɔ njáak paandaj (l)sŏmkhúan (m)kēŋ sŏmkhúan
(n)hàaj hέεŋ

243

CYCLE 54

M-1

<u>kin</u>   eat

   jāā kin lǎaj!   Don't eat too much!

<u>kháplōt wáj</u>   drive fast

   jāā kháplōt wáj lǎaj!   Don't drive too fast!

<u>fōt</u>   be noisy

   jāā fōt lǎaj!   Don't be too noisy!

<u>lùa</u>   misbehave

   jāā lùa lǎaj!   Behave yourself!

<u>khîikhàan</u>   be lazy

   jāā khîikhàan lǎaj!   Don't be too lazy!

<u>cōm</u>   complain, grumble

   jāā cōm lǎaj!   Don't complain too much!

M-2

<u>tɛ̂ʔtɔ̀ɔŋ</u>   touch (with hands)

   kárūnáa jāā tɛ̂ʔtɔ̀ɔŋ   Please don't touch.

<u>tan tháaŋ</u>   block the way

   kárūnáa jāā tan tháaŋ   Please don't block the way.

244

hēt sǐaŋ daŋ   make noise

    kárūnáa jāā hēt sǐaŋ daŋ   Please don't make noise.

lōpkuan   disturb

    kárūnáa jāā lōpkuan.   Please don't disturb (anyone).

jîap, njâa   step on, grass

    kárūnáa jāā jîap njâa   Please don't step on the grass.

sûup jaa   smoke

    kárūnáa jāā sûup jaa   Please don't smoke.

M-3

khâw   enter

    hâam khâw   Do not enter.

sûup jaa   smoke

    hâam sûup jaa   Do not smoke.

pêət   open

    hâam pêət   Do not open.

sūaŋ   pass, race

    hâam sūaŋ   Do not pass.

lūaŋlàm   trespass

    hâam lūaŋ làm   Do not trespass.

thîm khîi njŷa   dump trash

    hâam thîm khîi njŷa   No dumping.

dét dɔ̀ɔkmàj   pick flowers

    hâam dét dɔ̀ɔkmàj   Do not pick flowers.

C-1

    A. khɔ̌j bɔ̄ɔ jâak hâj láaw   I don't want him to eat
       kin lǎaj   too much.

       càw bɔ̀ɔk láaw hâj khɔ̌j   Would you please tell him
       dɛ̄ɛ   for me.

    B. jāā kin lǎaj   Don't eat too much.

C-2

    A. khácàw bɔ̀ɔk njǎŋ háw?   What did they tell us?

(tɛʔtɔ̀ɔŋ)   (touch)

    B. khácàw bɔ̀ɔk háw wāā   They told us. Please don't
       kárūnáa jāā tɛʔtɔ̀ɔŋ   touch.

C-3

(pàaj)   (sign)

    A. pàaj nàn bɔ̀ɔk njǎŋ?   What does that sign say?

(sûup jaa)   (smoke)

    B. hâam sûup jaa   No smoking.

_____

ການຝຶກຫັດເພີ່ມເຕີມສຳລັບຍົດບົກຫມັດຕົວາ ໃຫ້ນັກຮຽນບອກກັນບໍໃຫຣົ໌ຄສ່ວງໃຄສ່ວນງ ຫລືໃຫຂະເຈົ້າ
ປະຕິບັດຕາມຄຳບອກຂອງງມາຍຄຸ. ການຝຶກຫັດຄວນຈະໃຫເປັນໄປຄວຍຄວາມໄວຫັມມະຄາ.

NOTES

1) The request form in Lao is the Verb Phrase without NP (subject): paj kin khâw 'Go eat!' The request may be softened by putting kárūnáa (Lit. 'kindness') 'please' before NP, kárūnáa wàw sàa sàa 'Please speak slower' or by putting dɛɛ after VP: njāāŋ wàj wáj dɛɛ 'Walk faster, please.'

2) The negative request form is: jāā 'don't' + VP: jāā kin lăaj 'Don't eat too much.' This request form may also be softened by putting kárūnáa before it: kárūnáa jāā tan tháaŋ 'Please don't block the way.'

3) In written Lao hâam 'It is forbidden to' is normally used. One sometimes sees signs like this: hâam sûup jāā 'No Smoking'. hâam is rarely used in spoken Lao in this construction.

APPLICATION

1. Complete the following sentences using the English as a guide:

   (a) _____ jāā sûup jaa   (Please don't smoke.)

   (b) (A sign) _____ lūaŋlàm   (No Trespassing.)

   (c) jāā _____ lăaj   (Don't be too lazy.).

   (d) āān daŋ daŋ _____   (Read loudly, please.)

   (e) _____ wáj wáj   (Walk fast.)

   (f) _____ tɔ̂ɔp   (Don't answer that
       khámthăam khɔ̀ɔ nàn   question.)

Answers: (a)kárūnáa (b)hâam (c)khîikhàan (d)dɛɛ (e)njāāŋ
         (f)jāā

(g) (Sign) _____ thāaj   (No picture taking
    hùup jɯɯ nĭi   here.)

(h) jāā khúakin _____   (Don't cook too much.)

(i) _____ thée lóŋ jɯɯ hân   (Don't dump it out
                                        there.)

(j) wáaŋ wàj phùn _____   (Please put it over
                                        there.)

(k) (Sign): hâam _____   (Don't enter.)

(l) _____ kin aahăan phét   (Don't eat too much hot
    lăaj   spicy food.)

_____

Answers: (g)hâam (h)lăaj (i)jāā (j)dɛɛ (k)khâw (l)jāā

CYCLE 55

M-1

<u>săj</u>   where

   càw paj săj máa?   Where have you been (to)?

<u>njăŋ</u>   what

   càw paj hět njăŋ máa?   (You just come back) what
                        did you do?

M-2

<u>wăt</u>   pagoda, temple

   khɔ̌j paj wăt máa   I've been to the temple.

<u>kinkhâw</u>   to eat (meal)

   khɔ̌j paj kin khâw máa   I've been to eat.

<u>hăa mɔ̌ɔ</u>   see the doctor

   khɔ̌j paj hăa mɔ̌ɔ máa   I've been to see the doctor.

<u>sák jaa</u>   to get a shot

   khɔ̌j paj sák jaa máa   I've come back from getting
                        a shot.

<u>săaŋ kép khȳaŋ</u>   warehouse

   khɔ̌j paj săaŋ kép khȳaŋ   I've been to the warehouse.
   máa

249

C-1

    A. càw paj săj máa?   Where have you been?

(hóoŋhían)

    B. khɔ̃j paj hóoŋhían máa   I've been to school.

C-2

    A. càw paj hēt njăŋ máa?   (You just come back) What
                                did you do?

(kinkhâw)

    B. khɔ̃j paj kinkhâw máa   I've been to eat.

NOTES

1) The construction <u>paj</u> ... <u>máa</u> is used to indicate that someone
is returning from having been to some place or having done
something:

    <u>khɔ̃j</u> <u>paj</u> <u>wāt</u> <u>máa</u>   'I've just been to the temple!.

    <u>khɔ̃j</u> <u>paj</u> <u>kin</u> <u>khâw</u> <u>máa</u>   'I've been out to eat.'

The type of question may reflect the difference referred to
above:

    <u>càw</u> <u>paj</u> <u>săj</u> <u>máa</u>?   'Where have you been?'

    <u>càw</u> <u>paj</u> <u>hēt</u> <u>njăŋ</u> <u>máa</u>?   'What have you been doing?'

                            (Lit. What do you come from doing?

APPLICATION

1) Complete the following sentences:

   (a) khɔ̃j _____ kin khâw_____ (I've been to eat.)

   (b) càw paj _____ máa? (What have you been doing?)

   (c) khɔ̃j paj _____ máa (I've been to get a shot.)

2. Answer the following questions according to the actual situation:

   (d) càw paj hēt njǎŋ máa?

   (e) càw paj sǎj máa?

   (f) càw bɔ̄ɔ paj hēt njǎŋ máa bɔɔ?

   (g) càw bɔ̄ɔ paj sǎj máa bɔɔ?

3. Translate the following sentences into English:

   (h) láaw paj khǎj kácɛɛ pátuu nàn máa

   (i) phȳan khɔ̃j paj tiisək jūu páthèet wìat náam máa

   (j) láaw paj khâw thɛ̌ɛw sūamóoŋ khɔ̃ŋ

Answers: 1(a)paj ... máa 1(b)hēt njǎŋ 1(c)sák jaa
          2Your answers will depend on what you have been
          doing very recently. 3(a)He just come back from
          unlocking that door. 3(b)My friend has just come
          back from fighting in Vietnam. 3(c)He's been
          standing in a line for half an hour.

CYCLE 56

M-1

phùakcàw máa tɛɛ sǎj?	Where did you all come from?
pỳm, hǔa	book (classifier)-
pỳm hǔa nìi máa tɛɛ sǎj?	Where did this book come from
lŏt, khán	car (classifier)
lŏt khán nìi máa tɛɛ sǎj?	Where did this car come from?
hýabin, lám	airplane (classifier)
hýabin lám nìi máa tɛɛ sǎj?	Where did this airplane come from?
pyyn, kábɔ̀ɔk	gun (classifier)
pyyn kábɔ̀ɔk nìi máa tɛɛ sǎj?	Where did this gun come from?
cìa, phɛɛn	paper, sheet (classifier)
cìa phɛɛn nìi máa tɛɛ sǎj?	Where did this paper come from?
hýa, lám	boat (classifier)
hýa lám nìi máa tɛɛ sǎj?	Where did this boat come from?

252

M-2

tálâat	market
phùak khɔ̌j máa tɛɛ tálâat	We came from the market.
aw máa, hóoŋhían	bring, school
láaw aw pỳm hǔa nìi máa tɛɛ hóoŋhían	He brought this book from school.
pâaksán	Paksane
lõt khán nìi máa tɛɛ pâaksán	This car came from Paksane.
lǔaŋ phābaaŋ	Luang Phrabang
hỹa lám nìi máa tɛɛ lǔaŋ phābaaŋ	This boat came from Luang Prabang.
aw... máa, hóoŋkaan	bring, office building
khɔ̌j aw cìa phɛɛn nìi máa tɛɛ hóoŋkaan	I brought this piece of paper from the office.
tamlûat	policeman
tamlûat aw pyyn kábɔ̀ɔk nìi máa	The policeman brought this gun.

C-1

A. càw máa tɛɛ sǎj?	Where are you coming from?
(hỹan khɔ̌j)	(my house)
B. khɔ̌j máa tɛɛ hỹan khɔ̌j	I come from my house.

C-2

(hýabin lám nìi)   (this airplane)

    A. hýabin lám nìi máa   Where did this airplane come
        tɛ̄ɛ sǎj?   from?

(baaŋk3ɔk)   (Bangkok)

    B. máa tɛ̄ɛ baaŋk3ɔk   It came from Bangkok.

C-3

(pỳm hǔa nìi)   (this book)

    A. pỳm hǔa nìi máa tɛ̄ɛ   Where did this book come from?
        sǎj?

(hóoŋhían)   (school)

    B. kh3j aw máa tɛ̄ɛ   I brought it from school.
        hóoŋhían

ຈົ່ງສົມມຸດສະຖານະການຊ້ອມ ແລ້ວໃຫ້ນັກຮຽນເປັນຄົນສະແດງໂດຍການສົມມະບາດລິຖານເອົາລາຍລະອຽດ
ຕ່າງໆຈາກກັນແລະກັນ. ເປັນຕົ້ນວ່າຄົນສອງຄົນລົມກັນຢູ່ຄົນຍົນ, ຄົວຄົງໂດຍສານ ຕລອດການສະຖານຕີ
ອົນວິລົກ. ກ່ອນຈະໃຫ້ນັກຮຽນຝຶກຫັດໂດຍຂະເຈົ້າເອງ ຈົ່ງໃຫ້ແນໃຈວ່າທ່ານໂຄພາຂະເຈົ້າຝຶກຫັດຍົກຮຽນ
ຈົນຕົ້ນວ່າຄືສົມຄວນແລ້ວ; ບໍ່ດັ່ງນັ້ນ ອາດຈະເປັນການເສຍເວລາເປ່າໆ.

254

NOTES

tɛɛ + Location is used to refer to the point of origin of
something (i.e. the starting point of a trip, the place
where something was made, etc.). It is similar in usage
to câak. Neither câäk nor tɛɛ refer to the birthplace of
a person.

Q: hýabin lám nìi máa tɛɛ sǎj   'Where did the plane come
                                          from?'

A: máa tɛɛ baaŋkɔ̀ɔk   'It came from Bangkok.'

APPLICATION

1. How would you find out where certain things originated, such
   as Japanese cars, German beer, etc.?

2. How would you find out where a certain vehicle had just come
   from, such as an airplane, bus, etc.?

Answers: to both 1 and 2 are: ... máa tɛɛ sǎj

CYCLE 57

M-1

aw paj, kāj, khǎaj	take, chicken, sell
láaw si aw kāj paj khǎaj	He is taking the chickens to sell.
sỳy paj, āan	buy and take, read
láaw si sỳy pỳm paj āan	He is buying the book to read.
thěɛ, hǔa, bûat	shave, head, enter the priesthood
láaw si thěɛ hǔa bûat	He is having his head shaved to enter the priesthood.
tēɛŋtoo, bun	get dressed, festival
láaw si tēɛŋtoo paj bun	He is dressing up to go to the festival.
càaŋ, bɨŋ, lùuk	hire; look at, look after; offspring
láaw si càaŋ khón máa bɨŋ lùuk	He is hiring someone to come and look after his children.
hɔɔŋkhɔ̌ɔ, sɔɔj	request; help, assist
láaw si hɔɔŋkhɔ̌ɔ hâj khácàw máa sɔɔj	He is requesting them to come and help.
pót...ɔ̀ɔk, kɨ̂əp	remove, take off; shoe
láaw si pót kɨ̂əp ɔ̀ɔk wàj	He is removing his shoes and putting them away.
làaŋ, mýy	wash, hand
láaw si làaŋ mýy kin khâw	He is washing his hands in order to eat.

M-2

s̀yy, nàmsĭi	buy, paint
láaw si s̀yy námsĭi máa hēt njǎŋ?	What is he buying the paint for?
aw...máa	bring
láaw si aw khɔ̀j máa hēt njǎŋ?	What is he bringing me here for?
thɛ̌ɛ hǔa	shave one's head
láaw si thɛ̌ɛ hǔa hēt njǎŋ?	What is he having his head shaved for?
daŋfáj	build a fire
láaw si daŋfáj hēt njǎŋ?	What is he starting a fire for?
khŷn paj	go up
láaw si khŷn paj hēt njǎŋ?	What is he going up there for?
lóŋ máa	come down
láaw si lóŋ máa hēt njǎŋ?	What is he coming down here for?
cɔ̀ɔt lŏt	park a car
láaw si cɔ̀ɔt lŏt hēt njǎŋ?	What is he parking the car for?
nám { paj / máa	follow
láaw si nám khácàw paj hēt njǎŋ?	What is he following them for?

257

C-1

(tɛɛntoo)   (get dressed)

   A. láaw si tɛɛntoo hēt njǎŋ?   Why is he getting dressed?

(tɛɛntoo paj bun)   (get dressed to go to the
                            festival)

   B. láaw si tɛɛntoo paj   He is getting dressed to go
      bun   to the festival.

C-2

   A. càw si hēt njǎŋ?   What are you going to do?

(càaŋ khón)   (hire someone)

   B. khɔ̂j si càaŋ khón   I'm going to hire someone.

(máa)   (come)

   A. càw si càaŋ khón máa   What are you going hire
      hētnjǎŋ?   someone for?

(bəŋ)   (to look after the children)

   B. khɔ̂j si càaŋ khón máa   I'm hiring someone to come
      bəŋ lùuk   to look after my children.

C-3

   A. càw hēt njǎŋ ?   What are you doing?

(làaŋ mýy)   (washing my hands)

   B. khɔ̂j làaŋ mýy   I'm washing my hands.

(āan nǎŋsy̌y)   (to read)

   A. càw si làaŋ mýy paj   Are you washing your hands
      āan nǎŋsy̌y bɔɔ?   in order to read?

(kinkhâw)   (to eat)

 B. bɔɔ, khɔ̀j si làaŋ mýy No, I'm washing my hands in
  paj kinkhâw.   order to eat.

ໃນບົດຄວາມຄິວເຕີມແລ້ວວ່າ ເຮົາໃຊ້ຄຳກິຣິຍາຕລາຍຄຳຕິດຕໍ່ກັນ ເປັນຕົ້ນວ່າ:"ໄປລ້າງມືກ່ນເຂົ້າ".
ຈົ້ງຕາມຄຳຖາມທີນັກຣຽນຈະຕອບຕອບດ້ວຍປໂຍກທີ່ມີກິຣິຍາຕລາຍຄຳຕິດຕໍ່ກັນບໍ່ວຸດໆ!

NOTES

1) In English Verb Phrases of Purpose may be joined to other
  VP by <u>to</u>, as in:

     NP + VP + to - VP (Purpose)

     He brought chicken to sell.

  Compare this with Lao:

     NP + VP +   VP (Purpose)

     láaw <u>aw kāj máa</u>   <u>khǎaj</u>
       brought chicken (to) sell.'

2) <u>bûat</u> means 'to enter the Buddhist priesthood'. All young Lao
  men of the Buddhist religion are supposed to spend some period
  of time during their lives living as monks in a monastary.
  One's head is shaved and all worldly possessions are given
  away before entry.

3) a <u>bun</u> is a temple fair. Each temple has at least one <u>bun</u> a
  year as an occasion for reading certain Buddhist scriptures
  and also as a means of raising money to take care of temple
  needs. Many kinds of amusements (dances, songs, games, etc.)
  and many kinds of food are available.

APPLICATION

Complete the following sentences using the English as a guide:

(a) láaw si jyym pỳm khɔ̌j _____
(He will borrow my book to read.)

(b) jɯɯ hýan láaw bɔɔ míi nàm. láaw si _____ làaŋ
(There's no water in his house. He'll take his car out to wash it.)

(c) láaw si _____ sɔ̌ŋ paj hâj phỹan láaw.
(He'll take pictures to send to his friend.)

(d) láaw si pót kêəp khɯɯ mǎj _____
(He'll take off his new shoes to put them away.)

(e) láaw si _____ pɛɛ nǎŋsɣ̌y hâj láaw.
(He'll bring you to translate the book for him.)

(f) láaw si _____ kûat bəŋ wîak khɔ̌ŋ phùakháw.
(He'll come down to check our work.)

(g) láaw si _____ khón doojsǎan.
(He'll stop his bus to pick up passengers.)

(h) láaw jâak pen khúubaa. láaw si _____
(He would like to be a monk priest. He'll shave his head in order to enter the priesthood.)

(i) láaw bɔ̀ɔk hâj khɔ̌j _____ khúakin.
(He told me to build a fire to cook with.)

(j) láaw si khɣ̌n _____ jɯɯ sàn thíi sɔ̌ɔŋ.
(He'll go up to sleep on the second floor.)

Answers: (a)paj āan (b)aw lōt láaw paj (c)thāaj hùup (d)ɔ̀ɔk wàj (e)aw càw máa (f)lóŋ máa (g)cɔ̀ɔt lōt aw (h)thɛ̌ɛ hǔa bûat (i)daŋfáj (j)paj nɔɔn

CYCLE 58

M-1

kàw móoŋ, hâa móoŋ khǝ̄ŋ   9:00, 5:30

   tɛɛ kàw móoŋ hǎa hâa móoŋ   From nine to five-thirty.
   khǝ̄ŋ

wán can, wán súk   Monday, Friday

   tɛɛ wán can hǎa wán súk   From Monday through Friday.

sàw, khǎm   morning, night

   tɛɛ sàw hǎa khǎm   From morning to dark.

mỳy nîi, mỳy ɣyn   today, tomorrow

   tɛɛ mỳy nîi hǎa mỳy ɣyn   From today to tomorrow.

mýaŋ, wíaŋcan, lǔaŋphābaaŋ   city, Vientiane, Luang Phrabang

   tɛɛ mýaŋ wíaŋcan hǎa mýaŋ   From the city of Vientiane
   lǔaŋphābaaŋ   to Luang Phrabang.

hýan   house

   tɛɛ hýan khɔ̌j hǎa hýan càw   From my house to yours.

M-2

sǎj   where (question)

   tɛɛ sǎj hǎa sǎj?   From where to where?

mỳy, daj, mỳy daj   day, which (question), what day

   tɛɛ mỳy daj hǎa mỳy daj?   From what day to what day?

wéeláa, wéeláa daj   time, when (question)

     tɛ̄ɛ wéeláa daj hǎa wéeláa   From when to when?
     daj?

móoŋ, cák móoŋ   clock, watch, o'clock; what time?

     tɛ̄ɛ cák móoŋ hǎa cák móoŋ?   From what time to what time?

câak, thɤ̌ŋ   from; to reach, get to

     câak sǎj thɤ̌ŋ sǎj?   From where to where?

M-3

kháplōt   drive

     láaw si kháplōt $\begin{cases} \text{câak} \\ \text{tɛ̄ɛ} \end{cases}$ He is going to drive from
     wíaŋcan paj lǔaŋ   Vientiane to Luang Phrabang.
     phābaaŋ

khīi, hýabin   ride, airplane

     láaw si khīi hýabin $\begin{cases} \text{câak} \\ \text{tɛ̄ɛ} \end{cases}$ He is going to fly from
     wíaŋcan paj lǔaŋ   Vientiane to Luang Phrabang.
     phābaaŋ

lōtdoojsǎan   inter-city bus

     láaw si khīi   He is going to take an inter-
     lōtdoojsǎan $\begin{cases} \text{câak} \\ \text{tɛ̄ɛ} \end{cases}$ city bus from Vientiane to
     wíaŋcan paj   Luang Phrabang.
     lǔaŋ phābaaŋ

dəəntháaŋ   make a trip

    láaw si dəəntháaŋ $\begin{cases} \text{câak} \\ \text{tɛɛ} \end{cases}$ He is going to make a trip
    wíaŋcan paj lǔaŋ   from Vientiane to Luang
                                       Phrabang.
    phābaaŋ

M-4

hɔɔt, sâaŋ, thánǒn   reach, get to; build, street

    phən cá? sâaŋ thánǒn $\begin{cases} \text{câak} \\ \text{tɛɛ} \end{cases}$ They will build a road from
                                       this village to that village.
    bàan nìi paj $\begin{cases} \text{thǝ̌ŋ} \\ \text{hǎa} \\ \text{hɔɔt} \end{cases}$ bàan nàn

sɔɔmsɛ́ɛm   mend, repair, restore

    phən si sɔɔmsɛ́ɛm

    thánǒn $\begin{cases} \text{câak} \\ \text{tɛɛ} \end{cases}$ bàan   They will repair the road
                                       from this village to that
                                       one.
    nìi paj $\begin{cases} \text{thǝ̌ŋ} \\ \text{hǎa} \\ \text{hɔɔt} \end{cases}$ bàan nàn

phúun   pile up, heap up

    phən cá? phúun thánǒn $\begin{cases} \text{câak} \\ \text{tɛɛ} \end{cases}$ They are going to raise the
                                       level of the road from this
    bàan nìi paj $\begin{cases} \text{hɔɔt} \\ \text{hǎa} \\ \text{thǝ̌ŋ} \end{cases}$ bàan nàn   village to that one.

M-5

    khɔ̌j si kháp lōt cón $\begin{cases} \text{hɔɔt} \\ \text{thǝ̌ŋ} \end{cases}$ I'll drive until I get to
    lǔaŋ phābaaŋ   Luang Phrabang.

263

aanjūˀ, jɯɯ nám   age, live with

    láaw jɯɯ nám phɔɔmɛɛ láaw   He lived with his parents
    con $\begin{cases} \text{thɤ̌ŋ} \\ \text{hɔ̀ɔt} \end{cases}$ aanjūˀ láaw   until he reached the age of 2:

    dàj sáaw-ét pii

thâa, mýa (bàan)   wait for; go home, return home

    khɔ̌j si thâa láaw   I'll wait for him until it's
    con $\begin{cases} \text{hɔ̀ɔt} \\ \text{thɤ̌ŋ} \end{cases}$ wéeláa   time to go home.

    mýa bàan

phǎnjáanjáam, sútthàaj   try, attempt; last, final

    khɔ̌j si phǎnjáanjáam paj   I'll keep trying until the
    con $\begin{cases} \text{thɤ̌ŋ} \\ \text{hɔ̀ɔt} \end{cases}$ mỳy sútthàaj   last day.

C-1

    A. láaw kháp lɔ̌t tɛɛ sǎj   He drove from where to where?
       hǎa sǎj?

    B. láaw kháp lɔ̌t tɛɛ hýan   He drove from his house to
       láaw hǎa hóoŋkaan láaw   his office.

C-2

    A. càw si jɯɯ nìi tɛɛ mỳy   You will be here from what
       daj hǎa mỳy daj?   day to what day?

    B. khɔ̌j si jɯɯ nìi tɛɛ mỳy   I will be here from Monday
       wáncan hǎa mỳy wán aathít   to Sunday.

C-3

A. càw si kháplōt câak
   wíaŋcan paj thɤ̆ŋ sɤ̆j?

You are going to drive from
Vientiane to where?

B. khɔ̀j si kháplōt câak wíaŋcan
   paj thɤ̆ŋ lŭaŋ phābaaŋ

I'm going to drive from
Vientiane to Luang Phrabang.

A. lɛ̀ɛw càw si hēt njɤ̆ŋ?

Then what will you do?

B. khɔ̀j si khīī hýabin câak
   lŭaŋ phābaaŋ paj mýaŋ
   sĭŋ

I'll fly from Luang Phrabang
to Muong Sing.

C-4

A. càw si thâa láaw con thɤ̆ŋ
   cák·móoŋ?

Until what time are you going
to wait for him?

B. khɔ̀j si thâa con thɤ̆ŋ
   síp sɔ̆ɔŋ móoŋ

I'll wait for him until twelve
o'clock.

ຕລອດຈາກການຝຶກຫັດຈິນລະລົມກີແລວ ຕາມລອງຖາມນັກຮຽນເບິ່ງດຸ ຂະເຈົ້າຈະຮຽນພາສາລາວໄປຮອດ
ເດືອນໃດ? ຕລໍວ່າຂະເຈົ້າຈະຮຽນພາສາລາວຕກເດືອນໃດໄປຕາເດືອນໃດ? ແລະມນວ່າຂະເຈົ້າຮຽນຕກ
ຈັກໂມງຕາຈັກໂມງ? ປະຄົດເຮືອງປະກອບອນຕມອີກເບິ່ງດຸ! ຖາຕາກການຕກງເຮືອງຕເປັນຕນາສິນໃຈ
ອນ ມັນຈະຊ້ອຍໃນການຮຽນຂອງນັກຮຽນໄດຕລາຍຕສຸດ. ເຮືອງຕທານຕກງກຄວນມຍາຍາມໃຫມັນ
ຕມາະສົມກັບຍອງການອັນຕຈົງຂອງນັກຮຽນ. ເປັນຕນວ່າ ສໍລັບພວກຕເປັນນັກການທຸດ ທານກຄວນ
ຕກງເຮືອງຕກຽວກັບຍອງຮກຍານການເມືອງ; ຕຖາຕາກຂະເຈົ້າເປັນນັກທນາຍຄວນກຕກງໄປໃນຄານພາກ
ປຸກການຝັງແລະລຽງສັດ ແລະຄານການສາວຕ່າງໆ, ດ້ວຍຕອງໄປ.

NOTES

In Lao there are several ways to refer to an extent of space or period of time that is bounded on both ends.

1) t̄ɛɛ ... hǎa is used if 'static' space or duration of time time is referred to:

t̄ɛɛ mýaŋ wíaŋcan hǎa mýaŋ lǔaŋ phābaŋ   'From Vientiane to Luang Prabang.'

t̄ɛɛ kàw móoŋ hǎa hâa móoŋ khə̌ŋ   'from 9:00 a.m. to 5:30 p.m.'

2) If emphasis is on motion between two points in space, câak / t̄ɛɛ ... paj (hǎa) is used.

láaw si kháplōt { câak / t̄ɛɛ   wíaŋcan paj (hǎa) lǔaŋ phābaan

'He will drive from Vientiane to Luang Prabang.'

Frequently the means of transportation is indicated in constructions of this type (khīi hýa, etc.).

3) If emphasis is on reaching a certain limit or goal. thə̌ŋ 'to reach', hǎa 'to or towards', or hɔ̀ɔt 'to arrive at' may be used:

phə̌n cáʔ sâaŋ thánǒn { câak / t̄ɛɛ   bàan níi paj { thə̌ŋ / hǎa / hɔ̀ɔt   bàan nàn

'They will build a road from this village to that village' The reference is usually to a known goal or limit.

4) con ... { hɔ̀ɔt / thə̌ŋ   is used to indicate that some activity will proceed only until a certain limit is reached. It may not be known when that limit will be reached.

khɔ̌j si thâa láaw con { hɔ̀ɔt / thə̌ŋ   wéeláa mýa bàan

'I will wait for her until it's time to go home. (but no longer)'

266

APPLICATION

1. Complete the following sentences using the English as a guide:

   (a) khácàw hían _____ kàw móoŋ sàw _____ bāāj sīī móoŋ
       (They study from 9:00 to 4:00 p.m.)

   (b) jūū mýaŋ améelīkaa khón sūan màak hēt kaan tēē _____
       hǎa _____ ?
       (In America most people work from what day to what day?)

   (c) _____ tēē wíaŋcan hǎa lǔaŋ phābaaŋ kin wéeláa _____
       (It takes one hour to fly from Vientiane to Luang Prabang.)

   (d) càw dàj hían pháasǎa láaw _____ bóthían daj _____
       bóthían daj?
       (You studied Lao from what lesson to what lesson?)

   (e) càw si kháplōt _____ wíaŋcan _____ pâaksée bɔɔ,
       lỹy wāā càw si khīī hýa paj?
       (Are you going to drive a car or go by boat from
       Vientiene to Pakse?)

   (f) phùak khón ciin cáʔ sâaŋ thánǒn tēē mýaŋ khácàw paj _____
       mýaŋ daj?
       (The Chinese are going to build a road from their city
       to what city?)

Answers: 1(a)tēē... hǎa (b)mỳy daj... mỳy daj (c)khīī
hýabin... nȳŋ sūamóoŋ (d)tēē... hǎa
(e){cââk / tēē} ... paj (f){hɔɔt / thǒŋ}

(g) _____ wíaŋcan _____ mýaŋ phóon hóoŋ míi hók síp kiilóomɛ̄t

(It is 60 kilometers from Vientiane to Phonhong.)

(h) khón améelīkan baaŋkhón jūu nám phɔɔ̄mɛ̄ɛ khácàw _____ aanjū² dàj sáaw-ét pii

(Some Americans live with their parents up to age 21.)

(i) khácàw si nāŋ lîn jūu nìi _____ wéeláa mýa bàan

(They will sit here playing until it's time to go home. (and no longer).'

(j) khácàw si _____ phāk jūu mýaŋ nìi _____ sɔ̌ɔŋ aathīt

(They won't stay in this town as long as 2 weeks.)

Answers: (g) $\begin{cases} \text{tɛ̄ɛ} \\ \text{câak} \end{cases}$ ... paj hǎa   (h) con $\begin{cases} \text{hɔ̀ɔt} \\ \text{thə̆ŋ} \end{cases}$ (i) con $\begin{cases} \text{hɔ̀ɔt} \\ \text{thə̆ŋ} \end{cases}$

(j) bɔ̄ɔ... thə̆ŋ

CYCLE 59

M-1

cép thɔ̀ɔŋ	stomach ache
láaw cép thɔ̀ɔŋ	He has a stomach ache.
pûat hŭa	a headache
láaw pûat hŭa	He has a headache.
pen khâj	to have fever
láaw pen khâj	He has a fever.
pen wát	to have a cold
láaw pen wát	He has a cold.
thɔ̂ɔk thɔ̀ɔŋ	to have diarrhea
láaw thɔ̂ɔk thɔ̀ɔŋ	He has diarrhea.
pen aj	to have a cough
láaw pen aj	He has a cough.
wín hŭa	to be dizzy
láaw wín hŭa	He is dizzy.

M-2

pen njăŋ	what's wrong
láaw pen njăŋ?	What's wrong with him?
bɔ̃ɔ sábaaj	sick
láaw bɔ̃ɔ sábaaj bɔɔ?	Is he sick?

269

kháↄ khŷn   getting better

    láaw kháↄ (khŷn) dɛ̄ɛ
    lɛ̀ɛw bɔɔ?   Is he getting better?

aakaan   condition

    aakaan khɔ̌ɔŋ láaw pen
    nɛ́ɛwdaↄ?   How is his condition?

bɔ̄ɔ sábaaↄ lǎaↄ   very sick

    láaw bɔ̄ɔ sábaaↄ lǎaↄ bɔɔ?   Is he very sick?

hǎaↄ, sáw   recover

    láaw { hǎaↄ / sáw } lɛ̀ɛw bɔɔ?   Has he recovered?

M-3

    bɔ̄ɔ hàaↄ hɛ́ɛŋ paandaↄ!   Not very serious.
    hàaↄ hɛ́ɛŋ lǎaↄ!   Very serious (critical).
    dii khŷn dɛ̄ɛ lɛ̀ɛw   A little better!
    dii khŷn lǎaↄ lɛ̀ɛw!   Much better!
    sūt sóom lóŋ kwàākāw   Worse than before!
    phɔ́ɔpaan kāw   Still the same.

C-1

A. càw pen njăŋ?   What's wrong with you?

B. khɔ̀j cép thɔ̀ɔŋ   I have a stomach ache.

C-2

A. láaw bɔ̌ɔ sábaaj bɔɔ?   Is he sick?

B. mɛ́ɛn lɛ̀ɛw, láaw bɔ̌ɔ   Yes, he is sick; he has a
   sábaaj, láaw pen aj   cough.

ໃຕ້ນັກຮຽນສິນນຸດເອົາປ່ຽງຄູ່ວ່າ ຂະເຈົ້າໄປປ່ຽມຢ່າມເໝືອນຄົນບ່ວຫັກກໍລ້ວງນອນຮັກສາຕົວຢູ່ໂຮງໝໍ.
ໃຕ້ນັກຮຽນຄົນບ່ວສິນນຸດເປັນຄົນເຈັບຢູ່ຈະເປັນຜູ້ຕອບດຳຖາມກ່ຽວກັບອາການຂອງລາວ.

NOTES

1) cép means 'to hurt'. It is used to refer to the feeling one
   has right after an injury; hence it is usually temporary.
   pûat means 'to ache'. It normally refers to a more lasting
   sensation than cép. cép húa would refer to a bump on the head,
   whereas, pûat hŭa would refer to the 'headache' that might
   come from the bump. In some cases the above distinction
   doesn't exist and cép is one kind of painful sensation and
   pûat is another.

2) pen + name of disease may also be used to indicate what particular ailment one has, such as láaw pen wát 'He has a cold.'
   tít wát means 'to catch cold.'

3) wín 'to be dizzy' may be followed by hŭa 'head'. wín hŭa
   means 'to be dizzy (in the head)'. thɔ̌ɔk means 'to pour
   out (as with liquids, etc.)'; when thɔ̌ɔk occurs with thɔ̀ɔŋ
   it means 'dysentery, diarrhea'.

271

4) Either of the following may be used interchangeably to inquire about the health of a person:

láaw pen njăŋ?   'What's wrong with him?'

láaw bɔɔ sábaaj bɔɔ?   'Is he sick?'

aakaan khɔ̌ɔŋ láaw pen nɛɛwdaj?   'How is his condition?'

To inquire whether a person's sickness is subsiding:

láaw kháj (khŷn) dɛɛ lɛɛw bɔɔ?   'Is he getting better?'

láaw hǎaj (sáw) lɛɛw bɔɔ?   'Has she recovered?'

5) khŷn 'up, go up' and lóŋ 'down, go down' are both used after stative verbs to indicate a situation that is in process of change; khŷn indicates an 'upward' change (dii khŷn 'getting better'); whereas, lóŋ indicates a 'downward' change(sūt sóom lóŋ 'becoming worse, worsening'. kwāa kāw (lit. 'than old') 'than before' may occur after lóŋ or khŷn. phóopaan kāw (lit. equal in extent to old) 'still the same' is used to refer to conditions that have not undergone change.

APPLICATION

1. Complete the following sentences according to the English:

   (a) láaw _____ thɔɔŋ   (He has a stomach ache.)

   (b) khɔ̂j _____ sábaaj ____   (I'm very sick.)

   (c) _____ (The situation hasn't change

   (d) càw _____   (What's the matter with you?

   (e) láaw _____ aj _____   (Does he have a cough?)

   (f) _____ khâjwát (He has flu.)

Answers: 1(a)cep (b)bɔɔ... lǎaj (c)phóopaan kāw (d)pen njăŋ
           (e)pen ... bɔɔ (f)láaw pen

LAO BASIC COURSE

(g) láaw hăaj lɛ̀ɛw bɔɔ? _____

(Has he recovered yet? Not yet.)

(h) khɔ̂j pûat hŭa lǎaj _____

(My head hurts worse than before.)

(i) láaw _____ thɔ̀ɔŋ

(He doesn't have a stomach ache.)

(j) láaw máa hɛ̄t kaan bɔ̄ɔ dàj phɔ̄wáā láaw cép _____

(He. couldn't come to work because he had a bad stomach
ache.)

(k) wéeláa háw bɔ̄ɔ sábaaj háw khúan cā̌ʔ _____

(When we aren't well, we should go to the doctor's.)

(l) thāan mɔ̌ɔ bɔ̀ɔk wáā láaw _____, láaw âat cā̌ʔ tɔ̀ɔŋ
paj nɔ́ɔn jūu hóoŋmɔ̌ɔ

(The doctor said he was very sick. He may have to go to
the hospital.)

(m) háw bɔ̄ɔ khúan paj jūu kàj khón thɾ̄ɾ _____ phɔ̄wáā
háw âat cā̌ʔ _____.

(We shouldn't go stay with people who have colds because
we might catch cold.)

(n) mʏ̀y wáan nɪ̀i láaw pûat hŭa tɛɛ wáā láaw bɔ̄ɔ phākphɔ̄ɔn,
mʏ̀y nɪ̀i aakaan khɔ̌ɔŋ láaw _____.

(Yesterday he had a headache but he didn't rest. Today
his condition has become much more serious.)

___

Answers: (g)njáŋ (bɔ̄ɔ hǎaj) (h)kwáā kāw (i)bɔ̄ɔ cép (j)thɔ̀ɔŋ
lǎaj (k)paj hǎa mɔ̌ɔ (l)bɔ̄ɔ sabaaj lǎaj (m)pen wát...
tít wát (n)hàaj hɛ̀ɛŋ khʏ̂n

273

CYCLE 60

M-1

<u>máa kaan</u>   come to work

    pen njǎŋ láaw cỹŋ bɔɔ   Why doesn't he come to work?
    máa kaan?

<u>thǎam</u>   question, ask

    pen njǎŋ láaw cỹŋ thǎam?   Why did he ask?

<u>tɔ̂ɔp</u>   answer

    pen njǎŋ láaw cỹŋ bɔɔ   Why doesn't he answer?
    tɔ̂ɔp?

<u>phǎkphɔ̌ɔn</u>   take a rest

    pen njǎŋ láaw cỹŋ bɔɔ   Why doesn't he take a rest?
    phǎkphɔ̌ɔn?

<u>kin</u>   eat

    pen njǎŋ láaw cỹŋ kin?   Why did he eat (it)?

<u>dàj paj</u>   get to go

    pen njǎŋ láaw cỹŋ bɔɔ   Why didn't he get to go?
    dàj paj?

M-2

<u>bɔɔ sábaaj</u>   sick

    phɔwǎa láaw bɔɔ sábaaj   Because he is sick.

<u>khâwcaj</u>   understand

    phɔwǎa láaw bɔɔ khâwcaj   Because he doesn't understand

<u>hùu</u>   know

    phɔ́wáa láaw bɔ̀ɔ hùu   Because he didn't know.

<u>míi</u> <u>wéeláa</u>   have time

    phɔ́wáa láaw bɔ̀ɔ míi wéeláa   Because he doesn't have time.

<u>hǐw</u>   to be hungry

    phɔ́wáa láaw hǐw   Because he is hungry.

<u>máa</u> <u>sàa</u>   came late

    phɔ́wáa láaw máa sàa   Because he came late.

M-3

<u>sỳy</u>, <u>mǎj</u>, <u>míi</u>   buy, new, have

    láaw sỳy lŏt mǎj phɔ́wáa   He bought a new car because
    láaw míi ŋə́n lǎaj   he has a lot of money.

<u>khǎaj</u>, <u>kāw</u>   sell, old

    láaw sỳy lŏt mǎj phɔ́wáa   He bought a new car because
    láaw dàj khǎaj lŏt kāw   he has sold his old car.
    láaw

<u>aw</u>, <u>mía</u>   pick, get, take; wife

    láaw sỳy lŏt mǎj phɔ́wáa   He bought a new car because
    láaw si aw mía   he is getting married.

<u>tɛɛŋ</u> <u>ŋáan</u>   get married

    láaw sỳy lŏt mǎj phɔ́wáa   He bought a new car because
    láaw si tɛɛŋ ŋáan   he is getting married

dəəntháaŋ   travel

    láaw sỳy lŏt mǎj phɔ̌waǎ   He bought a new car because
    láaw si dəəntháaŋ   he is going to make a trip.

C-1

    A. pen njǎŋ láaw cȳŋ bɔ̌ɔ   Why didn't he come to work?
       máa kaan?

    B. phɔ̌waǎ láaw bɔɔ sábaaj   Because he is sick.

C-2

    A. pen njǎŋ láaw cȳŋ sỳy   Why did he buy a new car?
       lŏt mǎj?

    B. láaw sỳy lŏt mǎj phɔ̌waǎ   He bought a new car because
       láaw si aw mía   he is getting married.

C-3

    A. láaw hēt njǎŋ?   What did he do?

    B. láaw phākphɔ̌ɔn   He took a vacation.

    A. pen njǎŋ láaw cȳŋ   Why did he take a vacation?
       phākphɔ̌ɔn?

    B. láaw phākphɔ̌ɔn phɔ̌waǎ   He took a vacation because
       láaw míi wéeláa ..   he had the time.

_____

ຕົວປັນຕາສິມມຸກຂ້ນ ແລວໃຫ້ມັກຣຽນສ້ຳມສ່ຖຳມແລະໂຕວາຕິກັບເບຶ່ງຄູວາ ເປັນຫຍັງ? ຫລຶ ດວຍເຫດໃດ?
ເຫດການແນວໃດຈ່ວຂກິດຂ້ນ ຫລຶເປັນໄປໃນຫົນວຊຫຳວວ.

NOTES

1) The word order in the <u>pen njăn</u> type of question is:

> <u>pen njăn</u> + NP + <u>cȳn</u> + VP

> <u>pen njăn</u> + <u>láaw</u>   <u>cȳn</u>   <u>bɔɔ máa</u>
> (Why   he   then   not come)

> 'Why didn't he come?'

2) <u>pen njăn</u> is always in sentence initial position. <u>hēt njăn</u> 'Why, for what purpose' always comes after the MV <u>in</u> the sentence. <u>láaw si paj hēt njăn jūu hàan tát phŏm?</u>

3) The usual response to <u>pen njăn</u> + Sentence is <u>phɔwāa</u> + Sentence:

> Q: pen njăn láaw cȳn bɔɔ máa?   'Why didn't he come?'
> A: phɔwāa láaw bɔɔ sábaaj   'Because he was ill.'

> <u>cȳn</u> never occurs in responses with <u>phɔwāa</u>.

> In highly stylized spoken or written language the question may be answered as follows:

> Q: pen njăn láaw cȳn bɔɔ máa?   'Why didn't he come?'
> A: láaw bɔɔ sábaaj láaw cȳn bɔɔ máa 'He was ill; he, there-
>   fore, didn't come.'

APPLICATION

1. Complete the following sentences using the English as a guide:

> (a) mỳy nìi _____ láaw cȳn bɔɔ máa hóonhían
>   (Why didn't he come to school today?)

Answers: 1(a)pen njăn

(b) láaw bɔɔ tɔ̀ɔp khám thǎam khácàw _____ láaw bɔɔ hùu khám tɔ̀ɔp

(He didn't answer their question because he didn't know the answer.)

(c) láaw bɔɔ jâak míi mía láaw _____ bɔɔ tɛɛŋŋáan

(He doesn't want a wife, so he hasn't got married.)

(d) láaw bɔɔ thâa khácàw phɔwáa láaw _____, mɛɛn bɔɔ?

(He didn't wait for them, because he didn't have much time, is that so?)

(e) thâawáa láaw míi ŋə́n lǎaj _____ sì sɏ̀y lòt mâj

(If he had a lot of money, he'd buy a new car.)

(f) _____ láaw _____ thǎam hǎa khácàw?

(Why did he ask for them?)

(g) lòt khán nàn lɛɛn bɔɔ díi paandaj láaw cɏ̌ŋ _____

(That car doesn't run very well, so he's selling it cheap.)

(h) khácàw hét wɫak _____ khácàw cɏ̌ŋ bɔɔ phǎkphɔ̀ɔn.

(Their work is not yet finished, so they are not resting.)

(i) láaw kinkhâw lɛ̀ɛw _____ bɔɔ hǐw

(He's already eaten, so he isn't hungry.)

(j) _____ càw cɏ̌ŋ bɔɔ bɔ̀ɔk láaw, càw bɔɔ jâak hâj láaw hùu bɔɔ?

(Why didn't you tell him? Didn't you want him to know?)

Answers: (b)phɔwáa (c)cɏ̌ŋ (d)bɔɔ míi wéeláa lǎaj (e)láaw cɏ̌ŋ
(f)pen njǎŋ... cɏ̌ŋ (g)khǎaj thɏ̂yk (h)njáŋ bɔɔ lɛ̀ɛw
(i)láaw cɏ̌ŋ (j)pen njǎŋ

CYCLE 61

M-1

<u>iiduuton</u>   pity

    khɔ̌j iiduuton láaw   I pity him.

<u>hǎk</u>   love

    khɔ̌j hǎk láaw   I love her.

<u>jàan</u>   to be afraid

    khɔ̌j jàan láaw   I am afraid of him.

<u>hěn caj</u>   to empathize

    khɔ̌j hěn caj láaw   I empathize with him.

<u>aaj</u>   to feel bashful

    khɔ̌j aaj láaw   I feel bashful (in front of) him.

<u>sáŋ</u>   dislike, hate

    khɔ̌j sáŋ láaw   I hate him.

<u>keeŋcaj</u>   to have consideration for

    khɔ̌j keeŋcaj láaw   I have consideration for him.

M-2

<u>phūūsǎaw</u>   young unmarried girl

    càw míi khúam hùusýk néɛw   What kind of feelings do you
    daj tɔɔ phūūsǎaw phūū nìi?   have towards this young un-
                                     married girl?

náaj thāhǎan

   càw míi khúam hùusýk nέεw daj tɔɔ náaj thāhǎan phɯɯ nìi?

military officer

What kind of feelings do you have towards this military officer?

khónsàj

   càw míi khúam hùusýk nέεw daj tɔɔ khónsàj phɯɯ nìi?

servant

What kind of feelings do you have towards this servant?

nāk thòot

   càw míi khúam hùusýk nέεw daj tɔɔ nākthòot phɯɯ nìi?

prisoner

What kind of feelings do you have towards this prisoner?

khón khǒotháan

   càw míi khúam hùusýk nέεw daj tɔɔ khón khǒotháan phɯɯ nìi?

beggar

What kind of feelings do you have towards this beggar?

phɔɔkhàa

   càw míi khúam hùusýk nέεw daj tɔɔ phɔɔkhàa phɯɯ nìi?

merchant

What kind of feelings do you have towards this merchant?

thāān mǒɔ

   càw míi khúam hùusýk nέεw daj tɔɔ thāān mǒɔ phɯɯ nìi?

doctor

What kind of feelings do you have towards this doctor?

C-1

A. càw bɔɔ hěn caj láaw bɔɔ?

Don't you empathize with him?

B. khɔj hěn caj láaw

I empathize with him.

C-2

A. càw míi khúam hùusýk
nέεwdaj tɔɔ phɔɔkhàa
phūū nìi?

What kind of feelings do you
have towards this merchant?

B. khɔ̀j míi khúam hùusýk
hěncaj láaw

I have a feeling of empathy
with him.

ໃຫນັກຮຽນເລົ່າແອງຂອງບຸກຄົມຕາງໆທອະະເຈົ້າຮູ້ຈັກດີ ແລະໃຫະເຈົ້າບອກຖິ່ວຄວາມຮູ້ສຶກຂອງຂະເຈົ້າ
ເອງທມດບຸກຄົມເຕລ່ານັ້ນ ພອມດວຍເຫດຜົນວ່າເປັນຫຍັງຈ່ງເປັນດັ່ງນັ້ນ.

NOTES

1) Verbs of Emotion may be:

(a) Transitive Verb:

   khɔ̀j hāk láaw   'I love her.'
   càw sán khɔ̀j bɔɔ?   'Do you hate me?'

(b) Stative Verbs:

   láaw aaj càw   (She is shy of you.) 'Your presence
                            causes her to be shy.'

(c) Or compounds with -caj 'heart, soul, spirit':

   khɔ̀j hěncaj láaw   'I empathize with him'. (I associate
                            myself with his feelings.)

   khɔ̀j keeŋcaj láaw   'I have consideration for his feelings.'

   keeŋcaj may be used in the negative jāā keeŋcaj with the
   meaning 'Don't be afraid of imposing on me (by making a
   request, etc.)'

281

2) khúam is a noun formative (like -ness in English). Noun Compounds with khúam as the head of the compound are Abstract Nouns: khúam hùusýk 'feeling', khúamhǎk 'love', khúamhěncaj 'empathy', khúamaaj 'bashfulness', khúam penhǔaŋ 'concern', etc.

APPLICATION

1. Complete the following sentences:

(a) phùak khɔ̌j _____ láaw phɔ̌waā láaw pen khón khîi khàan

   (We don't pity him because he is a lazy person.)

(b) khácàw si tɛ̄ɛŋŋaan kan dyan nâa phɔ̌waā khácàw _____
   máa sɔ̌oŋ pii lɛ̀ɛw

   (They'll get married next month since they have been in love for 2 years.)

(c) láaw bɔ̄ɔ míi _____ njǎŋ _____ khácàw

   (He doesn't have any feelings toward them.)

(d) phȳan láaw _____ láaw tɛ̄ɛ khácàw sɔ̄ɔj njǎŋ láaw
   bɔ̄ɔ dàj

   (His friends empathize with him but they can't help him any.)

(e) láaw aw lŏt khɔ̌j paj sàj dooj bɔ̄ɔ _____

   (He took my car and used it without considering me.)

Answers: 1(a)bɔ̄ɔ iiduuton (b)hǎk kan (c)khúam hùusýk... tɔ̄ɔ
(d)hěn caj (e)keeŋcaj khɔ̌j

(f) _____ bɔɔ nǎpthỹy náaj khɔ̌oŋ khácàw

(Some servants don't respect their bosses.)

(g) náaj thīi dii cáʔ tɔ̀oŋ _____ khón khɔ̌oŋ láaw

(A boss that is good must love and empathize with his people.)

(h) láaw bɔ̀ɔk wāa láaw _____ phɔɔ khàa thīi bɔɔ sátsỹy

(He said he dislikes merchants that are not honest.)

(i) láaw _____ wāa khɔ̀j cáʔ hět hâj láaw _____

(He's afraid I will make him shy.)

(j) phǝn bɔ̀ɔk bɔɔ hâj láaw aaj _____ phǝn pen thāan mɔ̌ɔ

(He told her not to be shy because he is a doctor.))

2. Express how you feel about the following:

    (a) The President   (b) The Lao people (c) dogs

    (d) your wife or sister (e) your children

    (f) dishonest people   (g) your religion

    (h) meeting strangers

Answers: 1(f)khónsàj baaŋ khón (g)hǎk lɛ hěn caj (h)sǎŋ
(i)jàan... aaj (j)phɔ̄wāa 2Your answers will
depend on how you feel about each of these.

CYCLE 62

M-1

khĭt   think

    khɔ̃j khĭt wāā láaw bɔɔ máa   I didn't think he was coming.

hùu   know

    khɔ̃j hùu wāā láaw bɔɔ máa   I knew she wasn't coming.

khâwcaj   understand

    khɔ̃j khâwcaj wāā láaw bɔɔ   I understood he didn't come.
máa

dàj njín   hear

    khɔ̃j dàj njín wāā láaw   I heard he didn't come.
bɔɔ máa

wàw   say, speak

    khɔ̃j wàw wāā láaw bɔɔ máa   I said he didn't come.

bɔ̀ɔk   tell

    khɔ̃j bɔ̀ɔk wāā láaw bɔɔ máa   I told you he didn't come.

M-2

sȳa   believe

    càw sȳa wāā jāāŋ daj?   What do you believe?

tɔ̀ɔp   answer

    càw tɔ̀ɔp wāā jāāŋ daj ?   How did you answer?

284

thǎam | to question
càw thǎam wāā jāāŋ daj? | What did you ask?
hùusýk | feel
càw hùusýk wāā jāāŋ daj? | How do you feel about that?
sǒŋsǎj | suspect
càw sǒŋsǎj wāā jāāŋ daj? | What did you suspect?
thúaj | predict, guess
càw thúaj wāā jāāŋ daj? | What did you predict?

M-3

lỳaŋ, mýaŋ | about, story, matter; city, country
khɔ̌j hùu lỳaŋ mýaŋ láaw | I know about Laos.
kaan mýaŋ | politics
khɔ̌j hùu lỳaŋ kaan mýaŋ | I know about politics.
sǒŋkháam | war
khɔ̌j hùu lỳaŋ sǒŋkháam | I know about war.
pûuk, khâw | grow, raise; rice
khɔ̌j hùu lỳaŋ kaan pûuk khâw | I know about growing rice.

lìaŋ, sát | feed, nourish, raise; animal
khɔ̌j hùu lỳaŋ kaan lìaŋ sát | I know about raising animals.

C-1

    A. càw khǐt wāā láaw si   Do you think he will come?
       máa bɔɔ?

    B. khɔ̌j khǐt wāā láaw si   I think he will come.
       máa

C-2

    A. càw khâwcaj wāā jāandaj   How did you understand it?

    B. khɔ̌j khâwcaj wāā láaw   I understood he was not coming
       si bɔɔ máa

C-3

    A. càw hùu njǎŋ?   What do you know?

    B. khɔ̌j hùu lỳaŋ mýaŋ láaw   I know about Laos.

ຍົດມີຈຸດປະສົງຢາກໃຫ້ນັກຮຽນຮູ້ຈັກໃຊ້ຄຳວ່າ"ວ່າ" ເຮົາໃຊ້ຄຳນີ້ເວລາໃດ? ນັກຮຽນເອົາໃຈດີໆແລ້ວບໍ?

<u>NOTES</u>

1) Verbs of saying, thinking, etc. frequently have sentences as
complements; when they do, <u>wāā</u> occurs <u>obligatorily</u> as a connective:

   <u>khɔ̌j</u> <u>khǐt</u> <u>wāā</u> <u>láaw</u> <u>bɔɔ</u> <u>máa</u>   'I didn't think he was coming.'

   <u>láaw</u> <u>hùu</u> <u>wāā</u> <u>càw</u> <u>bɔɔ</u> <u>sábaaj</u>   'He knew you were very ill.'
   <u>lǎaj</u>

286

2) jáaŋ daj 'what, how, in what way' is the usual question form
   with sentences like those above:

   Q: càw tɔ̀ɔp wáa jáaŋ daj?   'What did you answer?'

   A: khɔ̀j tɔ̀ɔp wáa aw paj pá́,?   'I said, take it over there
      wàj phùn   and leave it.'

3) Although lỳaŋ 'story, matter' is a noun, it functions somewhat
   like a preposition in English when it occurs after hùu 'to know
   (a fact)', thus hùu lỳaŋ mýaŋ láaw (lit. know matter Laos)
   'to know about Laos'.

4) kaan is a Noun formative. Noun compounds with kaan are 'action
   nominals', i.e. they refer to actions and correspond roughly
   to the -ing form of the verb as in Singing songs is fun. kaan
   pûuk khâw 'Growing rice', kaan lìaŋ sàt 'Raising animals', etc.

5) khít 'to think' is sometimes pronounced khỹt.

APPLICATION

1. Complete the following sentences using the English as a guide:

   (a) khɔ̀j khít wáa càw míi khúam sǒncaj _____ mýaŋ láaw

       (I thought you had some interest in Laos.)

   (b) láaw _____ cá́? hèt njǎŋ dii

       (He doesn't know what he should do (what would be good
       to do)).

   (c) khɔj _____ pii nìi aahǎan cá́? phέɛŋ khỹn îik

       (I heard that food will become a little more expensive
       this year.)

Answers: 1(a)lỳaŋ (b)bɔ̀ɔ hùu wáa (c)dàj njín wáa

(d) phùak nāk-hían thǎam khɔ̌j _____ jʉ̄ʉ náj mýaŋ láaw
(The students asked me about raising animals in Laos.)

(e) khɔ̌j hùusýk wāa láaw _____ náj lỳaŋ nìi paandaj
(I don't feel he is very interested in this matter.)

(f) khácàw _____ láaw pen thāhǎan wîatnáam nyǎ.
(They suspect he is a North Vietnamese soldier.

(g) láaw hùu lýaŋ kaan mýaŋ tɛ̄ɛ wāa láaw bɔ̄ɔ hùu _____
(He knows politics but he doesn't know war.)

(h) _____ láaw âat cá? bɔ̄ɔ hùu lỳaŋ kaan lìaŋ sát
dìi paandaj
(The villagers suspect that he may not know much about
raising animals.)

(i) khɔ̌j bɔ̄ɔ _____ thǎam láaw phɔ̄wāa láaw bɔ̄ɔ hùu
lỳaŋ nìi
(I don't want to ask him because he doesn't know anything
about this.)

(j) (j) láaw _____ bɔ̄ɔ dàj _____ láaw bɔ̄ɔ míi wéeláa
(He was unable to answer that he didn't have time.)

Answers: (d)lỳaŋ kaan lìaŋ sát (e)bɔ̄ɔ sǒncaj (f)sǒŋsǎj wāa
(g)lỳaŋ sǒŋkháam (h)sáaw bàan sǒŋsǎj wāa (i)jâak
(j)tɔ̀ɔp... wāa

288

CYCLE 63

M-1

njàak   to be difficult, hard

   khɔ̌j khĭt wāā njàak lǎaj   I think it's very difficult.

sádûak   to be convenient

   khɔ̌j khĭt wāā sádûak lǎaj   I think it's very convenient.

njûŋ, njûŋ njàak   to be confused; to be complicated
                                            and difficult

   khɔ̌j khĭt wāā njûŋ njàak   I think it's very complicated.
   lǎaj

kandaan   to be dangerous (as of environment)

   khɔ̌j khĭt wāā kandaan lǎaj   I think it's very dangerous.

pɔ̂ɔt, pháj   to be free from, danger

   khɔ̌j khĭt wāā pɔ̂ɔt pháj   I think it's very safe.
   lǎaj

sòok, dii   luck; good, well

   khɔ̌j khĭt wāā sòok dii lǎaj   I think it's very good luck.

M-2

   njàak bɔɔ?   Is it difficult?
   sádûak bɔɔ?   Is it convenient?
   sa?âat bɔɔ?   Is it clean?
   pỳan bɔɔ?   Is it dirty?
   phéɛŋ bɔɔ?   Is it expensive?
   thŷyk bɔɔ?   Is it cheap?

289

M-3

<u>sɔ̄ɔj</u>

    mán njàak lǎaj láaw cȳŋ
háj khácàw máa sɔ̄ɔj

help, assist

    It's so difficult he let
them come help.

<u>phāk</u>

    mán sádûak lǎaj láaw cȳŋ
jâak máa phāk jūu nìi

stay (temporary)

    It's so convenient he wants
to come stay here.

<u>khǒo, njàaj, bɔ̄ɔn, ȳn</u>

    mán njûŋ njàak lǎaj láaw
cȳŋ khǒo njàaj paj bɔ̄ɔn
ȳn

ask, move, place, other

    The situation is so mixed
up he wants to move to
another place.

<u>sīaŋ</u>

    mán kandaan lǎaj láaw
cȳŋ bɔ̄ɔ sīaŋ

to take a risk

    The situation is so dangerous
he doesn't risk it.

<u>tɔ̀ɔŋkaan, thāhǎan</u>

    mán pɔ̀ɔtpháj lǎaj láaw
cȳŋ bɔ̄ɔ tɔ̀ɔŋkaan thāhǎan

need, soldier

    The situation is so safe he
doesn't need any soldiers.

<u>sȳy, îik, sɛ̂ɛp</u>

    mán sɛ̂ɛp lǎaj láaw cȳŋ
sȳy îik.

buy; more, again; delicious

    It was so delicious he
bought more.

M-4

<u>wlak</u>

    wlak nìi njàak bɔɔ?

task, work

    Is this job difficult?

290

hóoŋhéɛm, dàjhāp

    phāk jūu hóoŋhéɛm nìi
    dàjhāp khwáam sádûak bɔɔ?

hotel, receive

    Does this hotel have all
    the conveniences?

panhǎa

    panhǎa nìi njûŋ njàak bɔɔ?

problem, trouble

    Is this problem complex?

síiwɪt, théŋ, phúu

    síiwɪt jūu théŋ phúu
    kandaan bɔɔ?

life, on, mountain

    Is life in the mountains
    dangerous?

khêet, pótpɔɔj

    khêet pótpɔɔj nìi pɔɔt
    pháj bɔɔ?

area, liberate

    Is this liberated area safe?

aahǎan

    aahǎan nìi sɛɛp bɔɔ?

food

    Is this food delicious?

M-5

    wìak nìi njàak lǎaj láaw
    cȳŋ hâj khácàw máa sɔɔj

    This work is so complicated
    and difficult he had them
    come help.

    hóoŋhéɛm nìi hâj khwáam
    sádûak lǎaj láaw cȳŋ jâak
    máa phāk jūu nìi

    This hotel affords so many
    conveniences he likes to
    stay here.

    wìak nìi njûŋ jàak lǎaj
    láaw cȳŋ khɔ̌ɔ njàaj paj
    bɔɔn ȳyn

    The work here is so complicated
    he asked to move to another
    place.

    síiwɪt jūu théŋ phúu kandaan
    lǎaj láaw cȳŋ bɔɔ jâak sɪaŋ

    Life in the mountains is so
    dangerous he doesn't want
    to risk it.

khêet pótpɔ̌ɔj nìi pɔ̀ɔtpháj
lǎaj láaw cȳŋ bɔ̌ɔ tɔ̀ɔŋkaan
thāhǎan

This liberated area is so
safe he doesn't need any
soldiers.

khánǒm nìi sɛ̀ɛp lǎaj láaw
cȳŋ cá? sȳy îik

This cake is so delicious
he'll buy some more.

C-1

A. sádûak bɔɔ?

Is it convenient?

B. khɔ̂j khīt wāā sádûak lǎaj.

I think it's very convenient

C-2

A. aahǎan nìi sɛ̀ɛp bɔɔ?

Is this food delicious?

B. aahǎan nìi sɛ̀ɛp lǎaj láaw
cȳŋ cá sȳy îik

This food is so delicious
he'll buy some more.

C-3

A. wìak nìi njàak lǎaj láaw
cȳŋ hâj khácàw máa sɔ̌ɔj,
mɛ̄ɛn bɔɔ?

This work is so difficult
that he had them come and
help, didn't he?

B. mɛ̄ɛn lɛ̀ɛw, wìak nìi njàak
lǎaj láaw cȳŋ hǎj khácàw
máa sɔ̌ɔj

That's right, this work is
so difficult that he had
them come and help.

292

C-4

A. pen njăŋ láaw cȳŋ hâj   Why did he have them come
   khácàw máa sɔ̄ɔj?   to help?

B. láaw hâj khácàw máa sɔ̄ɔj   He had them come to help
   phɔwāā wìak nìi njàak lăaj   because this work is very
                              difficult.

ໃຕ້ມັກຣຽມຕິດໃຈຄືວິ່ຮສຄ (ວາຍ ຍາກ ແຊບ...)ຄວຍການຈຸແຈງຄືງສ້ວງຕາງໆ ຕຣິກຣິຍາອາການ
ຕາງໆ ພວມທ້ວຄວາມຮູ້ສຶກຂວງະເຈົາທັມຄສ້ວຍວງຕຣິກຣິຍາອາການຕາງໆຕຄລ້າມນ. ແລະເປັນຕຍ້ງ?

NOTES

1) The Subject is not expressed in Lao when the reference is to
a general situation, except in certain situations:

Q: kandaan bɔɔ?   'Is (it) dangerous?'
A: bɔ̄ɔ kandaan lăaj   '(It) isn't very dangerous.'

In more complex sentences mán 'it' must be used:

mán njàak lăaj láaw cȳŋ hâj   'It's so difficult he let
khácàw máa sɔ̄ɔj   them come help.'

2) The So + Adjective + that + Sentence construction in English
is expressed in Lao by:

       V_s + lăaj + NP (subject) + cȳŋ...

      njàak   lăaj   láaw   cȳŋ

(It is difficult   very   he   then...)

'It's so difficult that he... '

293

The <u>such</u> + Adjective + NP + <u>that</u> + S construction is expressed in Lao:

NP   + V_s +   lǎaj   +   NP (Subject) + cȳŋ...

wìak	nâasǒncaj	lǎaj	láaw	cȳŋ
(work	interesting	very	he	then...)

'such interesting work that he...)'

APPLICATION

1. Translate the following sentences into English:

(a) láaw khǐt wāā wìak nìi njàak lǎaj láaw cȳŋ jâak hâj càw sɔ̌ɔj láaw

(b) khɔ̌j khɔ̂ɔpcaj lǎaj lǎaj thīī càw hâj khwáam sáduak

(c) láaw míi wìak njûŋ lǎaj láaw cȳŋ bɔ̄ɔ hùu wāā cá? hēt njǎŋ kɔ̌ɔn

(d) khácàw bɔ̄ɔ jâak nāŋ kàj láaw phɔ̄wāā khȳaŋ nūŋ láaw bɔ̄ɔ sá?âat

(e) láaw khǐt wāā láaw sòok dii lǎaj phɔ̄wāā thāhǎan wìatkoŋ bɔ̄ɔ hěn láaw

---

Answers: 1(a)He thinks the work here is so hard that he would like to have you help him. (b)I am very appreciative that you have made it convenient. (c)He had such complicated work to do that he didn't know what to do first. (d)They don't want to sit near him because his clothes are dirty. (e)He thought he was very lucky because the Viet Cong didn't see him.

(f) kaan hēt wĺak jūū hóoŋkaan khɔ̀j bɔ̄ɔ sáduc 1ak dii paandaj

(g) thāhǎan bɔ̄ɔ hâj phùakháw paj phɔwā̄ tháaŋ sên nli bɔ̄ɔ
     pɔ̀ɔtpháj

(h) kaan dəəntháaŋ jūū náj khêet nli kandaan lǎaj

(i) aahǎan phɛ́ɛŋ phɔwā̄ bàan mýaŋ njûŋ njàak

(j) wéeláa kaan paj máa sáducâak thūk sɪŋ thūk jāāŋ kɔɔ thŷyk

---

Answers: (f)The work at my office is not very convenient.
          (g)The soldiers wouldn't let us go because this
          path is not safe. (h)Travelling in this area is
          very dangerous. (i)Food is expensive because the
          country is in a very precarious (difficult and
          dangerous) situation. (j)When going and coming are
          convenient everything is cheap.

CYCLE 64

M-1

<u>sȳa</u>   believe, trust

   càw sȳa wāā láaw si sānā?   You believe that he will win,
   sàn bɔɔ?   is that so?

<u>sárúp</u> (<u>aw</u>)   summarize, conclude

   càw sárúp aw wāā láaw si   You conclude that he will win
   sānā? sàn bɔɔ?   is that so?

<u>wǎŋ</u>   hope

   càw wǎŋ wāā láaw si sānā?   You hope that he will win,
   sàn bɔɔ?   is that so?

<u>ká?</u>   estimate, calculate, guess

   càw ká? wāā láaw si sānā?   You calculate that he will
   sàn bɔɔ?   win, is that so?

<u>fǎn</u>   to dream

   càw fǎn wāā láaw sānā?   You dreamed that he won,
   sàn bɔɔ?   is that so?

<u>thámnáaj</u>   foretell

   càw thámnáaj wāā láaw si   You foretell that he will
   sānā? sàn bɔɔ?   win, is that so?

<u>nɛ̄ɛcaj</u>   to be sure, certain, confident

   càw nɛ̄ɛcaj wāā láaw si   You are sure that he will
   sānā? sàn bɔɔ?   win, is that so?

M-2

sănā?   win

    wāā sàn lɛ̀ɛw, khɔ̌j sȳa wāā   That's how I see it. I
    láaw si sănā?.   believe that he will win.

sĕŋ, sĕŋdàj   take an exam, pass an exam

    wāā sàn lɛ̀ɛw, khɔ̌j sȳa wāā   That's the way I see it. I
    láaw si sĕŋdàj   believe that he will pass
                                   the exam.

dàj khŷn sàn, sàn   to be promoted; rank, grade,
                                   story, level

    wāā sàn lɛ̀ɛw, khɔ̌j sȳa   That's how I see it. I
    wāā láaw si dàj khŷn sàn   believe that he will be
                                   promoted.

dàjhāp, sămrēt   receive; complete, to be successful

    wāā sàn lɛ̀ɛw, khɔ̌j sȳa   That's how I see it. I
    wāā láaw si dàjhāp khwáam   believe that he will be
    sămrēt   successful.

phāājphɛ̀ɛ   to be defeated

    wāā sàn lɛ̀ɛw, khɔ̌j sȳa wāā   That's the way I see it.
    láaw si dàjhāp khwáam   I believe that he will be
    phāājphɛ̀ɛ   defeated.

sĕŋtók   to fail an exam

    wāā sàn lɛ̀ɛw, khɔ̌j sȳa   That's how I see it. I
    wāā láaw si sĕŋtók.   believe that he will not
                                   pass the examination.

M-3

khǐan

    khǐan cāŋ sǐi bɔɔ?

write

    You write it like this, huh?

tát

    tát cāŋ sǐi bɔɔ?

cut

    You cut it like this, huh?

hɔ̄ɔ

    hɔ̄ɔ cāŋ sǐi bɔɔ?

wrap, pack

    You pack it like this, huh?

pá? wàj

    pá? wàj cāŋ sǐi bɔɔ?

leave, abandon

    You leave it like this, huh?

aw jɔɔŋ kan khŷn

    aw jɔɔŋ kan khŷn cāŋ sǐi bɔɔ?

to stack something up

    You stack them up like this, huh?

kɔ́?, kan

    aw kɔ́? kan cāŋ sǐi bɔɔ?

to hook, each other

    You hook them together like this, huh?

M-4

khǐt

    khɔ̀j khǐt wāā (cāŋ) sàn lɛ̀ɛw

think

    I think so.

sȳa

    láaw sȳa wāā (cāŋ) sàn lɛ̀ɛw

to believe

    He believes it's that way.

298

sán̆ə   to propose

   khácàw sán̆ə wāā (cāŋ) sàn   That's what they proposed.
   lɛ̀ɛw

paakót   appear

   paakót wāā (cāŋ) sàn lɛ̀ɛw   It appears to be so.

hĕn   see

   khɔ̂j hĕn wāā (cāŋ) sàn lɛ̀ɛw   That's how I see it.

săŋkêet hĕn   observe, notice

   khɔ̂j săŋkêet hĕn wāā (cāŋ)   That's what I have noticed.
   sàn lɛ̀ɛw

C-1

   A. càw sȳa wāā láaw si sĕŋ   Do you believe he will pass
      dàj bɔɔ?   the exam?

   B. əə, khɔ̂j sȳa wāā láaw   Yes, I believe he will pass
      si sĕŋ dàj   the exam.

C-2

   A. càw thámnáaj wāā láaw si   You predict that he will get
      dàj khŷn sàn, sàn bɔɔ?   promoted, is that so?

   B. wāā sàn lɛ̀ɛw, khɔ̂j thámnáaj   Yes, I predict that he will
      wāā láaw si dàj khŷn sàn   certainly be promoted.
      jāāŋ nɛ̄ɛ nɔ́ɔn

C-3

    A. càw sárúp aw wāā jāāŋ daj?   What have you concluded?

    B. khɔ̂j sárúp aw wāā láaw si   I concluded that he will
       sěŋ dàj   pass the exam.

C-4

    A. càw sȳa wāā láaw bɔ̄ɔ máa   You believed that he wasn't
       sàn bɔɔ?   coming, huh?

    B. əə, khɔ̂j sȳa wāā (cāŋ) sàn   Yes. That's what I believed.
       lɛ̀ɛw

C-5

    A. càw si khǐan cāŋ sǐi bɔɔ?   You are going to write it
                                 like this, huh?

    B. bɔ̄ɔ, khɔ̂j si khǐan cāŋ sàn   No. I'm going to write it
                                 like that.

ສະແຄງໃຫ້ນັກຮຽນເບິ່ງວ່າ ຄວາມແຕກຕ່າງລະຫວ່າງ "ຈິ່ງຊັນ" ແລະ "ຈິ່ງຊີ" ມີຢ່າງໃດ. ແລະຄຳວ່າ
"ຊັນບໍ?" ແລະ "ວ່າຊັນແລວ" ຄຖ? ເຮົາໃຊ້ຄຳເຫລົ່ານີ້ໃນເວລາໃດ ແລະໃນກໍລະນີໃດ?

300

NOTES

1) <u>sàn</u> 'like that' occurs with <u>bɔɔ</u> after Sentences:

   <u>càw sỹa wāā láaw si sānā̌?sàn bɔɔ?</u>   'You believe he will win,
                                                   is that so?

   <u>sàn bɔɔ?</u> is similar in usage to <u>mɛ̄ɛn bɔɔ?</u> except that <u>mɛ̄ɛn</u>
   <u>bɔɔ?</u> is used primarily to check the truth value of statements;
   whereas, <u>sàn bɔɔ?</u> is used to check an opinion or a guess, and
   hence is more informal. The usual answer to <u>sàn bɔɔ?</u> questions
   is <u>wāā sàn lɛ̀ɛw</u> which means 'That's how I see it' or 'That's
   what I had in mind'.

2) <u>cāŋ sàn</u> 'like that' and <u>cāŋ sìi</u> 'like this' are used in statements and questions relating to how something is done.

   <u>khǐan cāŋ sìi bɔɔ?</u>   'You write it like this, huh?

   <u>khán sàn</u> means 'In that case'. It is heard often in conversation.

APPLICATION

(a) láaw bɔ̄ɔ hían khɔ̌j jàan wāā láaw si sěŋtók.

(b) khɔ̌j wǎŋ wāā sàn lɛ̀ɛw

(c) láaw sỹa wāā khwáam phānjáanjáam jūu sǎj khwáam sǎmrēt
    jūu hân

(d) mỳy khýynnìi càw fǎn wāā jāāŋ daj?

(e) khón láaw sūan lǎaj sỹa khwáam fǎn

Answers: 1(a)He doesn't study. I'm afraid he'll fail.
         (b)I hope so. (c)He believes that where there
         is striving (trying) there will be success.
         (d)What did you dream last night? (e)Most Laos
         believe in dreams.

(f) háw cá? sárúp aw bɔɔ dàj wāā wìak láaw cá? bɔɔ sămrèt

(g) thâawāā fāaj nyŋ sānā? ìik fāaj nyŋ kɔɔ cá? tɔɔŋ phāājphèɛ

(h) láaw sȳa wāā sájsānā? lɛ? khwáam phāājphèɛ pen khɔ̌ɔŋ khūu
kan

(i) pii kaaj nìi láaw sĕŋtók láaw nɛɛcaj wāā pii nìi láaw
si sĕŋdàj

(j) wāā sàn lɛɛw khɔ̂j sȳa wāā láaw si dàj khŷn sàn

Answers: (f) We can not conclude that his work will fail.
(g) If one side wins, the other side must lose.
(h) He believes that victory and failure are pairs.
(i) Last year he failed; he is certain he will pass
this year. (j) Certainly, I believe he will be promoted

302

CYCLE 65

M-1

láaw si paj tálâat, lɛ̀ɛw láaw si paj hóoŋmɔ̌ɔ	He will go to the market, then he will go to the hospital.
láaw si kinkhâw lɛ̀ɛw láaw si paj hēt kaan.	He will eat, then he will go to work.
láaw si ā̄an nǎŋ šyy lɛ̀ɛw láaw si paj nóɔn.	He will read, then he will go to bed.
láaw si sáw m̄yaj lɛ̀ɛw láaw si aâp nàm	He will rest, then he will take a shower.

M-2

<u>kya, mǔu</u>   feed (animal), pig

     láaw si kya mǔu lɛ̀ɛw láaw   He will feed the pigs, then
     si hēt njǎŋ?   what is he going to do?

<u>tát, njâa</u>   cut, grass

     láaw si tát njâa lɛ̀ɛw láaw   He will cut the grass, then
     si hēt njǎŋ?   what is he going to do?

<u>sāk khȳaŋnūŋ</u>   wash clothes

     láaw si sāk khȳaŋnūŋ   He will wash clothes, then
     lɛ̀ɛw láaw si hēt njǎŋ?   what is he going to do?

<u>jyym̀, ŋén</u>   borrow, money

     láaw si jyym ŋén lɛ̀ɛw láaw   He will borrow money, then
     si hēt njǎŋ?   what is he going to do?

pīan, phâa puu tó?   change, table cloth

   láaw si pīan phâa puu tó?   He will change the table cloth
   lɛ̀ɛw láaw si hēt nɟǎŋ?   then what is he going to do?

C-1

   A. càw si hēt nɟǎŋ dɛ̄ɛ?   What are you going to do?

   B. khɔ̂ɟ si paɟ kinkhâw   I will go to eat, then I will
      lɛ̀ɛw khɔ̂ɟ si máa sáw   come to rest.
      mȳaɟ

C-2

   A. càw si āan nǎŋsӳy lɛ̀ɛw   You will read, then what will
      càw si hēt nɟǎŋ?   you do?

   B. āan nǎŋsӳy lɛ̀ɛw khɔ̂ɟ si   After reading I will go feed
      paɟ kya mǔu   the pigs.

ຄຳວ່າ ແລວ ໃນຕົນ ຈິ່ງສອນແຕຄາມຄວາມໝາຍຕື້ນໆມີຢູ່ຕໍານັ້ນ! ປ່າຟ້າວອະຕິບາຍຄວາມໝາຍ
ຢ່າງອື່ນ. ເຮົາຈະຄອງໃຫະເຈົາຈຄໍ່ອລະຢ່າງ ອະເຈົາຈິ່ງຈະຮູ້ຈັກໃຊ້ຢ່າງຖືກຕ້ອງແລະກວ້ຍຄວາມ
ໝັ້ນໃຈ. ຈິ່ງຢູ່ ຄຳວ່າແລວມີຄວາມໝາຍຢ່າງອື່ນອີກ. ແຕເຮົາຢ່າເປັນຄອງໃຫະເຈົາຮູ້ຕົນມິດໃນ
ເວລານຄອກ. ໃນບົດຕໄປຍັງຈະມີອີກ.

NOTES

1) In the construction S^1 + lɛ̀ɛw + S^2 (láaw si paj tálâat lɛ̀ɛw láaw si paj hóoŋmɔ̌ɔ 'He's going to the market and then to the hospital.') lɛ̀ɛw is a sentence connective and there is an indication that the activity referred to in the first sentence preceded that of the second sentence.

2) dɛ̄ɛ in a question indicates that the questioner is expecting a multiple answer.

Q: láaw si hēt njǎŋ dɛ̄ɛ?   What (things) is he going to do?'

A: láaw si āan nǎŋšyy lɛ̀ɛw   'He'll read a book and then láaw si paj kin khâw   go eat.'

APPLICATION

1. Translate the following sentences into English:

(a) láaw kin khâw lɛ̀ɛw láaw si máa hǎa càw bɔɔ?

(b) taam thámmādaa mỹa càw kin khâw lɛ̀ɛw càw māk hēt njǎŋ?

(c) khácàw si paj bēŋ sínée lɛ̀ɛw khácàw si paj sǎj dɛ̄ɛ?

(d) càw si kháp lɔ̌t paj sỹy lɛ̀ɛw liaw sàaj mɛ̄ɛn bɔɔ?

(e) hían lɛ̀ɛw cỹŋ hāk, bɔ̌ɔ mɛ̄ɛn hāk lɛ̀ɛw cỹŋ hían

Answers: (a)Will he eat and then come to see you? (b)Usually when you have eaten, what do you like to do then? (c)They'll go to the movies and then where will they go? (d)You will drive straight ahead then you'll turn left, won't you? (e)Study then love; don't love and then study.

(f) thâawāā càw mȳaj kɔɔ phākphɔɔn sǎa, sáw mȳaj lɛ̀ɛw cȳŋ
paj- hēt wɫak îik

(g) mȳa háw lɫaŋ mǔu háw tɔ̀ɔŋ kya mán hâj īīm lɛ̀ɛw háw cá°
dàj láakháa dii

(h) láaw si pīan phâa puu tó° lɛ̀ɛw láaw cá° paj khúakin

(i) thâawāā càw jâak míi hȳan càw âat cá° tɔ̀ɔŋ jyym ŋə́n câak
thānáakháan

(j) láaw si tát njâa lɛ̀ɛw láaw si paj âap nàm

Answers: (f)If you're tired, rest; when you're rested, go
back to work. (g)When we raise pigs, we must feed
them full, then we'll get a good price (for them).
(h)She'll change the tablecloth then she'll go cook.
(i)If you want to have a house, you may have to borrow
money from the bank. (j)He'll cut the grass and then
go take a bath.

CYCLE 66

M-1

kûat, bə̄ŋ

   khɔ̌j njáŋ bɔ̄ɔ thán dàj
   kûat bə̄ŋ

check; look at

   I haven't got around to
   checking it yet.

sāk, khÿaŋ nūŋ

   khɔ̌j njáŋ bɔ̄ɔ thán dàj
   sāk khÿaŋ nūŋ

wash (cloth only), clothes

   I haven't got around to
   washing clothes yet.

pɛɛ

   khɔ̌j njáŋ bɔ̄ɔ thán dàj pɛɛ

translate

   I haven't got around to
   translating it yet.

khǐan, cótmǎaj

   khɔ̌j njáŋ bɔ̄ɔ thán dàj
   khǐan cótmǎaj

write, letter (epistle)

   I haven't got around to
   writing the letter yet.

sɔ̌ŋ

   khɔ̌j njáŋ bɔ̄ɔ thán dàj
   sɔ̌ŋ cótmǎaj

send

   I haven't got around to
   mailing the letter yet.

sýksǎa

   khɔ̌j njáŋ bɔ̄ɔ thán dàj
   sýksǎa bə̄ŋ

study

   I haven't got around to
   studying yet.

M-2

át, pátuu	close, door
caw át pátuu lɛɛw lўy njáŋ?	Did you close the door yet?
khǎj	open
caw khǎj pátuu lɛɛw lўy njáŋ?	Did you open the door yet?
làaŋ, mýy	wash, clean; hand
caw làaŋ mýy lɛɛw lўy njáŋ?	Did you wash your hands yet?
swāaj, nâa	wash (face or body only)
caw swāaj nâa lɛɛw lўy njáŋ?	Did you wash your face yet?
thǔu, khêɛw	to rub, scrub
caw thǔu khêɛw lɛɛw lўy njáŋ?	Did you brush your teeth yet
wǐi, phǒm	comb, hair (head only)
caw wǐi phǒm lɛɛw lўy njáŋ?	Did you comb your hair yet?
tyan	warn
caw tyan khácaw lɛɛw lўy njáŋ?	Did you warn them yet?

M-3

máa lɛɛw	Yes, (... already came.)
sáw lɛɛw	Yes, (... already stoped.)
mót lɛɛw	Yes. (... already gone. 'finished')

M-4

njáŋ   Not yet.

M-5

<u>lóm</u>, <u>káp</u>   to chat, talk; with

    càw thán dàj lóm káp láaw   Did you get a chance to chat
    bɔɔ?   with him?

<u>phɔ̀ɔ</u>   to meet, find

    càw thán dàj phɔ̀ɔ káp   Did you get a chance to meet
    láaw bɔɔ?   her?

<u>hěn</u>, <u>phǒn</u>   see, result

    càw thán dàj hěn phǒn   Were you able to see any
    njǎŋ bɔɔ?   results (in the time
                      available)?

<u>hūam</u>, <u>phīthíi</u>   to join, participate, attend;
                         ceremony

    càw thán dàj hūam phīthíi   Did you get to the ceremony
    bɔɔ?   in time to participate?

<u>fáŋ</u> <u>thèet</u>   to hear a sermon

    càw thán dàj fáŋ thèet   Did you get a chance to
    bɔɔ?   hear the sermon?

M-6

<u>āan</u>, <u>tɛ̄ɛ</u>, <u>pỳm</u>   read; only, but; book

    khɔ̂j thán dàj āan pỳm tɛ̄ɛ   I was able to read only two
    sɔ̌ɔŋ hǔa   books (in the time available).

wàw, nám, khám   speak; with, along; word

    khɔ̀j thán dàj wàw nám láaw   I had a chance to speak
    tɛɛ sɔ̌oŋ sǎam khám   only 2 or 3 words with him.

mɔ̀ot fáj, mâj   to put out a fire, burn

    khɔ̀j thán dàj mɔ̀ot fáj kɔɔn   I was able to put out the
    mán si mâj hýan   fire before the house
                                    burned down.

cáp mýy, káp { páj   to shake, hand, return
                   màa

    khɔ̀j thán dàj cáp mýy káp   I had a chance to shake
    phēn kɔɔn phēn si káp paj   hands with him before he
                                    returned.

C-1

    A. càw át pátuu lɛɛw ľyy njáŋ?   Did you close the door yet?

    B. át lɛɛw   Yes.

C-2

    A. càw khǐan cótmǎaj lɛɛw   Did you write the letter
       ľyy njáŋ?   yet?

    B. njáŋ.   Not yet.

C-3

    A. càw làaŋ mýy lɛɛw ľyy   Did you wash your hands
       njáŋ?   yet?

    B. làaŋ lɛɛw, khɔ̀j làaŋ mýy   Yes, I've already washed
       khɔ̀j lɛɛw   my hands.

310

C-4

   A. càw thán dàj phɔ̀ɔ káp   Did you get to meet him?
      láaw bɔɔ?

   B. thán, khɔ̀j thán dàj phɔ̀ɔ   Yes, I got to meet him before
      káp láaw kɔɔn láaw cá?   he returned.
      káp paj

C-5

   A. láaw kŷap bɔɔ dàj wàw nám   He almost didn't get to
      khácàw mɛɛn bɔɔ?   talk to them, isn't that so?

   B. mɛɛn lɛ̀ɛw, láaw thán dàj   That's right. He only got
      wàw nám khácàw tɛɛ sɔ̌ɔŋ   to say 2 or 3 words to them.
      sǎam khám

ໃນນິກຣົມຕາມກັນເບ່ງວ່າຜູ້ໃດກະຫາກຄວາມສ່ງໃຄແລວຄລຍ້ງ. ຖາຄຫຕອບແມນ "ບ່" ຕລ "ຍ່ງ" ກ່າງໃຄະເຈົາ
ໃຄເຕຄຜ່ນວ່າ ເປັນຫຍ້ງ? ຕລຖ້າຕອບວ່າ "ແລວ" ກ່າງຖາມວ່າ ກ່ໄປຣະເຈົາຈະເຣັຄຫຍ້ງ?

NOTES

1) **thán dàj** means 'to have been able to do something in the available time'. It may occur in the negative with the meaning 'not to have got something done when it was supposed to have been done.'

  khɔ̀j thán dàj mɔ̀ɔt fáj kɔɔn   'I was able to put out the
  mán si mâj hýan   fire before the house
                           burned down.'

  khɔ̀j njáŋ bɔɔ thán dàj ǎan   'I haven't got your book
  pỳm càw   read yet.'

  khɔ̀j thán dàj ǎan pỳm tɛɛ   'I've only got two books read.'
  sɔ̌ɔŋ hǔa

311

2) lɛ̀ɛw and njáŋ are 'aspect words', i.e., they indicate the state of an action, whether it is completed (lɛ̀ɛw) or whether it remains incomplete (njáŋ). njáŋ is a preverb and occurs before bɔ̀ɔ + VP:

khɔ̌j njáŋ bɔ̀ɔ thán dàj pɛɛ   'I haven't got around to translating it yet.'

njáŋ may occur alone in (a) responses to questions:

Q: càw wǐi phǒm lɛ̀ɛw lɣ̌y njáŋ   'Have you combed your hair yet?'

A: njáŋ 'Not yet.'   Or (b) in parallel sentences like the question above.

3) When an affirmative sentence with lɛ̀ɛw and the negative form of the same sentence with njáŋ are joined with lɣ̌y 'or', the negative sentence is reduced to njáŋ and follows the affirmative sentence:

Affirmative: càw thǔu khɛ̂ɛw lɛ̀ɛw 'You have brushed your teeth.

Negative: càw njáŋ bɔ̀ɔ thǔu   'You haven't brushed your
         khɛ̂ɛw   teeth yet.'

When combined with lɣ̌y: càw thǔu khɛ̂ɛw lɛ̀ɛw lɣ̌y njáŋ?
'Have you brushed your teeth yet or not?'

APPLICATION

1. Complete the following sentences using the English as a guide:

   (a) khɔ̌j _____ khǐan cótmǎaj hǎa phɣan khɔ̌j

       (I haven't had a chance to write a letter to my friend yet

   (b) láaw khǐan cótmǎaj _____ tɛɛ láaw _____ thán dàj sɔ̌r
       (He's written a letter, but he hasn't had a chance to mail it yet.)

Answers: 1(a)njáŋ bɔ̀ɔ thán dàj (b)lɛ̀ɛw... njáŋ bɔ̀ɔ

(c) càw dàjhāp khāāw câak khácàw _____?

(Have you had any news from them yet or not?)

(d) láaw njáŋ bɔɔ thán _____ phɔwāā láaw njáŋ bɔɔ thán dàj _____

(He hasn't been able to eat breakfast yet, because he's hasn't had a chance to wash his face yet.)

(e) láaw bɔɔ míi wǐi láaw _____ njáŋ bɔɔ thán dàj wǐi phǒm

(He hasn't got a comb so he hasn't yet been able to comb his hair.)

(f) láaw pɛɛ nǎŋsɣ̌y hâj khácàw lɛɛw tɛɛ wāā khácàw _____ aw ŋén hâj làaw

(He has already translated the book for them, but they haven't yet got around to paying him.)

(g) càw bɔ̀ɔk láaw át pátuu _____?

(Have you told him to close the door yet or not?)

(h) thâawāā pátuu _____ pɛɛ wāā làaw njáŋ bɔɔ thán máa

(If the door isn't opened yet, that means he hasn't arrived yet.)

(i) khɔ̀j njáŋ bɔɔ _____ khɔ̀j phɔwāā khɔ̀j njáŋ bɔɔ míi wéeláa

(I haven't yet been able to wash my clothes because I haven't had time yet.)

(j) láaw njáŋ bɔɔ thán dàj _____ khɣ̌oŋ khácàw

(He hasn't yet been able to come inspect their work.)

_____

Answers: (c)lɛɛw lɣ̌y njáŋ (d)kin khâw sàw... swāāj nâa (e)cɣŋ (f)njáŋ bɔɔ thán dàj (g)lɛɛw lɣ̌y njáŋ (h)njáŋ bɔɔ thán khǎj (i)thán dàj sāk khɣan nūŋ (j)máa kûat bəŋ wìak

313

CYCLE 67

M-1

pɛɛŋ, lōtdút	fix, repair; bulldozer
láaw pɛɛŋ lōtdút lɛ̀ɛw lɛ̀[ɛw] bɔɔ?	Has he finished fixing the bulldozer?
hâj sǎmphàat	to give an interview
láaw hâj sǎmphàat lɛ̀ɛw lɛ̀[ɛw] bɔɔ?	Has he finished giving the interview?
nāp, ŋə́n	to count, money
láaw nāp ŋə́n lɛ̀ɛw lɛ̀[ɛw] bɔɔ?	Has he finished counting money?
sŷypsǔan	to investigate
láaw sŷypsǔan lɛ̀ɛw lɛ̀[ɛw] bɔɔ?	Has he finished the investigation?
sɔ̂ɔpsǔan	to interrogate
láaw sɔ̂ɔpsǔan lɛ̀ɛw lɛ̀[ɛw] bɔɔ?	Has he finished the interrogation?
banthȳk, sǐaŋ	to record; sound, voice
láaw banthȳk sǐaŋ lɛ̀ɛw lɛ̀[ɛw] bɔɔ?	Has he finished recording?
màaŋ, pyyn	to dismantle, disassemble
láaw màaŋ pyyn lɛ̀ɛw lɛ̀[ɛw] bɔɔ?	Has he finished taking the gun apart?

M-2

lèɛw lèɛw	Yes, (he has) finished.
bɔ̃ɔ̃, njáŋ bɔ̃ɔ̃ lèɛw	No, (he has) not finished yet.
njáŋ, njáŋ bɔ̃ɔ̃ lèɛw	Not yet, (he has) not finished yet.

M-3

átsǐaŋ	to record sound
láaw átsǐaŋ lèɛw lè[ɛw]	He has finished recording.
èe	to decorate
làaw èe hýan lèɛw lè[ɛw]	He has finished decorating the house.
thǎaŋ, pāā	to clear (a forest), forest
láaw thǎaŋ pāā lèɛw lè[ɛw]	He has finished clearing the wood.
thǎj, náa	to plow, a plow, rice field
láaw thǎj náa lèɛw lè[ɛw]	He has finished plowing the rice field.
kǐaw, khâw	to cut (with a sickle), rice
láaw kǐaw khâw lèɛw lè[ɛw]	He has finished harvesting the rice.
fàat	to strike, slap, flail
láaw fàat khâw lèɛw lè[ɛw]	He has finished threshing the rice by hand.
khàat	harrow
láaw khàat náa lèɛw lè[ɛw]	He has finished harrowing the rice field.

315

M-4

tam   to pound (in a mortar)

    láaw tam khâw nján bɔ̄ɔ   He hasn't finished polishing
    lɛ̀ɛw   the rice.

hǔŋ, súk   cook by boiling; to be cooked,
                                                 ripe

    láaw hǔŋ khâw nján bɔ̄ɔ   He hasn't finished cooking
    súk   the rice.

nŷŋ   cook by steaming

    láaw nŷŋ khâw nján bɔ̄ɔ   He hasn't finished cooking
    súk   the (sticky) rice.

M-5

lɛ̌ɛm, sɔ̌ɔ   sharpen, sharp, crayon

    lɛ̌ɛm sɔ̌ɔ lɛ̀ɛw lɛ̀[ɛw]   What is he going to do after
    láaw si hēt njǎŋ?   he finishes sharpening the
                                                 pencils?

wǐi, nūŋ khȳaŋ   comb, get dressed

    wǐi phǒm lɛ̀ɛw lɛ̀[ɛw]   Is he going to get dressed
    láaw si nūŋ khȳaŋ bɔɔ?   after he finishes combing
                                                 his hair?

C-1

    A. càw pɛɛŋ lōt lɛ̀ɛw lɛ̀[ɛw]   Have you finished fixing your
       bɔɔ?   car?

    B. lɛ̀ɛw lɛ̀ɛw   Yes, I have.

316

C-2

    A. càw màaŋ pyyn càw lɛ̀ɛw   Have you finished taking
       lɛ̀[ɛw] bɔɔ?   your gun apart?

    B. bɔɔ, njáŋ bɔɔ lɛ̀ɛw   No, I haven't finished yet.

C-3

    A. càw āan cótmǎaj lɛ̀ɛw   Have you finished reading
       lɛ̀[ɛw] bɔɔ?   the letter?

    B. njáŋ, njáŋ bɔɔ lɛ̀ɛw   No, I haven't finished yet.

C-4

    A. càw kûat pỳm lɛ̀ɛw lɛ̀[ɛw]   Have you finished checking
       bɔɔ?   the book?

    B. əə, khɔ̀j kûat pỳm lɛ̀ɛw   Yes, I have finished checking
       lɛ̀[ɛw]   the book.

C-5

    A. láaw nŷŋ khâw súk lɛ̀ɛw   Has he finished cooking the
       bɔɔ?   rice?

    B. bɔɔ, láaw nŷŋ khâw njáŋ   No, he hasn't finished
       bɔɔ súk   cooking the rice.

C-6

    A. khúakin lɛ̀ɛw lɛ̀[ɛw] láaw   What is he going to do when
       si hēt njǎŋ?   he finishes cooking?

    B. khúakin lɛ̀ɛw lɛ̀[ɛw] láaw   When he finishes cooking he
       si əən háw máa kin khâw   will call us to the table.

317

NOTES

1) lɛ̀ɛw as an Aspect particle indicating 'action completed at a particular time' and as a secondary verb meaning 'to complete some activity' may occur in one sentence, thus

   láaw pɛɛ̌ŋ lǒt lɛ̀ɛw lɛ̀ɛw   'He has already finished making repairs on the car.

In normal speech the second lɛ̀ɛw occurs in reduced form as lɛ̀.

2) The response to ... lɛ̀ɛw lɛ̀[ɛw] bɔɔ? questions may be:

   Question: càw pɛɛ̌ŋ lǒt càw   'Have you finished fixing
              lɛ̀ɛw lɛ̀ɛw bɔɔ?   your car yet?'

   Affirmative
   Response: (a) lɛ̀ɛw lɛ̀[ɛw]   'Yes, I have.'

          (b) əə, khɔ̌j pɛɛ̌ŋ   'Yes, I've finished making
              lǒt lɛ̀ɛw lɛ̀ɛw   the repairs to my car
                        already.'

   Negative: (a) bɔɔ, njáŋ bɔɔ   'No, I haven't finished
              lɛ̀ɛw   yet.'

          (b) njáŋ, njáŋ bɔɔ   'No, I haven't finished
              lɛ̀ɛw   yet.'

3) VP + lɛ̀ɛw lɛ̀ɛw corresponds closely in meaning to English past participial constructions 'having...ed', etc. When VP + lɛ̀ɛw lɛ̀ɛw precedes NP + VP, there is an indication that the action referred to in the initial VP occurred before that in the second VP. Compare English and Lao:

   English: having done his work, he went to bed (or) After he did...

     Lao: hɛ̄t w̄ak lɛ̀ɛw lɛ̀ɛw, láaw paj nɔ́ɔn

318

APPLICATION

1. Complete the following sentences using the English as a guide:

    (a) tháaŋ _____ dút _____ phān cȳŋ bɔɔ hâj lōt thíaw
         (The road is not yet completed so they don't let cars
         pass through.)

    (b) mȳa njíŋ _____ phùak thāhǎan pháa kan màaŋ pyyn ɔ̂ok sēt
         lē sāj nàm mán
         (When the firing is over, the soldiers as a group take
         their guns apart and oil them simultaneously.)

    (c) phɔɔ náa thǎj náa _____ láaw cȳŋ _____ thán khàat
         (The farmer hasn't finished plowing so he hasn't started
         harrowing yet.)

    (d) mȳa kīaw khâw _____ phùak phɔɔ náa pháa kan fàat khâw
         (When the harvesting is done, the farmers as a group knock
         the heads off the rice stalks.)

    (e) mȳa wéeláa _____ mēē khàa nǎp bàŋ ŋén khɔ̌ɔŋ láaw
         (When everything is sold out, the female vendor counts her
         money [to see how much she took in]).

    (f) thâawāā láaw hēt wìak nìi _____ láaw si bɔɔ mȳa hȳan
         (If he hasn't finished doing this work, he will not go home.)

Answers: 1(a)njáŋ ... bɔɔ lɛ̀ɛw (b)lɛ̀ɛw (c)njáŋ bɔɔ lɛ̀ɛw ...
          njáŋ bɔɔ (d)lɛ̀ɛw lɛ̀ɛw (e)khǎaj khɔ̌ɔŋ mót lɛ̀ɛw (f)bɔɔ
          lɛ̀ɛw

(g) phȳa cá? hēt náa phə̄n tɔ̀ɔŋ thǎaŋ pāā, _____ phə̄n
     cȳŋ aw thǎj máa thǎj

(In order to farm one has to clear the forest; once the
forest is cleared, one brings a plough in and ploughs
[the land]).

(h) lǎŋ câak sɔ̂ɔpsǔan _____ tamlûat kɔɔ pɔ̄ɔj khácàw
     káp bàan

(After the interrogation is completed, the police lets
them go home.)

(1) sɔ̂ɔpsǔan _____, njáŋ cá? tɔ̀ɔŋ míi kạan banthȳk
     îik

(All aspects of the interrogation haven't been completed
yet, there still are more tape recordings that have to
be made.)

(j) mȳa èe hýan _____ láaw si sə̀ən mūū máa kin lìaŋ

(When the decoration of the house has been finished, she
will invite guests in to eat.)

Answers: (g)thǎaŋ pāā lèɛw (h)lèɛw lèɛw (1)lèɛw njáŋ bɔ̄ɔ lèɛw
          (j)lèɛw lèɛw

320

CYCLE 68

M-1

hē̃twìak	work
caw hē̃twìak hâj phăj?	Who do you work for?
khĭan pỳm	write the book for
caw khĭan pỳm hâj phăj?	Who do you write the book for?
kháp lŏt	drive the car
caw kháp lŏt hâj phăj?	Who do you drive the car for?
púk hýan	build the house
caw púk hýan hâj phăj?	Who do you build the house for?
tát phŏm	cut the hair
caw tát phŏm hâj phăj?	Who did you cut the hair for?
fâw hýan	watch the house
caw fâw hýan hâj phăj?	Who do you watch the house for?
phím năŋsўy	type the letter
caw phím năŋsўy hâj phăj?	Who do you type the letter for?

M-2

paj aw	going to get
khɔ̂j si paj aw hâj láaw	I am going to get (it) for him.
sōŋ năŋsўy	send the letter
khɔ̂j si sōŋ năŋsўy hâj láaw	I will send the letter for him.

321

pɛɛŋ lŏt	fix the car
khɔ̌j si pɛɛŋ lŏt hâj láaw	I will fix the car for him.
làaŋ lŏt	wash the car
khɔ̌j si làaŋ lŏt hâj láaw	I will wash the car for him.
khúakin	cook
khɔ̌j si khúakin hâj láaw	I will cook for him.
mìan pỳm	arrange the books
khɔ̌j si mìan pỳm hâj láaw	I will arrange the books for him.

M-3

kúlíi	the coolie
kúlíi si hɛ̄t njǎŋ hâj càw?	What is the coolie going to do for you?
khónsàj	the servant
khónsàj si hɛ̄t njǎŋ hâj càw?	What is the servant going to do for you?
sāaŋmàj	the carpenter
sāaŋmàj si hɛ̄t njǎŋ hâj càw?	What is the carpenter going to do for you?
léekhǎanūkaan	the secretary
léekhǎanūkaan si hɛ̄t njǎŋ hâj càw?	What is the secretary going to do for you?

322

<u>náajsāāŋ</u>   the mechanic

 náajsāāŋ si hēt njǎŋ hâj   What is the mechanic going
 càw?   to do for you?

<u>sāāŋtátphǒm</u>   the barber

 sāāŋtátphǒm si hēt njǎŋ   What's the barber going to
 hâj càw?   do for you?

C-1

 A. càw si pɛɛŋ lōt hâj phǎj? Who are you going to fix the
            car for?

 B. khɔ̂j si pɛɛŋ hâj láaw   I will fix (the car) for him.

C-2

 A. phǎj si aw paj hâj càw? Who will take it for you?

 B. khónsàj si aw paj hâj khɔ̂j The servant will take it for
            me.

C-3

 A. náajsāāŋ si hēt njǎŋ hâj What's the mechanic going
   càw?   to do for you?

 B. láaw si pɛɛŋlōt hâj khɔ̂j He will fix the car for me.

ຍົດນກໍ່ມີຈຸດປະສິງທີ່ຈະສອນການໃຊ້ຄຳວ່າ "ໃຫ້". ຢ່າລືມອຍາຍການຝຶກຫັດໃນພາກ C ແລະຖ້າມໍ່ເຮັດ
ໂກກໍ່ຈົງປະຕິດເຮືອງນອກເບິ່ງດູ!

NOTES

1) hâj in the construction VP + hâj + NP indicates that the
   activity referred to in VP is either done (a) for the benefit
   of, or (b) in place of the person(s) referred to in NP.

   láaw kháp lōt hâj khɔ̄j   'He drives for me (in place
                                           of me).'

   láaw tát phǒm hâj khɔ̄j   'He cuts my hair (for my
                                           benefit).'

   hâj has many other meanings but the most of them relate in some
   way to one or the other of the two categories stated above.
   hâj parallels English for in only a few instances.

2) hâj kan indicates that some activity is carried out for the
   mutual benefit of the parties participating in it. khácàw
   khúakin hâj kan 'They cook for each other'.

3) hâj + NP may contrast with eeŋ 'oneself' in use.

   khɔ̄j sì khúakin hâj láaw phōwāā   'I'll cook for him, because
   láaw khúakin eeŋ bɔ̄ɔ dàj   he can't cook for himself.'

4) pháa kan + VP is used to indicate that all the members of a
   group engage in simultaneous and identical action.

   phɔ̄ɔ náa pháa kan fàat khâw   'All the farmers flail rice
                                           stalks at the same time.'

5) khǎw occurs in informal usage for khácàw 'they'. It is commonly
   used with children. It may also be used for unidentified person
   phēn is also used for 'they', but it is used only for persons of
   higher status. It also means 'he, she'.

APPLICATION

1. Complete the following sentences using the English as a guide:

(a) láaw wàw wāā láaw jâak máa hētwìak _____
   (He said he would like to come work for me.)

(b) khón kháplōt khôj si paj kháplōt _____ sɔ̌ɔŋ mỳy
   (My chauffeur will go drive for him two days.)

(c) phùak nāk-hían bɔ̄ɔ jâak sǐa ŋén khāā tátphǒm khácàw
   cɣ̄ŋ tátphǒm _____
   (Students don't like to spend money on haircuts, so they
   cut each other's hair.)

(d) léekhǎanūkaan bɔ̀ɔk wāā láaw si phím nǎŋsʌ̌y _____
   mỳy nìi
   (The secretary said she would finish typing the letter
   for me today.)

(e) khôj si khúakin _____ phɔ̄wāā láaw khúakin _____
   _____ bɔ̄ɔ pen
   (I'll cook for her because she doesn't know how to cook
   herself.)

(f) láaw pɛɛŋ lōt bɔ̄ɔ pen láaw cɣ̄ŋ si càan náajsāāŋ _____
   (He doesn't know how to fix a car himself, so he will hire
   a mechanic to come fix it for him.)

Answers: 1(a)hâj khôj (b)hâj láaw (c)hâj kan (d)hâj khôj
hâj lɛɛw (e)hâj láaw... een (f)máa pɛɛŋ hâj láaw

(g) sāaŋmàj si _____ khɔ̂j kɔɔ bɔ̌ɔ hùu

(I don't know what the carpenter is going to do for me either.)

(h) khɔ̂j si aw khɔ̌oŋ nìi sāj lŏt paj khǎaj _____

(I'll put these things in the car and go sell them for her.)

(i) déknɔ̀ɔj _____ làaŋ lŏt _____ phɔ̄wāā khǎw ˙jâak hâj khɔ̂j pháa paj sǔan sát

(The children all pitch in and wash the car for me because they want me to take them to the zoo.)

(j) khɔ̂j bɔ̌ɔ diicaj njɔ̀ɔn wāā sāaŋ tátphǒm tátphǒm _____ sân phòot

(I'm not happy due to the fact that the barber cut my hair too short.)

Answers: (g)hēt njǎŋ hâj khɔ̂j (h)hâj láaw (i)pháa kan...
hâj khɔ̂j (j)hâj khɔ̂j

CYCLE 69

M-1

<u>hētkaan</u>	to work
kh3j jâak hētkaan	I want to work.
<u>míi ŋén lăaj</u>	to have a lot of money
kh3j jâak míi ŋén lăaj	I want to have a lot of money.
<u>lîn kíláa</u>	to engage in sport
kh3j jâak lîn kíláa	I want to engage in sports.
<u>tii pɪ̂ŋpɔ̌ŋ</u>	play table tennis
kh3j jâak tii pɪ̂ŋpɔ̌ŋ	I want to play table tennis.
<u>lɛɛn</u>	to run
kh3j jâak lɛɛn	I want to run.
<u>hěn lăaj mýaŋ</u>	to see many cities
kh3j jâak hěn lăaj mýaŋ	I want to see many cities.
<u>fáŋ phéeŋ</u>	to listen to the song
kh3j jâak fáŋ phéeŋ	I want to listen to the song.

M-2

<u>máa</u>	to come
kh3j jâak hâj láaw máa	I want him to come.
<u>jūu nám kh3j</u>	to stay with me
kh3j jâak hâj láaw jūu nám kh3j	I want him to stay with me.

tɛ̄ɛŋŋáan | to get married

  khɔ̌j jâak hâj láaw tɛ̄ɛŋŋáan | I want him to get married.

tàŋcaj hían | to concentrate on studying

  khɔ̌j jâak hâj láaw tàŋcaj hían | I want him to concentrate on studying.

sáw sûup jaa | to stop smoking

  khɔ̌j jâak hâj láaw sáw sûup jaa | I want her to stop smoking.

lə̀əm hētkaan | to begin working

  khɔ̌j jâak hâj láaw lə̀əm hētkaan | I want him to begin working.

pen thāhǎan | to become soldier

  khɔ̌j jâak hâj láaw pen thāhǎan | I want him to become soldier

M-3

náajkhúu

  náajkhúu jâak hâj càw hēt njǎŋ? | What does the teacher want you to do?

rāthābaan | the government

  rāthābaan jâak hâj càw hēt njǎŋ? | What does the government want you to do?

khúubaa   the monk

     khúubaa jâak hâj càw hēt njǎŋ?   What does the monk want you to do?

(aàj) cua   the monk novice

     (aàj) cua jâak hâj càw hēt njǎŋ?   What does the monk novice wants you to do?

déknòoj   the children

     déknòoj jâak hâj càw hēt njǎŋ?   What do the children want you to do?

lùuk càw   your children

     lùuk càw jâak hâj càw hēt njǎŋ?   What do your children want you to do?

C-1

     A. càw jâak hēt njǎŋ?   What do you want to do?

     B. khòj jâak fáŋ phéeŋ   I want to hear the songs.

C-2

     A. càw jâak hâj khòj hēt njǎŋ?   What do you want me to do?

     B. khòj jâak hâj càw jūu nám láaw   I want you to stay with him.

329

C-3

A. náaɟkhúu ɟâak hâɟ càw
   hēt nɟǎŋ?

What does the teacher want
you to do?

B. phēn ɟâak hâɟ khɔ̌ɟ
   tàŋcaɟ hían

He wants me to concentrate
on studying.

ຂະວັງຢ່າງປ່ອຍໃຫ້ນັກຮຽນໃຈຄໍວ່າ "ຢາກ" ຢ່າງຜິດພາດ. ສວນມາກຂະເຈົ້ານັກເວົ້າວ່າ "ຂອຍຢາກລາງ
ໄປຕລາດ" ແທນຫ່ະເວົ້າວ່າ "ຂອຍຢາກໃຫ້ລາວໄປຕລາດ". ທ່ານກໍຍອມພາສາຂອງຂະເຈົ້າ.

NOTES

1) **ɟâak** + VP means 'to want, would like (to do something)'.

   khɔ̌ɟ ɟâak míi ŋén lǎaɟ   'I would like to have lots
                                      of money.'

   When the Subject of the sentence and the person performing the
   action are not the same person, **ɟâak hâɟ** + VP is used.

   khɔ̌ɟ ɟâak hâɟ láaw pen náaɟ   'I want her to be a teacher.'
   khúu

2) **phɔ̀ɔm kan** means 'simultaneously' or 'at the same time'.

   khɔ̌ɟ khīt wāā khácàw si bɔ̌ɔ   'I don't think they will
   máa hɔ̀ɔt phɔ̀ɔm kan   arrive simultaneously.'

3) **ton** 'oneself, itself, themselves' is used in place of **láaw** or
   khácàw when the subject of the sentence and the person(s)
   referred to later are the same person:

   phɔ̌ɔmēē thūk khón kɔɔ ɟâak hâɟ   'All parents would like to
   lùuk khɔ̌ɔŋ ton tàŋcaɟ hían   have their children concen-
   nánsɣ̌y   trate on studying.' (**phɔ̌ɔmēē**
                                            and **ton** refer to the same
                                            people.)

330

APPLICATION

1) Complete the following sentences using the English as a guide:

(a) aanjūʔ láaw njáŋ bɔɔ thə̌ŋ síp pɛ̂ɛt pii tɛ̄ɛ láaw kɔɔ _____
    hēt kaan lɛ̀ɛw
    (She isn't 18 yet, but she would like to get a job.)

(b) láaw _____ tɛ̄ɛ wāa súkháphàap láaw bɔɔ dii.
    (He would like to engage in sports, but his health isn't
    good.)

(c) thâawāa phūu nȳŋ _____ phūu nȳŋ _____ khácàw
    âat cáʔ bɔɔ paj hòot _____
    (If one person wants to walk and another wants to run,
    they may not arrive at the same time.)

(d) khɔ̂j _____ láaw máa hěn khwáam cáréən khɔ̌ɔŋ bàan mýaŋ
    (I would like to have him come see the growth and progress
    in the country.)

(e) phɔɔmɛ̄ɛ thūk khón tāaŋ kɔɔ _____ lùuk khɔ̌ɔŋ ton
    tàŋcaj hían nǎŋsȳy
    (Each individual parent would like to have his children
    concentrate on their studies.)

Answers: 1(a)jâak (b)jâak lȋn kíláa (c)jâak njāaŋ... jâak
         lɛ̄ɛn... phɔ̀ɔm kan (d)jâak hâj (e)jâak hâj

(f) khɔ̀j wǎŋ dii tɔ̄ɔ láaw khɔ̀j cŷŋ ＿＿＿＿＿＿＿＿＿ sûup jaa

(I wish him well, so I would like to have him stop smoking.)

(g) phɔ̄ɔmɛ̄ɛ baaŋkhón ＿＿＿＿＿＿＿＿＿ tɛ̄ɛŋŋáan phʸa cá? dàj
mót khwáam pen hûaŋ

(Some parents want their daughters to get married so as to
get rid of worrying [about them]).

(h) khɔ̀j ＿＿＿＿＿＿ láaw ＿＿＿＿＿＿ tɔ̄ɔ paj njɔ̀ɔn wāa láaw
hían njáŋ bɔ̄ɔ cóp

(I would like to have him continue staying with me due to
the fact that he hasn't finished his studies yet.)

(i) láthábaan ＿＿＿＿＿＿ pásáasón míi khwáam jūu dii kin dii

(The Government would like for the people to have a good
standard of living.)

(j) khúubaa ＿＿＿＿＿＿＿ àaj cua phānjáanjáam hāmhían aw khwáam
h̥ùu (The monk told the novice to study hard to gain knowled

―――――――――――――――――――

Answers: (f)jâak hâj láaw sáw (g)jâak hâj lùuksǎaw khǒoŋ ton
(h)jâak hâj... jūu nám khɔ̀j (i)jâak hâj (j)bɔ̀ɔk hâj

CYCLE 70

M-1

<u>khúakin</u>   cook

    khɔ̌j hâj láaw khúakin hâj   I $\left\{ \begin{array}{l} \text{had} \\ \text{let} \end{array} \right.$ her cook for me.
    (khɔ̌j)

<u>phát kə̂əp</u>   shine (my) shoes

    khɔ̌j hâj láaw phát kə̂əp   I $\left\{ \begin{array}{l} \text{had} \\ \text{let} \end{array} \right.$ him shine (my) shoes
    hâj (khɔ̌j)   for me.

<u>làaŋ thûaj sáam</u>   wash dishes

    khɔ̌j hâj láaw làaŋ thûaj   I $\left\{ \begin{array}{l} \text{had} \\ \text{let} \end{array} \right.$ him wash dishes for
    sáam hâj (khɔ̌j)   for me.

<u>phím nǎŋšyy</u>   type the letter

    khɔ̌j hâj láaw phím nǎŋšyy   I $\left\{ \begin{array}{l} \text{had} \\ \text{let} \end{array} \right.$ her type the letter
    hâj (khɔ̌j)   for me.

<u>bə̄ŋ lùuk</u>   watch the children

    khɔ̌j hâj láaw bə̄ŋ lùuk   I $\left\{ \begin{array}{l} \text{had} \\ \text{let} \end{array} \right.$ her watch the
    hâj (khɔ̌j)   children for me.

<u>fâw hýan</u>   watch the house

    khɔ̌j hâj láaw fâw hýan   I $\left\{ \begin{array}{l} \text{had} \\ \text{let} \end{array} \right.$ him watch the house
    hâj (khɔ̌j)   for me.

333

M-2

<u>kháp lŏt</u>   drive the car

    càw si hâj phǎj kháp lŏt   Who will you $\begin{Bmatrix} \text{have} \\ \text{let} \end{Bmatrix}$ drive
    hâj (càw)?   for you?

<u>làaŋ lŏt</u>   wash the car

    càw si hâj phǎj làaŋ lŏt   Who will you $\begin{Bmatrix} \text{have} \\ \text{let} \end{Bmatrix}$ wash the
    hâj (càw)?   car for you?

<u>kûat</u>   check

    càw si hâj phǎj kûat   Who will you $\begin{Bmatrix} \text{have} \\ \text{let} \end{Bmatrix}$ check it
    hâj (càw)?   for you?

<u>tὲεm</u>   draw

    càw si hâj phǎj tὲεm   Who will you $\begin{Bmatrix} \text{have} \\ \text{let} \end{Bmatrix}$ draw it
    hâj (càw)?   for you?

<u>cāaj</u>   pay

    càw si hâj phǎj <u>cāaj</u> Who will you $\begin{Bmatrix} \text{have} \\ \text{let} \end{Bmatrix}$ pay it
    hâj (càw)?   for you?

<u>tàjfáj</u>   turn on.

    càw si hâj phǎj tàjfáj   Who will you $\begin{Bmatrix} \text{have} \\ \text{let} \end{Bmatrix}$ turn on
    hâj (càw)?   the light for you?

<u>mòɔtfáj</u>   turn off

    càw si hâj phǎj mòɔtfáj   Who will you $\begin{Bmatrix} \text{have} \\ \text{let} \end{Bmatrix}$ turn off
    hâj (càw)?   the light for you?

C-1

    A. láaw si hâj càw hēt njǎŋ
       hâj (láaw)?

          What will he have you do
          for him.

    B. láaw si hâj khɔ̂j phát kêǝp
       hâj (láaw)

          He will have me shine shoes
          for him.

C-2

    A. khácàw si hâj phǎj bɔ̄ŋ
       lùuk hâj khacàw?

          Who will they have look after
          their children for them?

    B. khácàw si hâj phȳan bàan
       khácàw bɔ̄ŋ hâj

          Their neighbor.

C-3

    A. càw wāā si hâj láaw hēt
       njǎŋ hâj càw?

          What were you going to have
          him do for you?

    B. khɔ̂j wāā si hâj láaw phím
       nǎŋsȳy hâj khɔ̂j

          I was going to have him
          type letters for me.

ໃນບົດກັບມນກາານໃຊ້"ໃຫ້"ສອງຕ໌. ຫານຈິ່ວພາານັກຮຽນລອມຄົນເບົ່ງດູວ່າ ມີຫຍ້ງແຕກຕ່ະເຈ້ຈ່າຍ້ຍຍ່ຈ ຕລ
ຍ່ວໃຊ່ຍ່າງຜິດຖາຫກ. ຖ້າຫາກມີກຈິ່ວຊ້ອມຄືນໃຫມ່ອີກ.

NOTES

1) hâj frequently occurs twice in a sentence, once with the meaning 'on behalf of, for the benefit of' (benefactive meaning as in Cycle 68) and once with the meaning 'to have, let, cause (someone to do something)' (causative meaning as in Cycle 69):

khôj hâj láaw khúakin hâj (khôj)   'I had her cook for me.'

NP after hâj (benefactive) may be omitted if it has the same referent as NP (Subject), as in the example above and in this example:

phùak náaj khúu hâj láaw kháp   'The teachers let him drive
lōt hâj (khácàw)   for them.'

APPLICATION

1. Translate the following sentences into English and check your answers:

   (a) thâwāā láaw khúakin pen khôj si hâj láaw khúakin hâj khôj

   (b) càw si hâj láaw bēŋ lùuk hâj càw bɔɔ?

   (c) phăj si hēt wîak hâj phăj khôj kɔɔ njáŋ bɔɔ hùu thȳa

   (d) wéeláa càw bɔɔ jūu càw si hâj phăj fâw hýan hâj càw

   (e) mȳy wáan nîi láaw hâj déknɔɔj làaŋ lōt hâj láaw, càw
       hùu bɔɔ láaw aw ŋén hâj khăw thāwdaj?

Answers: (a) If she can cook, I will have her cook for me.
          (b) Are you going to have her babysit for you?
          (c) I have no idea yet who will work for who.
          (d) When you're not home, who will you have watch
              the house for you?
          (e) Yesterday he had the children wash the car for him
              do you know how much money he gave them?

(f) khɔ̃j jâak hâj láaw máa kûat bɛ̄ŋ cák lŏt hâj khɔ̃j phɔ̄wāa
diawnìi lŏt khɔ̃j lɛ̄ɛn bɔ̄ɔ khɔ̄ɔj dii paandaj

(g) láaw bɔ̄ɔ khə́əj hâj khón ɣ̃yn hɛ̄t wìak hâj láaw phɔ̄wāa láaw
bɔ̄ɔ sȳa caj khácàw

(h) thâawāa càw jâak hâj láaw lɛ̄ɛn wìak hâj càw, càw tɔ̀ɔŋ sȳy
lŏt hâj láaw

(i) khɔ̃j si hâj láaw khăaj khŏɔŋ nìi hâj khácàw phɔ̄wāa khácàw
bɔ̄ɔ míi wéeláa paj khăaj een

(j) kaan hâj khón ɣ̃yn títtɔ̄ɔ káp càw khŏɔŋ thīi din âat cá?
bɔ̄ɔ dàj phŏn dii thɔ̄ɔ kaan thīi háw paj títtɔ̄ɔ een

Answers: (f) I would like for him to come check the motor of
my car for me because my car isn't running very
well at present.
(g) He has never had other people work for him before,
because he doesn't trust them.
(h) If you want her to run errands for you, you have
to buy her a car.
(i) I'll have him sell these things for them because
they don't have time to go sell (them) themselves.
(j) Having other people contact the owner of the land
may not get as good results as if we went to
contact (him) ourselves.

II. Translate the above English sentences back into Lao and
check your answers. Since your translation may differ
at some points from the original, you should check with
the instructor about these differences.

CYCLE 71

M-1

<u>tó?</u>   table

    tó? nìi hēt duàɟ nɟăŋ?   What is this table made of?

<u>wātcánáanūkom</u>   dictionary

    wātcánáanūkom hŭa nìi hēt   What is this dictionary made
    dùaɟ nɟăŋ?   of?

<u>tùu</u>   cabinet

    tùu nìi hēt dùaɟ nɟăŋ?   What is this cabinet made of?

<u>dɔ̀ɔk fáɟ</u> fàa   light bulb

    dɔ̀ɔk fáɟ fàa hēt dùaɟ   What is the light bulb
    nɟăŋ?   made of?

<u>săaɟ sôo</u>   chain

    săaɟ sôo nìi hēt duàɟ nɟăŋ?   What is this chain made of?

<u>sábuu</u>   soap

    sábuu hēt dùaɟ nɟăŋ?   What is soap made of?

M-2

<u>săaɟsɔ̀ɔɟ</u>   chain(jewelry)

    săaɟsɔ̀ɔɟ nìi hēt dùaɟ khám   This chain is made of gold.

<u>săaɟ ɛɛw</u>   belt

    săaɟ ɛɛw nìi hēt dùaɟ năŋ   This belt is made of leather.

338

pɔɔŋjìam   window

    pɔɔŋjìam nìi hēt dùaj kὲεw   This window is made of glass.

pháathâat   tray

    pháathâat nìi hēt dùaj ŋə́n   This tray is made of silver.

mìittát, lék   scissors, iron

    mìittát nìi hēt dùaj lék   These scissors are made of iron.

sǎajfáj, thɔ́ɔŋdεεŋ   wires, copper

    sǎajfáj nìi hēt dùaj   These wires are made of copper.
    thɔ́ɔŋdεεŋ

cɔ̂ɔk, plastík   cups, plastic

    cɔ̂ɔk nìi hēt dùaj plastík   These cups are made of plastic.

sábuu, khȳan khéemíi   soap, chemical substances

    sábuu hēt dùaj khȳaŋ   Soap is made of chemical substances.
    khéemíi

M-3

thúŋ, cìa, thúŋcìa   flag, paper, paper flag

    thúŋ thīī hēt dùaj cìa   A flag which is made of
    əən wāā thúŋcìa   paper is called a paper flag.

sỳak, níilóŋ, sỳakníilóŋ   rope, nylon, nylon rope

    sỳak thīī hēt dùaj níilóŋ   A rope which is made of
    əən wāā sỳakníilóŋ   nylon is called a nylon rope.

339

khȳaŋnūŋ, khǒnsát   clothes, fur

    khȳaŋnūŋ thīī hēt dùaj
    khǒnsát ə̀ən wāā
    khȳaŋnūŋkhǒnsát

          Clothes which are made of
          fur are called fur clothes.

tiaŋ, màj, tiaŋmàj   bed, wood, wooden bed

    tiaŋ thīī hēt dùaj màj
    ə̀ən wāā tiaŋmàj

          A bed which is made of
          wood is called a wooden bed.

M-4

kə̀əp, jaaŋ   shoes, rubber

    háw ə̀ən kə̀əp thīī hēt dùaj
    jaaŋ wāā jáāŋ daj?

          What do we call shoes that
          are made of rubber?

mɔ̂ɔ, din   pot, earthı

    háw ə̀ən mɔ́ɔ thīī hēt dùaj
    din wāā jáāŋ daj?

          What do we call pots that
          are made of earth(enware)?

phâaphɛ́ɛ, mǎj   scarves, silk

    háw ə̀ən phâaphɛ́ɛ thīī hēt
    dùaj mǎj wāā jáāŋ daj?

          What do we call scarves that
          are made of silk?

C-1

    A. tùu nūaj nìi hēt dùaj
       njǎŋ?

          What is this table made of?

    B. tùu nūaj nìi hēt dùaj
       lék

          This table is made of metal
          (iron).

340

C-2

A. háw ə̀ən thúŋ thīī hēt
   dùaj cìa wāā jāāŋ daj?

What do we call flags that
are made of paper?

B. háw ə̀ən thúŋ thīī hēt
   dùaj cìa wāā thúŋcìa

We call them paper flags.

C-3

A. sỳakmǎj mēēn sỳak thīī
   hēt dùaj màj, mēēn bɔɔ?

Silk rope is rope that
is made of wood, is that
right?

B. bɔɔ mēēn, sỳakmǎj mēēn
   sỳak thīī hēt dùaj mǎj

No that's not right, silk
rope is rope made of silk.

C-4

A. sỳakmǎj mēēn sỳak thīī
   hēt dùaj njǎŋ?

What's a silk rope made of?

B. sỳakmǎj mēēn sỳak thīī
   hēt dùaj mǎj

Silk rope is rope made of
silk.

ຄ່ານນັກຣຽນເບິ່ງຄວາ ອັນໃດເຮັດດ້ວຍຫຍັງ? ແລະເຮົາເອມມັນວ່າຢ່າງໃດ? ລອງໃຫ້ນັກຣຽນທຽບຄຸນ
ພາບຂອງສິ່ງຂອງຕ່າງໆເບິ່ງດຸ! ເຮັ່ນ: ໂຕະໄມ້ຄົກວ່າໂຕະເຫລັກບໍ? ຫລືວ່າແນວໃດ ດ້ວນ.

NOTES

1) hēt dùaj means 'to be made of'. The response to the question
... hēt dùaj njǎŋ 'What is...made of?' is some type of material,
such as glass, paper, iron, etc.

Q: tùu nìi hēt dùaj njǎŋ?   'What is this cabinet made of?

A: tùu nìi hēt dùaj màj   'This cabinet is made of wood.

2) thīi 'that, which, who' functions as a Noun Phrase substitute
and as a connective in NP+thīi+VP constructions: thúŋ thīi
hēt dùaj cìa 'A flag (that is) made of paper'.

3) háw əən ... wāa jāaŋ daj? (Lit. how do we call) 'What do we
call...?' is used in requesting the name of something háw əən
kəəp thīi hēt dùaj jaaŋ wāa jāaŋ daj? 'What do we call shoes
that are made of rubber?'

APPLICATION

Complete the following sentences.

(a) wēēntaa hēt dùaj _____
    (Eye glasses are made of glass.)

(b) tóʔ hēt dùaj _____ lɛ̄ʔ lék
    (Tables are made of metal and wood.)

(c) móoŋ hēt dùaj _____
    (Watches are made of silver.)

(d) lōt _____ lék
    (Cars are made of iron.)

Answers: 1(a)kɛ̀ɛw (b)màj (c)ŋén (d)hēt dùaj

(e) jaaŋ lōt hēt dùaj _____
(Car tires are made of rubber.)

(f) syak thīī hēt dùaj mǎj ə̀ən wāā _____
(Rope that is made of silk is called silk rope.)

(g) pátuu thīī _____ ə̀ən wāā pátuu kɛ̀ɛw
(Doors that are made of glass are called glass doors.

(h) kátāā thīī hēt dùaj wǎaj ə̀ən wāā _____
(Baskets that are made of rattan are called rattan baskets.)

(i) kə̄əp _____ ə̀ən wāā kə̄əp nǎŋ.
(Shoes that are made of leather are called leather shoes.)

(j) thǒŋ thīī hēt dùaj plaastík _____ thǒŋ plaastík
(Bags that are made of plastic are called plastic bags.)

2) Answer the following questions:

(a) háw ə̀ən mɔ̄ɔ thīī hēt dùaj thɔ́ɔŋ αɛɛŋ wāā jāāŋ daj? _____
(What do we call a pot that is made of copper?)

(b) háw ə̀ən wɛ̌ɛn thīī hēt dùaj khám wāā jāāŋ daj? _____
(What do we call rings that are made of gold?)

(c) háw ə̀ən pâakkaa thīī hēt dùaj plaastík wāā jāāŋ daj??
_____ (What do we call pens that are made of plastic?)

Answers: 1(e)jaaŋ (f)syak mǎj (g)hēt dùaj kɛ̀ɛw (h)kátāā wǎaj
(i)thīī hēt dùaj nǎŋ (j)ə̀ən wāā 2(a)mɔ̄ɔ thɔ́ɔŋdɛɛŋ
(b)wɛ̌ɛn khám (c)pâakkaa plaastík

343

(d) háw èən kápaw thīī hēt dùaj năŋ waā jāaŋ daj? _____
(What do we call bags that are made of leather?)

(e) háw èən hýan thīī hēt dùaj màj phāj waā jāaŋ daj? _____
_____ (What do we call houses that are made of bamboo?)

(f) háw èən tāŋ ìi thīī hēt dùaj wăaj waā jāaŋ daj? _____
(What do we call a chair that is made of rattan?)

(g) háw èən sáam thīī hēt dùaj lék waā jāaŋ daj? _____
(What do we call a dish that is made of metal?)

(h) háw èən thŏŋ thàw thīī hēt dùaj fâaj waā jāaŋ daj? _____
(What do we call socks that are made of cotton?)

(i) háw èən sŷa thīī hēt dùaj măj waā jāaŋ daj? _____
(What do we call a blouse that is made of silk?)

(j) háw èən sáam thīī hēt dùaj cìa waā jāaŋ daj? _____
(What do we call plates that are made of paper?)

Answers: 2(d)kápaw năŋ (e)hýan màj phāj (f)tāŋ ìi wăaj
          (g)sáam lék (h)thŏŋthàw fâaj (i)sŷa măj (j)sáam cìa

CYCLE 72

M-1

khĭan   write

  láaw khĭan dùaɟ nɟăŋ?   What did he write with?

tát   cut

  láaw tát dùaɟ nɟăŋ?   What does he cut (it) with?

khút   dig

  láaw khút dùaɟ nɟăŋ?   What did he dig with?

māt   tie

  láaw māt dùaɟ nɟăŋ?   What did he tie with?

khâam mɛɛnàm   cross the river

  láaw khâam mɛɛnàm dùaɟ
  nɟăŋ?   What did he cross the river
                                             with?

dəəntháaŋ   travel

  láaw dəəntháaŋ dùaɟ nɟăŋ?   How did he travel?

M-2

tát, lῩaɟ   cut, saw

  khácàw sì tát dùaɟ lῩaɟ   They will cut with saws.

māt, wăaɟ   tie, rattan

  khácàw sì māt dùaɟ wăaɟ   They will tie (it) with rattan.

khút, cók   dig, hoe

  khácàw sì khút dùaɟ cók   They will dig with hoes.

345

khâam mɛɛnàm, thɔɔnmàj   cross the river, logs

    khácàw si khâam mɛɛnàm   They will cross the river
    dùaj thɔɔnmàj   with logs.

dəəntháaŋ, khɣaŋ bin   travel, airplanes

    khácàw si dəən tháaŋ dùaj   They will travel with
    khɣaŋ bin   airplanes.

thǎj náa, thǎj   plow the rice field, plows

    khácàw thǎj náa dùaj thǎj   They plow the ricefield
                           with plows.

pháaj hɣa, màj pháaj   paddle the boat, paddle

    khácàw pháaj hɣa dùaj   They paddle the boat with
    màj pháaj   paddles.

C-1

    A. càw si khɣan dùaj njǎŋ?   What will you write with?

    B. khɔj si khɣan dùaj pâakkaa I will write with a pen.

C-2

    A. láaw si tát màj dùaj cók,   He will cut wood with a hoe,
       mɛɛn bɔɔ?   is that right?

    B. bɔɔ mɛɛn, láaw si tát màj   No, he will cut wood with
       dùaj lɣaj   a saw.

ຈົງສົມມຸດປັນຫາຂ້ນ ແລ້ວໃຫ້ນັກຣຽນແກ້ປັນຫາສາລາວຢ່ອງໆ! ຖ້າຫາກວ່າການກະທຳສິ່ງໃດສິ່ງນື່ງ
ດ້ວຍວັດຖຸໃດຫນຶ່ງ ບໍ່ສາເຣັດຜົນ ຂະເຈົ້າຄິດວ່າຈະມີຫາງແກ້ໄຂໄດ້ຢ່າງໃດ?

NOTES

1) VP + <u>dùaj</u> + NP (Instrument) is used to indicate what device or means is used to perform some activity:

<u>khácàw tát màj dùaj lyaj</u>   'They cut the wood with a saw.'

<u>khácàw si māt dùaj wǎaj</u>   'They'll tie it up with rattan.'

APPLICATION

1. Translate the following sentences into English:

(a) láaw bɔɔ míi pâakkaa láaw cỹŋ khǐan dùaj sǒodam.

(b) din jūu nìi khěeŋ lǎaj cá? khút dùaj njǎŋ kɔɔ bɔɔ dàj

(c) thâawāa tát dùaj lyaj-thámmādaa bɔɔ dàj láaw si tát dùaj lyaj-tát-lék

(d) kaan dəən tháaŋ dùaj lŏt cāak wíaŋcan paj hǎa lǔaŋ phābaaŋ bɔɔ pɔɔtpháj

(e) phɔɔ náa jūu mýaŋ láaw thǎj náa dùaj thǎj nɔɔj

(f) láaw sɔɔk hǎa hýa bɔɔ hěn láaw cỹŋ khâam mɛɛ nàm dùaj thɔɔn màj

---

Answers: 1(a)He didn't have a pen so he wrote with a pencil (b)The earth here is too hard to be able to be dug with anything. (c)If it can't be cut with an ordinarv saw, he will cut it with a hacksaw. (d)Traveling by car from Vientiane to Luang Prabang is not safe. (e)Rice farmers in Laos plow their fields with small plows. (f)He wasn't able to find a boat, so he crossed the river on a log.

(g) dəən tháaŋ dùaj khҳaŋ bin wáj kwāa kaan dəəntháaŋ dùaj lōt

(h) láaw bɔɔ hùu wāa cá? mɛ̄t dɔ̀ɔk màj nìi dùaj njǎŋ

(i) thâawāa háw bɔɔ míi màj-pháaj háw si tɔ̀ɔŋ pháaj hҳa dùaj m

(j) láaw njáŋ bɔɔ hùu wāa diaw nìi háw át sҳaŋ dàj dùaj khҳaŋ
     át sҳaŋ

2. Complete the following sentences using the English as a guide:

(a) láaŋ khón kinkhâw dùaj _____
     (Some people eat with their hands.)

(b) khɔ̀j hɔɔ _____ plaastík.
     (I wrapped it with sheets of plastic.)

(c) láaw aw nîip sāj kan _____ lék nîip clà
     (He attached it with a paper clip.)

(d) láaw hāp fáŋ khāaw_____
     (He received the news by radio.)

(e) yàj khɔ̀j cá? dəəntháaŋ káp bàan _____
     (My older sister will return by train.)

Answers: 1(g)Traveling by plane is faster than by ear. (h)He
didn't know what he would tie up the flowers with.
(i)If we don't have any paddles, we'll have to paddle
the boat by hand. (j)He isn't yet aware that now we
can record sound with a tape recorder.
2(a)mýy (b)dùan phēēn (c)dùaj (d)dùaj wīthānjū?
(e)dùaj lōt fáj

(f) khón ciin _____ màj-thɯɯ
     (Chinese eat with chopsticks)

(g) khácàw khón _____ bɯaŋ
     (They stir it with a spoon.)

(h) sét ɔ̂ok dùaj _____
     (Wipe it off with a soft cloth.)

(i) njōk lōt khỹn _____ mɛɛ héɛŋ
     (Raise the car with a jack.)

(j) dyŋ _____ sǎaj sôo
     (Pull it with a chain.)

(k) māt dùaj _____
     (Tie it with a rope.) ·

(l) thǔu ɔ̂ok _____
     (Clean it with a brush.)

(m) _____ dùaj nàm jaa làaŋ pâak
     (Wash out your mouth with mouth wash.)

(n) _____ dùaj kɛ́ɛs
     (Cook with gas.)

_____

Answers: 2(f)kin khâw dùaj (g)dùaj (h)phâa ɔ̄ɔn ɔ̄ɔn (i)dùaj
          (j)dùaj (k)sỳak (l)dùaj pɛɛŋ (m)làaŋ pâak (n)khǔakin

349

(o) _____ dùaj lék khǎj kápɔɔŋ
(Open it with a can opener.)

(p) láaw thȳyk māt taa _____ phâa _____
(His eyes were bound with a black cloth.)

(q) tháa _____
(Paint it with yellow paint.)

(r) sēt thûaj sáam _____
(Dry the dishes with a cloth.)

(s) phát _____
(Polish it with a cloth.)

(t) tɔ̂ɔk tápuu _____ khɔ̀ɔn tii
(Drive the nail with a hammer.)

(u) tít taam bəŋ _____ khȳaŋ léedàa
(Track it by radar.)

(v) lɛɛn _____ kásɛ̌ɛ _____
(Run it on electrical current.)

(w) _____ khwáam ót thón
(Work with patience.)

(x) _____ dùaj khwáam pámâat
(Don't drive carelessly.)

Answers: (o)khǎj (p)dùaj... sǐi dam (q)dùaj sǐi lȳaŋ (r)dùaj p
(s)dùaj phâa (t)dùaj (u)dùaj (v)dùaj...fájfàa (w)hɛt
wìak dùaj (x)jàa kháp lōt

350

CYCLE 73

M-1

daŋ-fáj   to make a fire

   càw si sàj njăŋ daŋ-fáj?   What will you use for making
                            a fire?

hɔ́ɔŋ, nāŋ   to underlay, place beneath; sit

   càw si sàj njăŋ hɔ́ɔŋ nāŋ?   What will you use to sit on?

lābaaj, nàm   to control the flow, water

   càw si sàj njăŋ lābaaj nàm?   What will you use to control
                            the water flow?

sămlûat, bəŋ   survey, inspect, look at, see

   càw si sàj njăŋ sămlûat   What will you use for
   bəŋ?   inspecting?

lʸak, mâak màj   select, choose; fruit

   càw si sàj phăj lʸak   Who will you use to select
   mâak màj?   fruit?

kinkhâw   to have one's meal

   càw si sàj njăŋ kinkhâw?   What will you use to eat with?

phán, mýy   to wrap around, hand

   càw si sàj njăŋ phăn mýy ?   What will you use to wrap
                            around your hand?

M-2

thāan	charcoal
khɔ̌j si sàj thāan daŋ-fáj	I'll use charcoal for making a fire.
cìa	paper
khɔ̌j si sàj cìa hóoŋ nāŋ	I'll use paper to sit on.
kɔ̀oŋsɔ̄ɔŋ	binoculars
khɔ̌j si sàj kɔ̀oŋsɔ̄ɔŋ sǎmlûat bəŋ	I'll use binoculars for inspection.
déknɔ̀oj	children
khɔ̌j si sàj déknɔ̀oj lȳak mâak màj	I'll use children to select fruit.
būaŋ, sɔ̂ɔm	spoon, fork
khɔ̌j si sàj būaŋ sɔ̂ɔm kin khâw	I'll use a spoon and fork to eat with.
khȳaŋcák	machine, engine, motor
khɔ̌j si sàj khȳaŋcák lābaaj nàm	I'll use a machine for controlling the flow of the water.
phâa	cloth
khɔ̌j si sàj phâa phán mýy	I'll use a cloth to wrap around my hand.

C-1

    A. càw sì sàj njăŋ daŋ-fáj?   What will you use for
                                            building fire?

    B. khɔ̌j sì sàj thāan daŋ-fáj   I'll use charcoal for a fire.

C-2

    A. càw sì sàj cìa hēt njăŋ?   What will you use paper for?

    B. khɔ̌j sì sàj cìa hɔ́ɔŋ nāŋ   I'll use paper to sit on.

ເວລາກະທ່ວຽຮກການສ່ວງໃຄສ່ວນໆ ແລະຫາວາງນ່ຫຼຽອງໃຮຫມວໃຄແມວນໆ ຂະເຈ້າຈະໃຊຫຍ່ວງແຫນ?
ເປັນຕົມວາ ເມວຍມຽອມຫລັຍວງເຮົາກັຫລວງໃຮຽມກັນເຮົາ. ແລະອ້ຽງອັກໃນຫຼັຍອວງກຽອຫັນ.

NOTES

1) <u>sàj</u> 'to use' + NP + VP may be used in a similar way to <u>dùaj</u>
   + NP, i.e. to indicate the means or device used for accom-
   plishing something. Compare the two sentences:

   <u>khɔ̌j</u> <u>sàj</u> <u>būaŋ</u> <u>sɔ̂ɔm</u> <u>kin</u> <u>khâw</u>   (Lit. I use spoon fork to eat.)
                                    'I eat with a spoon and fork.'

   <u>khɔ̌j</u> <u>kin</u> <u>khâw</u> <u>dùaj</u> <u>būaŋ</u> <u>sɔ̂ɔm</u>   'I eat with a spoon and fork.'

   <u>sàj</u> may be used with persons as well as things, but should
   only be used by a person of superior status to one of lower
   status.

   <u>khɔ̌j</u> <u>sàj</u> <u>lùuk</u> <u>khɔ̌j</u> <u>paj</u> <u>s̄yy</u>   'I have my child go shopping
   <u>khɔ̌ɔŋ</u> <u>hâj</u>   for me.'

                                    (I use my child go buy things
                                    for.)

353

APPLICATION

1) Complete the following sentences using the English as a guide:

   (a) láaw _____ pyyn khūū khón khîi-lāk
   (He uses a gun to scare off thieves.)

   (b) khácàw sàj mìit-thɛ̆ɛ _____ hâj kan
   (They used razors to shave their heads with.)

   (c) láaw _____ khwáam phānjáanjáam hɛ̄t wìak con sǎmrēt
   (He uses effort to work until he is successful.)

   (d) láaw bɔ̄ɔ sálâat phɔwāā láaw _____ hǔa khɔ̆ɔŋ láaw
   hâj pen pánjôot
   (He is not clever since he has never used his head to
   advantage.)

   (e) láaw _____ pen khȳaŋ-mȳy khɔ̆ɔŋ láaw
   (He uses money as a tool.)

   (f) wéeláa láaw pɛɛ nǎŋsȳy láaw _____ wātcánáanūkom
   (He didn't use a dictionary while translating the book.)

   (g) láaw sàj _____ phán bâat-phɛ̆ɛ láaw
   (He used a clean cloth to wrap his wounds with.)

   (h) khɔ̂j bɔ̄ɔ khéəj sàj ŋén dooláa khɔ̂j khéəj _____ ŋén kīip
   (I've never used dollars. I've only used kips.)

Answers: 1(a)sàj (b)thɛ̆ɛ hǔa (c)sàj (d)bɔ̄ɔ khéəj sàj (e)sàj
ŋén (f)bɔ̄ɔ sàj (g)phâa sá?âat (h)sàj tɛɛ

354

LAO BASIC COURSE

(i) láaw _____ bɔɔ phían mán cʏ̄ŋ phée jɯ̄ɯ lʏ̀aj
(He doesn't use his car carefully so it's always out of fix.)

(j) láaw _____ khón-sàj láaw paj sʏ̀y khɔ̌ɔŋ
(He uses his servant for (to go) shopping.)

(k) láaw sàj kɔ̀ɔŋ-thāāj-hùup _____ láaw cʏ̄ŋ _____ hùup
(He doesn't know how to use a camera so he didn't get any pictures.)

(l) láaw _____ khón-sàj phɔ̄wāā láaw bɔɔ jâak hăp sàj khón ʏ̌yn
(He doesn't want to be a servant since he doesn't want to be used by others.)

(m) _____ phɛ̌ɛn-thīī sămlăp wáaŋ phɛ̌ɛnkaan
(Use a map for laying plans.)

(n) khón láaw _____ náa
(Laotians used water buffaloes for plowing.)

(o) láaw _____ Parker
(He uses a Parker pen.)

(p) láaw _____ sɛ̌ɛŋ-taa sákót cít
(He uses his eyesight to hypnotize.)

(q) lŏt khán nìi _____ phɔ̄wāā khʏ̄a?cák mán taaj
(This car can't be used since its motor is dead.)

(r) thūk khón _____ thīī míi khúnnāphàap dii
(Everybody likes to use things that are of good quality.)

(s) láaw bɔɔ hùucák _____
(He doesn't know how to use it.)

Answers: (i)sàj lŏt (j)sàj (k)bɔɔ pen... bɔɔ dàj (l)bɔɔ jâak pen (m)sàj (n)sàj khwáaj thăj (o)sàj pâakkaa (p)sàj (q)sàj bɔɔ dàj (r)māk sàj khɔ̌ɔŋ (s)sàj

355

2) Translate the following sentences into English:

(a) khɔ̌j māk sàj thāān khúakin phɔwāā mán sádûak dii

(b) khácàw bɔɔ míi tāŋ ìi khácàw cȳŋ sàj cìa hɔ́ɔŋ nāŋ

(c) sáaw bàan jūū náj mýaŋ láaw sàj tɛ̄ɛ būaŋ kinkhâw

(d) mȳa wéeláa fǒn bɔɔ tók phùak phɔɔ náa sàj khȳaŋcák lābaaj nàm khâw náa

(e) khɔ̌j si sàj láaw paj tálâat hâj khɔ̌j phɔwāā khɔ̌j míi wìak lǎaj

(f) láaw sàj khɔ̌ɔŋ lāw nìi bɔɔ pen mán cȳŋ phée

(g) kaan sàj déknɔ̀ɔj hēt wìak khɔ̌ɔŋ phūu njāj njɔ̄ɔm pen kaan kátham thīī bɔɔ lɔ̀ɔpkhɔ̀ɔp

(h) sáaw bàan pháa kan sàj phâa phán hǔa phɔwāā dɛ̂ɛt hɔ̀ɔn lǎaj

(i) thâawāā bɔ̌ɔn nāŋ pȳan khácàw si tɔ̀ɔŋ sàj nɛ́ɛwdaj nɛ́ɛwnȳŋ hɔ́ɔŋ nāŋ

(j) kaan sàj sīŋkhɔ̌ɔŋ tāāŋ jāāŋ ɒɔɔ thȳyk tɔ̀ɔŋ taam phǒnpánjôc knɔ̌ɔŋ mán âat cá? nám phǒn sǐa hǎaj máa sūū phūu sàj

Answers: 2(a)I like to use charcoal for cooking because it's nice and convenient. (b)They don't have chairs so they use paper to sit on. (c)Villagers in Laos use only spoons to eat with. (d)When there is no rain, rice farmers use an irrigating machine to bring water into the rice fields. (e)I'll have (lit. make use of) him go to the market for me since I have a lot of work. (f)He doesn't know how to use these things so they break down.(g)Using children to do the work of adults is not a circumspect act(is not advisable). (h)Villagers as a group wrap cloth around their heads because the sun is so hot. (i)If the seats are dirty, they'll have use something or other to sit on. (j)Incorrect use of thing may bring poor results to the user.

CYCLE 74

M-1

| pátíthín | a calendar |

pátíthín míi wàj sǎmlāp
njǎŋ?

What's a calendar for?

móoŋ

a clock, watch

móoŋ míi wàj sǎmlāp njǎŋ?

What is a watch for?

sǎaj ɛɛw

a belt

sǎaj ɛɛw míi wàj sǎmlāp
njǎŋ?

What is a belt for?

pyyn

a gun

pyyn míi wáj sǎmlāp njǎŋ?

What's a gun for?

kɔɔŋthāp

an army, armed forces

kɔɔŋthāp míi wàj sǎmlāp
njǎŋ?

What's an army for?

lōt-dáp-phəəŋ

a fire engine

lōt-dáp-phəəŋ míi wàj
sǎmlāp njǎŋ?

What's a fire engine for?

lōt- hóoŋmɔ̌ɔ

an ambulance

lōt-hóoŋmɔ̌ɔ míi wàj sǎmlāp
njǎŋ?

What's an ambulance for?

M-2

banthūk, khóncép	to load on, transport; patient
lõt-hóoŋmɔ̃ɔ míi wàj sǎmlāp banthūk khóncép	An ambulance is for transporting sick persons.
bɔ̃ɔk, wéeláa	tell, time
móoŋ míi wàj sǎmlāp bɔ̃ɔk wéeláa	A clock is for telling time.
hāt	fasten
sǎaj-ɛɛw míi wàj sǎmlāp hāt	A belt is for fastening.
wánthíi	date
pátíthín míi wàj sǎmlāp bɔ̃ɔk wánthíi	A calendar is for giving the date.
pɔ̀oŋkan, páthèet	defend, country
kɔɔŋthāp míi wàj sǎmlāp pɔ̀oŋkan páthèet	An armed force is for defending the country.
mɔ̀ɔt fáj	to put out fire
lõt-dáp-phéəŋ míi wàj sǎmlāp mɔ̀ɔt fáj	A fire engine is for putting out fires.

C-1

A. pyyn míi wàj sǎmlāp njǎŋ?	What's a gun for?
B. pyyn míi wàj sǎmlāp njíŋ	A gun's for shooting.

358

LAO BASIC COURSE

C-2

A. háw míi lōt-hóoŋmɔ̌ɔ wàj
sǎmlāp njǎŋ?

What do we use an ambulance
for?

B. háw míi lōt-hóoŋmɔ̌ɔ wàj
sǎmlāp̄ banthūk khón cép

We use an ambulance for
transporting sick persons.

C-3

A. kɔɔŋthāp míi wàj sǎmlāp
mɔ̀ɔt fáj mɛɛ̄n bɔɔ?

Is it true that an army is
for putting out fires?

B. bɔɔ mɛɛ̄n, kɔɔŋthāp míi wàj
sǎmlāp pɔ̀ɔŋkan páthèet

No, an army is for defending
a country.

ຈົ່ງໃຫ້ນັກຮຽນຊຸແຈງເຖິງພັນປໂຍກອອສ່ວອອງແຕລະຢ່າງເບົ້ງກຸວ່າ ອັນໃດນີໄວ້ສຳລັບຫຍັງ? ຕລມີ
ປໂຍກຢ່າງໃດ? ແຕງເຮືອງປະກອບຂນອິກ ໂດຍພຍາຍາມໃຫ້ນັກຮຽວອອງກັບວຊກການທີ່ແຕຫ່ອອງນັກຮຽນ.

NOTES

1) <u>míi wàj sǎmlāp</u> 'to be on hand for use as' occurs in the
construction:

NP + <u>míi wàj sǎmlāp</u> + VP

<u>móoŋ</u>   <u>míi wàj sǎmlāp</u>   bɔ̀ɔk wéeláa
'A watch   is for telling time.'

The negative of this construction seldom occurs. It is

NP + <u>bɔɔ mɛɛ̄n</u> + <u>míi wàj sǎmlāp</u> ....

<u>kə̀əp</u>   <u>bɔɔ mɛɛ̄n</u>   <u>míi wàj sǎmlāp</u> ....
'Shoes are not for .....'

359

APPLICATION

1. Translate the following sentences into English.

(a) khȳaŋcák nìi míi wàj sămlāp njăŋ khɔ̌j kɔɔ bɔɔ hùu

(b) pâakkaa mɛɛn khɔ̌ɔŋ thɪɪ háw míi wàj sămlāp khĭan

(c) pyyn míi wàj sămlāp pɔ̀ɔŋkan tua

(d) aahăn míi wàj sămlāp lìaŋ síiwɪt khɔ̌ɔŋ khón lɛ? sát

(e) ŋúa lɛ? khwáaj sŭan màak jɯɯ náj eesía míi wàj sămlāp sàj wìak

(f) pỳm ǎan míi wàj sămlāp ǎan lɛ? pỳm khĭan míi wàj sămlāp khĭan

(g) pỳm lāw nìi míi wàj sămlāp cêɛk-jaaj hâj nàk-hían thāw nǎ

(h) kə̂əp bɔɔ mɛɛn míi wàj sămlāp sàj hŭa tɛɛ míi wàj sămlāp sàj tiin

(i) sɔ̌ɔ-khăaw míi wàj sămlāp khĭan sàj kádaan

(j) màj banthāt míi wàj sămlāp khîit sên

Answers: 1(a)What this machine is for I don't know. (b)A pen is a thing that we have (on hand) for writing. (c)A gun is for defending oneself with. (d)Food is for nourishing life of people and animals. (e)In Asia most cattle and water buffaloes are for working. (f)A reading book is for reading and a writing book (notebook) is for writing in. (g)These books are for distribution to the students only. (h)Shoes aren't f« wearing on your head but are for wearing on your fee (i)Chalk is for writing on the blackboard. (j)A rule: is for drawing lines.

CYCLE 75

M-1

tɛ̄ɛkɔ̄ɔn	in the past, previously
tɛ̄ɛkɔ̄ɔn càw jūū sǎj?	Where were you previously?
tɛ̄ɛkìi	in the past, previously
tɛ̄ɛkìi càw jūū sǎj?	Where were you previously?
njáam	time, period
njáam khɔ̌j bɔ̄ɔ sábaaj càw jūū sǎj?	Where were you at the time that I was sick?
mỹa, kɔ̄ɔn	when; before, first
mỹa sɔ̌ɔŋ pii kɔ̄ɔn càw jūū sǎj?	Where were you two years ago?
mỳy, khýyn, mỳy khýyn nìi	day, time; night, last night
mỳy khýyn nìi càw jūū sǎj?	Where were you last night?
lɛ̀ɛw	finish, over, last
mỳy wáncan lɛ̀ɛw nìi càw jūū sǎj?	Where were you last Monday?

M-2

pátcúban, pácam	the present, nowadays; to be stationed at
pátcúban nìi láaw thŷyk sɔ̌ŋ paj pácam jūū pâaksée	Presently he is being sent to be stationed at Pakse.

m͞ɔɔ, m͞ya m͞ɔɔ m͞ɔɔ nɪ̀i   near, close; recently

    m͞ya m͞ɔɔ m͞ɔɔ nɪ̀i láaw thŷyk   Recently he was sent to be
    sɔ̆ŋ paj pácam jʉʉ pâaksée   stationed at Pakse.

don, m͞ya bɔɔ don nɪ̀i   long time, not long ago

    m͞ya bɔɔ don nɪ̀i láaw thŷyk   Not long ago he was sent to
    sɔ̆ŋ paj pácam jʉʉ pâaksée   be stationed at Pakse.

kaaj, pii kaaj nɪ̀i   pass, go past; last year

    pii kaaj nɪ̀i láaw thŷyk   Last year he was sent to be
    sɔ̆ŋ paj pácam jʉʉ pâaksée   stationed at Pakse.

diaw nɪ̀i   now, at the present time

    diaw nɪ̀i láaw thŷyk sɔ̆ŋ   Now he is being sent to be
    paj pácam jʉʉ pâaksée   stationed at Pakse.

C-1

    A. diaw nɪ̀i láaw pácam jʉʉ   Where is he stationed now?
       sǎj?

    B. diaw nɪ̀i láaw pácam jʉʉ   Right now he is stationed
       pâaksée   at Pakse.

C-2

    A. tɛ̆ɛkɔ̆ɔn láaw jʉʉ sǎj?   Where was he before?

    B. tɛ̆ɛkɔ̆ɔn láaw jʉʉ m͞yaŋ láaw   Before he was in Laos.

A. láaw hēt njǎŋ jūū hân?   What was he doing there?

B. láaw thŷyk sōŋ paj pácam   He was sent to be stationed
   jūū hân   there.

ໃຫ້ນັກຮຽນຖາມກັນເຖິງເບື້ອງຫລັງຂອງອະເຈົ້າເບິ່ງຄວາ ເວລາໃດຜູ້ໂດຍຣັດທະຍັງຢູ່ໃສ? ແລະຄິນປານ
ໃດ? ຕລີວ່າເຫດການຕ່າງໆເປັນໄປໃນທາຫນອງໃດ? ຕລອດຫົວປະສືບປະການຕ່າງໆຂອງອະເຈົ້າ.

NOTES

1) The following list of time expressions is given for your
   convenience:

   (a) Days of the week in order: wán-can, wán-aŋkháan, wán-phūt
       wán-phāhát, wán-súk, wán-sǎw, wán-aathīt.

   (b) Months of the year in order: mōkkáráa, kumpháa, míináa,
       méesǎa, phȳtsápháa, mīthúnáa, kɔɔrākádaa, sǐŋhǎa, kan-
       njáa, túláa, phȳtsácíkaa, thánwáa.

   (c) mỳy nìi 'today', mỳy wáan nìi 'yesterday', mỳy ȳyn
       'tomorrow', mỳy hýy 'day after tomorrow', mỳy sýyn 'day
       before yesterday'.

   (d) $\left.\begin{array}{l} \text{tɛɛ kɔɔn} \\ \text{tɛɛ kìi} \end{array}\right\}$ 'previously', 'before', sɔ̌ɔŋ pìi kɔɔn '2 years
       ago'.

       aathīt lɛ̀ɛw nìi 'a week ago', mȳa mɔɔ mɔɔ nìi 'recently',
       mȳa bɔɔ don máa nìi 'not long ago', mỳy wán-aŋkháan lɛ̀ɛw nìi
       'last Tuesday', mỳy wán-sùk nâa 'next Friday', pìi kaaj
       nìi 'last year', $\left.\begin{array}{l} \text{diaw nìi} \\ \text{pátcúban nìi} \end{array}\right\}$ 'now', pìi nâa 'next year',
       náj wéeláa nàn 'at that time'.

(e) náj dyan mīthúnáa pii phán kàw hɔ̀ɔj hóksíp hâa 'in June
1965', mȳa wéeláa khɔ̌j jūu... 'when I was living in...',
etc.

APPLICATION

1. Complete the following sentences using the English as a guide:

(a) _____ pii 1967 khɔ̌j jūu mȳaŋ wíaŋcan.
(In August 1967 I was living in Vientiane.)

(b) _____ láaw paj jìam-jaam phȳan láaw jūu hóoŋmɔ̌ɔ
(Last Thursday he went to visit his friend in the hospital

(c) khɔ̌j dàj hùucák káp ȳaj láaw mȳa _____ nǎŋsȳy
jūu sájŋɔ̌ɔn
(I met his older sister when I was studying in Saigon.)

(d) _____ láaw kamláŋ āan pȳm thīi nâa sǒncaj hǔa nȳ
(He is reading an interesting book at the present time.)

(e) _____ khɔ̌j dàj khīi hȳa paj pâaksée
(Not long ago I went to Pakse by boat.)

(f) _____ khɔ̌j njáŋ thāaj-hùup bɔ̌ɔ pen.
(Last year I still didn't know how to take pictures.)

_____

Answers: 1(a)mȳa dyan sǐŋhǎa (b)mȳy wánphāhát lɛ̀ɛw nìi
(c)wéeláa khɔ̌j hían (d)pátcúban nìi (e)mȳa bɔ̌ɔ
don máa nìi (f)pii kaaj nìi

(g) càw ká? wāā cá? púk hýan _____ bɔɔ?
(Do you expect to build a house next month?)

(h) _____ láaw pháa khácàw paj lǐn náj mýaŋ
(Last night he took them out on the town.)

(i) _____ khâw khɔ̂j bɔɔ njáŋ cák mēt. diaw nìi
khɔ̂j míi hók thǒŋ
(Two weeks ago I didn't have any ric(left. Now I have six bags.)

(j) sǎn-njáa nìi dàj sén kan _____
(This contract was signed not long ago.)

(k) _____ láaw njáŋ thŷyk khǎn jūū bɔɔ?
(Was he still locked up last Tuesday?)

(l) _____ láaw dàj sàj nǐi khɔ̌ɔŋ láaw con mót
(Recently he paid off all his debts.)

(m) khɔ̂j dàj ɔ̀ɔk câak thāhǎan _____ 1945.
(I left military service on September 19, 1945.)

(n) khácàw thŷyk pɔ̀ɔj tua mỳy khýyn nìi _____
(They were released last night at 10:30 p.m.)

Answers: (g)náj dyan nâa nìi (h)mỳy khýyn nìi (i)mýa sɔ̌ɔŋ aathīt kɔ̀ɔn (j)mýa bɔɔ náan máa nìi (k)mỳy wán aŋkháan lɛ̀ɛw nìi (l)mýa mɔ̀ɔ mɔ̀ɔ máa nìi (m)mýa wanthíi síp kàw kan-njáa (n)wéeláa síp móoŋ khə̄ŋ

(o) _____ khɔ̌j bɔ̌ɔ míi wlak hēt

(I was out of work last year.)

(p) _____ láaw hētkaan jūū sáthǎanthùut ámée̷elīkan
jūū mýaŋ wíaŋcan

(At present he works at the American Embassy in Vientiane

(q) àaj láaw sǐa síiwɪt mȳa _____ pii kaaj ǹìi

(Her older brother died in July last year.)

(r) _____ khɔ̌j _____ déknɔ̀ɔj khɔ̌j māk hían wɪ́ʔsáa
phúumɪsâat

(When I was a child, I like to study geography.)

(s) _____ khɔ̌j njáŋ hían nǎŋšy jūū thɪ̄ɪ māhǎawɪ́thā-
njáaláj óplóm khúu

(At that time I was still studying at the teacher trainin
college.)

(t) _____ mēē khɔ̌j dàj máa jaam phùak khɔ̌j

(The day before yesterday my mother came to visit us.)

(u) _____ khɔ̌j khâw nɔ́ɔn wéeláa síp móoŋ khə̌ŋ

(Every night I go to bed at 10:30 p.m.)

_____

Answers: (o)pii kaaj ǹìi (p)pátcúban ǹìi (q)dyan kɔɔrākádaa
(r)mȳa wéeláa... njáŋ pen... (s)wéeláa nàn (t)mỳy
sýyn (u)thūk thūk khýyn

(v) khɔ̀j si dàj phɔ̀ɔ láaw jūū thīī mýaŋ síkháakoo náj _____
_____ nâa
(I'll get to meet her in Chicago next December.)

(w) mȳa wéeláa bāāj sɔ̌ɔŋ móoŋ láaw _____ nóɔn _____
(He was still asleep at 2:00 p.m.)

(x) hàan-khǎaj-khɔ̌ɔŋ jūū náj mýaŋ wíaŋcan pə̀ət wéeláa kàw
móoŋ sàw _____
Shops in Vientiane open at 9:00 a.m. every day.)

(y) khɔ̀j hǎp cɔɔŋ nǎŋsɥ̌y phím _____ nȳŋ sábáp
(I subscribe to a weekly newspaper.)

Answers: (v)dyan thán wáa (w)njáŋ... jūū (x)thūk thūk mɥ̀y
(y)pácam sápádaa

367

CYCLE 76

M-1

<u>lǎŋ</u> <u>câak</u>, <u>njàaj</u>   after, move

    lǎŋ câak nàn láaw sì dàj   After that he will get to
    njàaj ɔ̀ɔk paj jǖu bàan nɔ̀ɔk   move out to the countryside.

    lǎŋ câak nìi láaw sì dàj   After this he will get to
    njàaj ɔ̀ɔk paj jǖu bàan nɔ̀ɔk   move out to the countryside.

    lǎŋ câak pii phán kàw hɔ̀ɔj   After 1960 he got to move
    hóksíp láaw dàj njàaj ɔ̀ɔk   out to the countryside.
    paj jǖu bàan nɔ̀ɔk

<u>tɔ̌ɔ</u>, <u>tɔ̌ɔ</u> { <u>paj</u> / <u>máa</u> }   join, extend; next, later on

    tɔ̌ɔ máa láaw dàj njàaj   Later on he got to move out
    ɔ̀ɔk paj jǖu bàan nɔ̀ɔk   to the countryside.

    tɔ̌ɔ paj láaw sì dàj njàaj   Then he will get to move out
    ɔ̀ɔk paj jǖu bàan nɔ̀ɔk   to the countryside.

M-2

<u>tɛ̌ɛ</u>, <u>tɛ̌ɛ</u> <u>nàn</u> <u>máa</u>   from, since; since then

    tɛ̌ɛ nàn máa láaw dàj njàaj   From that time on did he get
    paj sǎj bɔɔ?   to move anywhere?

<u>tɛ̌ɛ</u> <u>nìi</u> <u>paj</u>   from now on

    tɛ̌ɛ nìi paj láaw sì dàj   From now on will he get to
    njàaj paj sǎj bɔɔ?   move anywhere?

con, thə̆ŋ   until; reach, to get to

     con thə̆ŋ pátcúban láaw   Until now did he get to
     dàj njàaj paj sǎj bɔɔ?   move anywhere?

náj mɔɔ mɔɔ nìi   soon

     náj mɔɔ mɔɔ nìi láaw si   Soon will he get to move
     dàj njàaj paj sǎj bɔɔ?   anywhere?

ánáakhōt, kàj   future, near

     náj ánáakhōt an kàj nìi   In the near future will he
     láaw si dàj njàaj paj   get to move anywhere?
     sǎj bɔɔ?

wáj, náj wáj wáj nìi   fast, in the very near future

     náj wáj wáj nìi láaw si   In the very near future will
     dàj njàaj paj sǎj bɔɔ?   he get to move anywhere?

C-1

     A. tɔɔ máa láaw dàj njàaj   Later on did he get to move
        paj sǎj bɔɔ?   anywhere?

     B. dàj njàaj, tɔɔ máa láaw   Yes. Later on he got to
        dàj njàaj ɔ̀ɔk paj jūū   move out to the countryside.
        bàan nɔ̀ɔk

C-2

     A. láaw si thŷyk njàaj náj   He will be transferred very
        wáj wáj nìi, mɛɛn bɔɔ?   soon, is that right?

     B. mɛɛn lɛɛw, láaw si thŷyk   That's right, he will be
        njàaj náj wáj wáj nìi   transferred very soon.

A. láaw si thŷyk njàaj paj sǎj?   Where will he be transferred to?

B. láaw si thŷyk njàaj ɔ̀ɔk paj pácam jūū bàan nɔ̀ɔk   He will be transferred out and stationed in the country-side.

ການຝຶກຊ້ອມຫັດຢ່າງນ້ວຣຫໍລັຍຍົກຣຽນນກໍຄ ການຕຖວຽເຮອງປະກອບ ເພາະມິດາຫັຽກຽງທັຍເວລາ
ຫລາຍຄຳ. ທ່ານຈະສາມາກເລ້າເຮອງຕ້ວແຕ່ອະດິດໄປຈົນຖຶງວະນາຄິດໄດ້ຢ່າງບໍ່ບັນຫາເລຍ.

NOTES

1) Certain types of time expressions can only be explained with reference to the 'present time'. On the diagram below 'present time' is represented by the line in the center of the page.

'past'	'present'	'future'

tɛɛ nàn máa   tɛɛ nìi paj
'from that time on'   'from now on'

tɔɔ máa   tɔɔ paj
'later on'   'then'

lǎŋcâak nàn   lǎŋcâak nìi
'after that'   'after this'

     *náj mɔɔ mɔɔ nìi

con thǒŋ pátcúban   'soon'
'until now'   *náj ánáakhòt an kàj nìi
     'in the near future'
     *náj wáj wáj nìi
     'in the very near future'

APPLICATION

1) Read the sentences below carefully and supply the time expression that fits best. In some cases more than one answer is acceptable.

(a) láaw jūu hýan lǎŋ nìi máa tàŋ tɛɛ mỳy láaw kə̀ət _____
    _____ láaw kɔɔ njáŋ bɔɔ dàj njàaj paj sǎj

(b) láaw khə́əj thỹyk tamlûat cáp thỹa nỹŋ _____
    láaw bɔɔ kàa¹ kháp lōt wáj

(c) láaw bɔɔ khə́əj tàŋcaj hían láaw cỹŋ sěŋ bɔɔ dàj. mỳy nìi
    láaw dàj bɔ̀ɔk káp phɔɔ mɛɛ láaw wāā _____ láaw s
    tàŋcaj hían lǎaj kwāā tɛɛ kɔɔn

(d) mỹa sīī pii kɔɔn láaw dàj paj kamkáp² wìak jūu tháaŋ
    phàak nỹa _____ láaw dàj thỹyk njàaj lóŋ paj
    phàak tàj lɛ? diaw nìi láaw kɔɔ njáŋ jūu hân

(e) diaw nìi láaw kamláŋ hían kaan hāksǎa khwáam sá?-âat
    khỹaŋcák _____ láaw cá? dàj hían kaan sɔ̀ɔmpɛɛŋ

(f) wéeláa khɔ̌j paj jìam jaam láaw mỹa sɔ̌ɔŋ dyan kɔɔn láaw
    bɔɔ sábaaj lǎaj lɛ? wéeláa khɔ̌j câak láaw máa láaw kɔɔ
    njáŋ bɔɔ sáw _____ sɔ̌ɔŋ aathīt láaw kɔɔ mót
    bun³

---

¹dare ²supervise ³die

Answers: 1(a)con thə̌ŋ pátcúban (b)tàŋ tɛɛ nàn máa (c)tɛɛ
nìi paj (d)tɔɔ máa (e)tɔɔ paj (f)lǎŋ câak nàn máa

(g) lōt fáj khán nìi máa wēē nìi mỳy nìi pen thȳa sútthàaj
_____ khácàw si bɔɔ aw mán lēēn îik

(h) khɔ̀j dàj hǎp cótmǎaj câak phȳan khɔ̀j mỳy sàw nìi, láaw
khǐan bɔ̀ɔk khɔ̀j wāā _____ láaw si pháa khɔ̀ɔp-
khúa láaw máa jaam khɔ̀j, baaŋthíi âat cá? mēēn aathít nâa

(i) dìaw nìi mía láaw kamláŋ thȳy-pháa[4] _____ láaw
kɔɔ cá? dàj pen phɔɔ khón

(j) láaw sɔ̀ɔkhǎa khón kháplōt khɔ̌ɔŋ láaw phɔ̄wāā phȳan láaw
sȳŋ máa câak tāāŋ páthèet cá? máa hɔ̀ɔt dēēn-njón[5] _____
_____, láaw hɔ̀oncaj[6] phɔ̄? láaw jàan wāā cá? paj sàa

---

[4]to be pregnant [5]airport [6]anxious, uneasy

Answers: (g)lǎŋ câak nìi paj (h, i, j)náj mɔɔ mɔɔ nìi (or)
naj ánáakhōt an kàj nìi (or) náj wáj wáj nìi

372

CYCLE 77

M-1

îik don paandaj	how much longer
caw si jūu nîi îik don paandaj?	How much longer will you be here?
îik cák pii	how many more years
caw si pen thāhǎan îik cák pii?	How many more years will you be in the service?
îik kaj paandaj	how much farther
caw si njāaŋ paj îik kaj paandaj?	How much farther will you walk?
îik cák mỳy	how many more days
caw si nóon jūu hóoŋmɔ́ɔ îik cák mỳy?	How many more days will you be confined in the hospital?
îik cák sūamóoŋ	how many more hours
caw si hētwlak jūu nîi îik cák sūamóoŋ?	How many more hours will you be working here?
îik cák pii	how many more years
caw si aasǎj jūu nîi îik cák pii?	How many more years will you live here?

M-2

| îik sɔ̌ɔŋ aathīt | two more weeks |
| khɔ̌j si hían pháasǎa láaw îik sɔ̌ɔŋ aathīt | I will study Lao language for two more weeks. |

373

îik cák sɔ̌ɔŋ sǎam mỳy	about two or three more days
kh3j si phǎk jɯɯ nîi îik cák sɔ̌ɔŋ sǎam mỳy	I will stay here for about two or three more days.
îik pámáan hók cét dyan	about six or seven more months
kh3j si hētkaan jɯɯ nîi îik pámáan hók cét dyan	I will be working here for about six or seven more months
nākhían îik náj láaw síp khón	approximately ten more students
kh3j si míi nākhían îik náj láaw síp khón	I will have approximately ten more students.
náj lāwāaŋ síphâa hǎa sáaw hǔa	between 15 to 20 books
kh3j si sỳy pỳm dàj îik náj lāwāaŋ síphâa hǎa sáaw hǔa	I will be able to buy between 15 to 20 more books.

M-3

ɔ̌ɔk câak thāhǎan	leave the military service
njáŋ îik don paandaj láaw [cȳŋ] si dàj ɔ̌ɔk câak thāhǎan?	How much longer before he gets to leave the service?
dàj hāp ŋéndyan	receive salary
njáŋ îik cák aathīt láaw [cȳŋ] si dàj hāp ŋéndyan?	How many more weeks before he gets his salary?

374

máa hɔ̀ɔt — arrives

njáŋ ȋik pámáan cák sนamóoŋ láaw [cຈŋ] sì máa hɔ̀ɔt
— About how many more hours before he arrives?

hían, sǎmlēt — study; complete, finish

njáŋ ȋik náj láaw cák pii láaw [cຈŋ] sì hían sǎmlēt?
— Approximately how many more years before he finishes his studies?

khâw pen thāhǎan — join the military service

njáŋ ȋik cák dyan láaw [cຈŋ] sì khâw pen thāhǎan?
— How many more months before he joins the service?

câak paj — leave, go away

njáŋ ȋik cák náathíi láaw [cຈŋ] sì câak càw paj?
— How many more minutes before he leaves you?

pɛɛŋ — fix, repair

njáŋ ȋik cák m̀yy láaw [cຈŋ] sì pɛɛŋlōt lɛ̀ɛw?
— How many more days before he finishes fixing cars?

M-4

sȋȋ, sนamóoŋ — four, hour

njáŋ ȋik pámáan sȋȋ sนamóoŋ — In about four more hours.

bɔ̄ɔ don paandaj — not a very long time

njáŋ ȋik bɔ̄ɔ don paandaj — In not much longer.

bɔ̄ɔ lǎaj sนamóoŋ — not many hours

njáŋ ȋik bɔ̄ɔ lǎaj sนamóoŋ — In not many more hours.

sīī hâa mỳy	four or five days
njáŋ îik sīī hâa mỳy	In four or five days.
bɔ̄ɔ thɛ̌ŋ dyan	less than a month
njáŋ îik bɔ̄ɔ thɛ̌ŋ dyan	In less than a month.
bɔ̄ɔ kəən sǎam aathīt	not more than three weeks
njáŋ îik bɔ̄ɔ kəən sǎam aathīt	In not more than three weeks.
khɛ̄ŋ sūamóoŋ phɔ́ɔdii	exactly half an hour
njáŋ îik khɛ̄ŋ sūamóoŋ phɔ́ɔdii	In exactly half an hour.

C-1

A. càw si hían pháasǎa láaw îik don paandaj?

How much longer will you be studying the Lao language?

B. khɔ̂j si hían pháasǎa láaw îik sǎamsíp aathīt

I'll be studying Lao for thirty more weeks.

C-2

A. càw si pen thāhǎan îik pámáan cák pii?

About how many more years will you be in the service?

B. khɔ̂j si pen thāhǎan îik pámáan sɔ̌ɔŋ pii

I'll be in the service for about two more years.

C-3

A. càw si njāāŋ paj ʈik náj
láaw cák sūamóoŋ?

Approximately how many more
hours will you walk?

B. khɔ̀j si njāāŋ paj ʈik
náj láaw sɔ̌ɔŋ sūa móoŋ

I'll walk for approximately
two more hours.

C-4

A. càw si jūū nám láaw ʈik
cák aathɪt?

How many more weeks will
you be with her?

B. khɔ̀j si jūū nám láaw ʈik
cák sɔ̌ɔŋ sǎam aathɪt

I'll be with her about two
or three more weeks.

C-5

A. njáŋ ʈik cák sūamóoŋ
láaw [cȳŋ] si máa hɔ̀ɔt?

How many more hours before
he arrives?

B. njáŋ ʈik bɔ̄ɔ lǎaj sūamóoŋ

In not many more hours.

C-6

A. njáŋ ʈik don paandaj láaw
[cȳŋ] si dàj hāp ŋə́ndyan?

How much longer before he
gets his salary?

B. njáŋ ʈik bɔ̄ɔ kəən sɔ̌ɔŋ
aathɪt.

In not more than two weeks.

C-7

   A. njáŋ îik cák dyan láaw
      [cȳŋ] si dàj ɔ̀ok thāhǎan?

                How many more months before
                he gets out of the service?

   B. njáŋ îik bɔ̄ɔ thěŋ dyan

                In less than a month.

C-8

   A. njáŋ îik don paandaj láaw
      [cȳŋ] si paj thěŋ?

                How much longer before he
                arrives (there)?

   B. njáŋ îik pámáan sūamóoŋ
      khə̄ŋ

                In one and a half more hours.

ถ้าว่า ยัง มีบักธรมทักโตธรมมากกอมแลว มิแຕ อิก ถ้ามันตอะเจ้าจะกอງตักใจ. จิງใถมัก

ธรมฦามทันว่า ยัງอิกถัมปานใถใฟสิเธิถทย็ງ? ตลิถถทามแมอใถจะเทิถธบ? และกันมไปถก?

NOTES

1) îik means 'to be more, additional'. When it is followed by
Time Expressions, it refers to a period of time beginning
at the present and continuing. The focus is on the amount
of time involved.

   khɔ̀j si <u>pen</u> thāhǎan îik
   hók pii

                'I will be a soldier for
                six more years.'

2) njáŋ îik + Time Expressions also refers to a period of time
beginning at the present time and continuing, but the focus
is on <u>an event</u> which will take place after a certain period
of time.

   njáŋ îik hók pii khɔ̀j (cȳŋ)
   si dàj ɔ̀ok thāhǎan

                'In 6 more years I'll get
                out of the service.'

378

njáŋ ꞌ̂ik + Time Expression comes at the beginning of the sentences; whereas, ꞌ̂ik + Time Expression comes at the end.

APPLICATION

1. Fill in the blanks below using the English as a guide:

(a) láaw si jyyn jūū hân _____

(How many more minutes will she stand there?)

(b) khɔ̌j si sɔ̌ɔn jūū hóoŋhían nìi _____

(I'll teach at this school for approximately 3 more years.)

(c) láaw si tɔ̀ɔŋ tii-cák _____

(How much longer will she have to type?)

(d) _____ khâw-cꞮꞮ láaw kɔɔ si mót

(In about 2 more days he will be out of bread.)

(e) láaw si nɔ́ɔn _____

(How much longer will she be asleep?)

(f) láaw khóŋ cá? sūaŋsáw pháaj náj wéeláa _____

(It will not be more than 3 weeks before he recovers.)

(g) khɔ̌j si bɔ̄ɔ thâa jūū nîi _____

(I will not wait here many minutes more.)

Answers: 1(a)ꞌ̂ik cák náathíi (b)ꞌ̂ik náj láaw sǎam pii (c)ꞌ̂ik don paandaj (d)ꞌ̂ik pamáan sɔ̌ɔn mỳy (e)ꞌ̂ik don paandaj (f)bɔ̄ɔ kəən sǎam aathꞮt (g)ꞌ̂ik lǎaj náathíi

(h) _____ hók sūamóoŋ khɔ̀j kɔɔ si mýa bàan

(In less than 6 hours more I'll go home.)

(i) _____ láaw kɔɔ si lə̀ək kaan

(In about 10 minutes more he'll be out of work.)

(j) _____ pỳm kɔɔ si lɛ̀ɛw

(In about 5 or 6 more days the book will be finished.)

(k) _____ láaw cȳŋ si thȳyk keen khâw pen thāhǎan

(How many more weeks before he gets drafted into the army?)

(l) càw ká? wāā cá? jūu nîi _____ ?

(How much longer do you plan to stay here?)

(m) _____ mỳy khɔ̀j kɔɔ si dàj phɔɔ láaw

(In less than half a day I will meet her.)

(n) _____ khɔ̀j kɔɔ si ɔ̀ok kin bìa bamnáan

(It will not be very many more years before I retire.)

(o) càw si paj tiisék jūu náj wîatnáam _____ ?

(How many more weeks will you go fight in Vietnam?)

_____

Answers: (h)njáŋ îik·bɔ̀ɔ kəən (i)njáŋ îik síp náathíi (j)njáŋ
îik hāa hók mỳy (k)njáŋ îik cák aathīt (l)îik don
paandaj (m)njáŋ îikbɔ̀ɔ thə̆ŋ khəŋ (n)njáŋ îik bɔ̀ɔ
lǎaj pii (o)îik cák aathīt

380

(p) _____ khɔ̌j kɔɔ siipaj nɔ́ɔn dàj

    (It will not be many more hours before I can go to bed.)

(q) càw si sɣ̀y pɣ̀m _____

    (How many more books will you buy?)

(r) háw njáŋ míi wéeláa hían _____

    (How much more time do we have to study?)

2) Cover the Lao and see if you can translate the English back into Lao.

Answers: (p)njáŋ îik bɔ̀ɔ lǎaj sūamóoŋ (q)îik cák hǔa
(r)îik lǎaj paandaj

CYCLE 78

M-1

taamthámmādaa   normally

     taamthámmādaa khácàw māk kin aahăan nέεw daJ?   What kind of food do they normally like to eat?

sŭanmàak   mainly

     sŭanmàak khácàw māk kin aahăan nέεw daJ?   What kind of food do they mainly like to eat?

láaŋ thȳa   sometimes

     láaŋ thȳa khácàw māk kin aahăan nέεw daJ?   What kind of food do they like to eat sometimes?

láaŋ mȳy   somedays

     láaŋ mȳy khácàw māk kin aahăan nέεw daJ?   What kind of food do they like to eat somedays?

dooJ thŭa paJ lὲεw   generally

     dooJ thŭa paJ lὲεw khácàw māk kin aahăan nέεw daJ?   What kind of food do they like to eat generally?

dooJ sáphɔ̃ʔ lὲεw   in particular

     dooJ sáphɔ̃ʔ lὲεw khácàw māk kin aahăan nέεw daJ?   What kind of food do they like to eat in particular?

baaŋ wéeláa.   sometimes

     baaŋ wéeláa khácàw māk kin aahăan nέεw daJ?   What kind of food do they like to eat sometimes?

M-2

aahǎan phét   spicy food

 taamthámmadaa khácàw māk They normally like to eat
 kin aahǎan phét   spicy food.

aahǎan khém   salty food

 sūanmàak khácàw māk kin They mainly like to eat
 aahǎan khém   salty food.

khǒoŋwǎan   sweets

 láaŋthȳa khácàw māk kin Sometimes they like to have
 khǒoŋwǎan   sweets.

aahǎan sôm   sour food

 láaŋ mỳy khácàw māk kin Somedays they like to eat
 aahǎan sôm   sour food.

aahǎan cŷyt   bland food

 dooj thūa paj lɛ̀ɛw khácàw Generally they like bland
 māk kin aahǎan cŷyt   food.

aahǎan phỳyn mýaŋ   native food

 dooj sáphɔ́ʔ lɛ̀ɛw khácàw Particularly they like to
 māk kin aahǎan phỳyn mýaŋ eat native food.

aahǎan tāaŋ páthèet   exotic food

 baaŋ wéeláa khácàw māk Sometimes they like to eat
 kin aahǎan tāaŋ páthèet exotic food.

C-1

    A. taamthámmādaa càw māk kin   Normally what kind of food
        aahǎan nέεw daj?   do you like to eat?

    B. taamthámmādaa khɔ́j māk kin   Normally I like spicy food.
        aahǎan phét

C-2

    A. càw si kin aahǎan nέεw   What kind of food will you
      ` daj?   have?

    B. khɔ́j si kin aahǎan jīīpūn   I will have Japanese food.

    A. aahǎan jīīpūn cŷyt, mε̄ε̄n   The Japanese food is bland,
        bɔɔ?   isn't it?

    B. mε̄ε̄w lέεw, taamthámmādaa   That's right, normally the
        khón jīīpūn māk kin   Japanese like to eat bland
        aahǎan cŷyt   food.

ຂໍ້ມແຄວງປະກອບຂນອີກ ໂດຍຂໍຂຍາຍເຖີງນິສັຍຂອງຍຸກຄົນທີ່ສັມພຸດຂນຜູ້ນ່ວງຈາ ລາງເຖືອລາວມັກຄຶດ
ຫຍັງ? ແລະບາງເວລາອົນອີກຄຄ? ດ້ວນຄວງໄປ. ຄຣອນນັກຣຽນຂອງທ່ານກໍ່ຄວນຈະເວົ້າພາສາລາວໄດ້
ຫລາຍຄຶບແລວ. ສະນນ ຕາມຈິງຕນັນຄວນຂະເຈ້າຄຸຍແຄວງຕ່າງໆທີ່ເກີດຂນປະຈ່ວິນ ໂດຍໃຫ້ຂະເຈ້າ
ມີໂອກາດໄດ້ເວົ້າຫລາຍທີ່ສຸດ. ຕ້ວນຄໍ່ໃຫ້ຂະເຈ້າເກີດຄວາມຄຶຍຈິນໃນການສະແດງທີ່ສມະຂອງຂະ
ເຈ້າເປັນພາສາລາວ. ຕໍ່ໄປຂະເຈ້າກໍ່ຈະຄ່ອຍໆມີຄວາມຄຸ່ອທນ່ນໃນຕິນຄວງຍ່ວຂນ.

APPLICATION

1. Fill in the blanks using the English as a guide:

(a) _____ síp móoŋ khɔ̌j cɣ̄ŋ lūk câak bɔ̃ɔn nɔ́on

(Normally I don't get up until 10 o'clock.)

(b) _____ láaw bɔ̄ŋ thóorāthāt jūū con dǝ̀k
(Sometimes she stays up late watching TV.)

(c) _____ lɛ̀ɛw mía khɔ̌j bɔ̃ɔ mǎk mǎa
(My wife dislikes dogs in particular.)

(d) náj rāduu nǎaw _____ fǒntók mót m̀yy
(Some days in Winter it rains all day.)

(e) sáaw náa _____ sàj khwáaj thǎj náa khácàw
(Most farmers use water buffaloes for plowing rice fields.)

(f) _____ kinkhâw thīaŋ phūū diaw
(I usually eat lunch by myself.)

(g) _____ khɔ̌j hɛ̄t wìak náj m̀yy wán-sǎw
(Normally I work on Saturday.)

(h) _____ khácàw kin paa lɛ̄ʔ aahǎan thālée
(They mainly eat fish and sea food.)

Answers: 1(a)taamthámmādaa (b)láaŋ thɣa (c)dooj sáphɔ́ʔ
(d)láaŋ m̀yy (e)sūan màak (f)taamthámmādaa khɔ̌j
(g)taamthámmādaa (h)sūan màak

(i) _____ láaw wàw pháasǎa aŋkít

(Normally he speaks English.)

(j) _____ khɔ̂j tɔ̀ɔŋ thâa láaw káp bàan thə̌ŋ

sɔ̌ɔŋ sūa móoŋ

(Sometimes I have to wait 2 hours for her to come
home.)

(k) _____ lɛ̀ɛw láaw māk máa sàa sáaw hǎa

sǎamsíp náathíi

(She generally comes 20 to 30 minutes late.)

(l) _____ lɛ̀ɛw khɔ̂j māk khɔ̌ɔŋ wǎan

(I like desserts in particular.)

CYCLE 79

M-1

cá?tɔ̀ɔŋ   must

    thâawāā láaw si paj láaw   If he is going, he must
    cá?tɔ̀ɔŋ lỳak aw náaj tháaŋ   choose a guide.

khúan cá?   ought to

    thâawāā láaw si paj láaw   If he is going, he ought to
    khúan cá?lỳak aw náaj tháaŋ   choose a guide.

âat cá?   might

    thâawāā láaw si paj láaw   If he is going, he might
    âat cá? lỳak aw náaj tháaŋ   choose a guide.

khýy si   be likely

    thâawāā láaw si paj láaw   If he is going, he will be
    khýy si lỳak aw náaj tháaŋ   likely to choose a guide.

campen tɔ̀ɔŋ   it will be necessary for

    thâawāā láaw si paj láaw   If he is going, it will be
    campen tɔ̀ɔŋ lỳak aw náaj   necessary for him to choose
    tháaŋ   a guide.

khóŋ cá?   probably

    thâawāā láaw si paj láaw   If he is going, he will
    khóŋ cá? lỳak aw náaj   probably choose a guide.
    tháaŋ

M-2

thŷyk lāɟ ɔ̂ok   be fired

    kɔɔn láaw si paɟ láaw âat   Before he goes, he might
    cá? thŷyk lāɟ ɔ̂ok   be fired.

tēēŋ tàŋ, hŭa nâa   to appoint; chief, boss

    kɔɔn láaw si paɟ láaw âat   Before he goes, he might be
    cá? thŷyk tēēŋ tàŋ pen hŭa   appointed to be a chief.
    nâa

thŷyk lỳak khŷn pen pátháan   be chosen to be the chairman

    kɔɔn láaw si paɟ láaw âat   Before he goes, he might be
    cá? thŷyk lỳak khŷn pen   chosen to be the chairman.
    pátháan

tátsĭncaɟ hâɟ càw ɟùū   decide to let you stay

    kɔɔn láaw si paɟ láaw âat   Before he goes, he might
    cá? tátsĭncaɟ hâɟ càw ɟùū   decide to let you stay.

hĕndii hâɟ càw láa phāk   consent to letting you take leave

    kɔɔn láaw si paɟ láaw âat   Before he goes, he might
    cá? hĕndii hâɟ càw láa phāk   consent to letting you take
                                            leave.

ɔ̂ok khám sāŋ hâɟ cáp láaw   issue an order to arrest him

    kɔɔn láaw si paɟ láaw âat   Before he goes, he might
    cá? ɔ̂ok khám sāŋ hâɟ cáp   issue an order to arrest
    láaw   him.

tóklóŋcaɟ hâɟ pɔɔɟ khácàw   agree to free them

    kɔɔn láaw si paɟ láaw âat   Before he goes, he might
    cá? tóklóŋcaɟ hâɟ pɔɔɟ khácàw   agree to free them.

388

C-1

A. thâawāā láaw si paj láaw
si hēt njǎŋ?

What is he going to do before
he goes?

B. láaw si lỳak aw náaj tháaŋ

He will choose a guide.

C-2

A. kɔ̄ɔn láaw si paj láaw âat
cá? hēt njǎŋ bɔɔ?

Might he do something before
he goes? (is it probable)

B. kɔ̄ɔn láaw si paj láaw âat
cá? tátsǐncaj pɔ̄ɔj khácàw

Before he goes, he might
decide to free them.

C-3

A. kɔ̄ɔn láaw si paj láaw si
campen tɔ̀ɔŋ hâj càw láa
phǎk bɔɔ?

Before he goes, will it be
necessary for him to let you
take leave?

B. mɛ̄ɛn lɛ̀ɛw, kɔ̄ɔn láaw si
paj láaw campen tɔ̀ɔŋ hâj
khɔ̌j láa phǎk

Yes, before he goes, it is
necessary for him to let
me take leave.

ຍ້ວອິກຍຕໃຄຍໍຄຣຸມ ປົມຕົວມກ໌າຈະຈຶບແລວ. ສະນັນຈ້ວຕມັ່ນພາກນັກຣຸມລົມຄົນເລອຍ໗.ແລະຖາຄຕົມວາ໗
ຂະເຈ້າຍ້ວອອນຢູຕອມໃຄ ກ໌າຈ໌ພາຂະເຈ້າຝຶກຊ້ອມອອກ. ເມ໌ອມິກ້ານສຶມຕະບາກັບ ຕ້ານກໍ່ອາຄຈະຈ້າເປ໌ນ
ຕອງໃຊ໌ຄ້າໃຕມຼເປ໌ນບາ໗ຄ້າ. ແຕກ້ານຈິຄຄ້າໃຕມ໌ໃຕມິກຣຸມຈະເປ໌ນກ້ານຄສ໌ຮຄວລາຄປ້າ໗ ແລະອາຄ
ຈະເຮຶຄໃຕມິກຣຸມເກິຄຄວາມຕໍ່ຖອຍ.

389

NOTES

1) Words which occur in the position between NP (Subject) and MV are called 'preverbs'. One of the most important groups of preverbs are the 'modals': tɔ̀ɔŋ, khúan, âat, khýy, campen tɔ̀ɔŋ, khóŋ, etc. Each of these words is used in a wide range of situations, and there is some overlap in their usage in Lao. It is, therefore, difficult to indicate their meaning briefly. The following description is meant as a general guide only. The only good way to learn how to use them is to observe the situations in which Lao speakers use each of them and to imitate their usage.

   (a) (cá²/ si) tɔ̀ɔŋ 'must, have to'. The situation requires it

        háw tɔ̀ɔŋ s̆ia khaa fáj fàa   'We have to pay our electric
                                       bill.'

   (b) khúan (cá²/ si) 'should, ought to'. Social or moral
        obligation or expectation.

        càw bɔ̄ɔ khúan cá² kin l̆aj   'You shouldn't eat too much.'

   (c) âat (cá²/ si) 'may, might'. Likelihood, expectation,
        possibility.'

        láaw âat cá²bɔ̄ɔ sábaaj l̆aj   'He may be very ill.'

   (d) khýy (si / cá²) 'may, might'. Similar to âat

        khýy si mɛ̄ɛn   'It may be so.'

   (e) khóŋ (cá²/ si) 'it is likely'. Probability.

        láaw khóŋ cá²bɔ̄ɔ hùu   'It is likely that he doesn't
                                   know.'

390

APPLICATION

1. Complete the following sentences using the English as a guide:

    (a) láaw _____ khǎaj khɔ̌ɔŋ bɔ̌ɔ mót dɔ̂ɔk phɔ̌waā mỳy nìi
         bɔ̌ɔ míi khón paj tálâat lǎaj paandaj.

         (She probably won't sell out her goods, since there
         aren't very many people going to the market today.)

    (b) khácàw bɔ̌ɔ míi lōt lɛ́ʔ tháaŋ sên nìi bɔ̌ɔ míi lōt thíaw
         khácàw _____ njāaŋ paj

         (They don't have a car and there are no cars on this
         road. They must necessarily walk.)

    (c) láaw _____ máa phɔ̌waā láaw si hēt wìak lɛ̀ɛw mỳy nìi

         (He may come since he will have finished his work today.)

    (d) kaan hāksǎa pīn pua hâj jūū sábaaj mɛ̄ɛn sīŋ thīī háw
         _____ hēt

         (Maintaining good health is the thing we must do.)

    (e) diaw nìi mán kaaj wéeláa máa dàj sɔ̌ɔŋ sūa móoŋ lɛ̀ɛw láaw
         _____ bɔ̌ɔ máa dɔ̂ɔk

         (It's two hours past the time now. He must not be coming
         at all.)

    (f) láaw _____ cāaj ŋén khāā hýan thūk thūk tòn dyan

         (He has to pay the rent on his house at the beginning
         of each month.)

    (g) láaw _____ paj hāp aw mía láaw kɔ̌ɔn láaw si paj
         kinkhâw

         (He will have to go pick up his wife before going to eat.)

Answers: 1(a)khýy si (b)si campen tɔ̀ɔŋ (c)âat cáʔ (d)campen
          tɔ̀ɔŋ (e)khón cáʔ (f)tɔ̀ɔŋ (g)si tɔ̀ɔŋ

(h) thâawāā càw khɔ̌ɔ thòot nám láaw láaw _____ áphái
hâi càw

(If you apologize to him, he may forgive you.)

(i) láaw pai dài sīī sūa móoŋ lɛ̀ɛw, paan nìi láaw _____
hɔ̀ɔt lɛ̀ɛw

(He's been going for 4 hours already. He must have
arrived by now.)

(j) mɣa hùu wāā mán bɔɔ dii lɛ̀ɛw phùakháw kɔɔ bɔɔ _____hɛ̆t

(If (we) know it's not good, we shouldn't do it.)

(k) phɛ̄n _____ bɔɔ kin phɔwāā aahǎan nìi phét lǎai

(He may not eat since the food is very hot.)

(l) dék nɔ̀ɔi _____ sɣa fáŋ khám sāŋsɔ̌ɔn khɔ̌ɔŋ phɔɔ mɛɛ

(Children should listen to the advice of their parents.)

(m) mɣa wéeláa láaw bɔɔ míi kaan hɛ̆t láaw kɔɔ _____ hǎa
ŋén dùai wíthíi dai wíthíi nɣ̄ŋ

(During the times when he is out of work, he must seek
money by any means or other.)

(n) láaw _____ taai phɔwāā thāān mɔ̌ɔ bɔɔ míi jaa cáʔ
hāaksǎa láaw

(He may die since the doctor doesn't have any medicine
to cure him.)

(o) láaw _____ pai sɣ̀y khɣaŋkin jūū tálâat phɔwāā láaw
bɔɔ míi aahǎan

(He will have to go buy food at the market because he
doesn't have any food.)

Answers: (h)âat cáʔ (i)khón cáʔ (j)khúan (k)âat cáʔ (l)khúan
(m)campen tɔɔŋ (n)âat cáʔ (o)si tɔɔŋ

(p) m̄ya wéeláa láaw míi ŋə́n láaw kɔɔ _____ thɔ̀ɔn ŋə́n
wàj sǎmlắp wéeláa campen

(When he has money, he should save it for time of need.)

(q) diaw nı̀i láaw thūk lǎaj láaw _____ khɔ̌otháan kin

(Now he's very poor. He has to beg for food.)

(r) nàm mán lǒt bɔɔ lǎaj háw _____ paj bɔɔ hɔ̀ɔt

(There's not much gas in the car, we may not get there.)

(s) khɔ̌j khīt wāa láaw _____ paj bɔɔ dàj dɔ̀ok phɔ̄wāa
láaw míi wı̀ak lǎaj

(I think he may not be able to go at all because he has
a lot of work.)

(t) khácàw hāk kan lǎaj khɔ̌j khīt wāa m̄ya wéeláa tɛɛŋ ŋáan
kan lɛ̀ɛw khácàw _____ míi khwáam súk nám kan

(They're very much in love. I think they should be very
happy after they get married.)

(u) khɔ̌j dàj njín wāa láaw jâak paj bəŋ síinée tɛɛ don lɛ̀ɛw
thâawāa càw súan láaw láaw _____ paj

(I heard she has been wanting to go to the movies for a
long time, if you ask her, she may go.)

(v) láaw si _____ paj sɔ̀ok hǎa khácàw phɔ̄wāa láaw
tɔ̀ɔŋkaan khácàw

(He will have to go look for them because he needs them.)

(w) phɔɔ mɛɛ _____ sāŋsɔ̌on lùuk khɔ̌oŋ ton phya njāj máa
khácàw cá? pen khón dii

(Parents should train their children so that when they
grow up they'll be good people.)

Answers: (p)khúan (q)campen tɔ̀ɔŋ (r)khýy si (s)khýy si (t)khóŋ
cá? (u)khýy si (v)tɔ̀ɔŋ (w)khúan cá? - khýy and âat
are practically interchangeable and cá? and si are.

CYCLE 80

M-1

<u>paj, mýaŋ láaw</u>   to go, Laos

    càw khə̀əj dàj paj mýaŋ   Have you ever been to Laos?
    láaw bɔɔ?

<u>hěn, sát, pálâat</u>   see, animal, strange

    càw khə̀əj hěn sát pálâat   Have you ever seen a strange
                                         animal?

<u>síim, sìin, khwáaj</u>   taste, meat, flesh, water buffalo

    càw khə̀əj síim sìin   Have you ever tasted
    khwáaj bɔɔ?   water buffalo meat?

<u>āan, nǎŋ sỹy phím</u>   read, newspaper

    càw khə̀əj dàj āan nǎŋ sỹy   Have you ever read the Sat
    sỹy phím sàat láaw bɔɔ?   Lao Newspaper?

<u>títian</u>   criticize

    càw khə̀əj dàj thŷyk   Have you ever been criticized?
    títian bɔɔ?

<u>njɔ̀ɔŋ</u>   compliment

    càw khə̀əj dàj thŷyk   Have you ever been complimente
    khácàw njɔ̀ɔŋ njóo bɔɔ?   by them?

<u>thŷyk keen pen thāhǎan</u>   to be drafted

    càw khə̀əj dàj thŷyk keen   Have you ever been drafted?
    pen thāhǎan bɔɔ?

M-2

khə́əj	Yes. (I have...)
bɔ̄ɔ, njáŋ bɔ̄ɔ khə́əj	No. (I have never...)

M-3

dàj paj mýaŋ láaw   to have been to Laos

khə́əj, khɔ̀j khə́əj dàj paj
mýaŋ láaw lǎaj thӯa lὲεw

Yes, I have been to Laos
many times already.

thōtlóoŋ   experiment

khə́əj, khɔ̀j khə́əj dàj
thōtlóoŋ lǎaj thӯa lὲεw

Yes, I have experimented
many times already.

M-4

sàj nέεw nìi   use this kind

bɔ̄ɔ, khɔ̀j njáŋ bɔ̄ɔ khə́əj
dàj sàj nέεw nìi cákthӯa

No, I have never used this
kind at all.

sûup, jaa fīn   smoke, opium

bɔ̄ɔ, khɔ̀j njáŋ bɔ̄ɔ khə́əj
dàj sûup jaa fīn cákthӯa

No, I have never smoked opium
at all.

khīt, tὲεŋ ŋáan   think, get married

bɔ̄ɔ, khɔ̀j njáŋ bɔ̄ɔ khə́əj
khīt cá? tὲεŋ ŋáan cákthӯa

No, I have never thought of
getting married at all.

395

C-1

   A. càw khə́əj dàj thŷyk   Have you ever been criticized?
      títian bɔɔ?

   B. khə́əj   Yes.

C-2

   A. láaw khə́əj dàj paj mýaŋ   Has he ever been to Laos?
      láaw bɔɔ?

   B. bɔ̌ɔ, njáŋ bɔ̌ɔ khə́əj   No.

C-3

   A. càw khə́əj dàj āan nǎŋšyy   Have you ever read the Sat
      phím sàat láaw bɔɔ?   Lao Newspaper?

   B. khə́əj, khɔ̌j khə́əj dàj āan   Yes, I have read the Sat Lao
      nǎŋšyy phím sàat láaw   Newspaper two or three times
      sɔ̌ɔŋ sǎam thȳa lɛ̀ɛw   already.

C-4

   A. càw khə́əj dàj thŷyk   Have you ever been arrested
      tamlûat cáp bɔɔ?   by the police?

   B. bɔ̌ɔ, khɔ̌j njáŋ bɔ̌ɔ khə́əj   No, I have never been arrested
      dàj thŷyk tamlûat cáp   by the police.
      cákthȳa

ໃນບົດກ່ມແຕ່ໄຕ່ຕາມມັກຣອມເບິ່ງກ່ຽວກັບການໃຊ້ຄຳວ່າ "ຄືຍ". ຂະເຈົ້າເຄີຍຕລົບຄືຍເຮັດຕຍ້ງ?

NOTES

1) khə́əj + VP is used to indicate that someone has experienced
    something.

    khɔ̌j khə́əj paj páthèet láaw   'I have been to Laos.'

    càw khə́əj pen wát bɔɔ?   'Have you ever had a cold?'

2) thŷyk + VP corresponds roughly to the passive in English. It
    occurs only with a very limited number of verbs, most of which
    have unpleasant connotations.

    càw thŷyk títian bɔɔ?   'Were you criticized?'

    If an Agent is indicated, it occurs after thŷyk before VP:

    láaw thŷyk tamlûat cáp   (He was by a policeman
                                         arrested.)

                                        'He was arrested by the
                                         policeman.'

3) The two constructions above frequently occur together:

    càw khə́əj dàj thŷyk khǎŋ bɔɔ?   'Have you ever been locked
                                         up?'

APPLICATION

1. Complete the following sentences using the English as a guide:

    (a) tàŋ tɛɛ khɔ̌j kə̀ət, máa khɔ̌j _____ hěn khón phūū
         nàn cák thɣa
         (I have never seen that man before in my life.)

    (b) càw _____ tamlûat cáp cák thɣa bɔɔ?
         (Were you ever arrested by the police?)

    (c) nɔ̀ɔŋ sǎaw khɔ̌j khə́əj _____ kát sǎam thɣa lɛ̀ɛw
         (My younger sister was bitten 3 times by a dog.)

    (d) lùuk sáaj kók láaw _____ khâa taaj (sǐa síiwɪt)
         jūū náj sǒŋkháam wîatnáam
         (Her oldest son was killed in the War in Vietnam.)

    (e) khácàw _____ paj jūū mɣ́aŋ lǔaŋ phābaaŋ
         (They have never lived in Luang Prabang.)

    (f) pii kaaj nìi láaw pen khâj wát njāj _____
         (Last year she had the flu 2 times.)

    (g) láaw _____ wāāŋ ŋáan cák thɣa
         (He has never been out of a job.)

___

Answers: 1(a)njáŋ bɔɔ khə́əj (b)khə́əj thɣ̂yk (c)thɣ̂yk mǎa
          (d)thɣ̂yk (e)njáŋ bɔɔ khə́əj (f)sɔ̌ɔŋ thɣa (g)bɔɔ
          khə́əj

(h) càw khéəj dàj paj tiisék cák thӯa bɔɔ? bɔɔ, _____
     (Have you ever been to war? Not yet.)

(i) càw _____ keen khâw pen thāhǎan bɔɔ? _____
     (Were you drafted? Yes, I was.)

(j) càw dàj āan nǎŋsӯy phím mỳy nìi _____ bɔɔ? āan
     lὲεw _____
     (Have you read today's newspaper? Yes, 2 or 3 times.)

(k) láaw _____ sàj nìi mót cák thӯa
     (He has never been completely out of debt.)

(l) khɔ̂j _____ dàj hían pɛɛŋ lõt
     (I have never learned how to repair cars.)

Answers: (h)njáŋ bɔɔ khéəj (i)khéəj thӯyk... khéəj (j)lὲεw...
          sɔ̌ŋ sǎam thӯa (k)bɔɔ khéəj (l)njáŋ bɔɔ khəəj

399

CYCLE 81

M-1

paj nám khɔ̌j   go with me

    míi phǎj si paj nám   Is there anybody going
    khɔ̌j bɔɔ?   with me?

míi, ŋə́n   have, money

    míi phǎj míi ŋə́n bɔɔ?   Is there anybody who has
                                    money?

nǎpthy̌y sâatsánǎaphūt   believe in Buddhism

    míi phǎj nǎpthy̌y sâat-   Is there anyone that believes
    sánǎaphūt bɔɔ?   in Buddhism?

lɛ̂ɛk (aw), ŋə́n doolàa   to exchange for, dollars

    míi phǎj jâak lɛ̂ɛk aw   Is there anybody who wants
    ŋə́n doolàa bɔɔ?   to exchange (other money)
                                    for dollars?

títtaam, khǎaw nìi   follow, keep up; news

    míi phǎj jâak títtaam   Is there anybody who wants
    khǎaw nìi bɔɔ?   to keep up with the news?

phūu taaŋnâa   representative

    míi phǎj jâak pen phūu   Is there anybody who wants
    taaŋnâa phùakháw bɔɔ?   to be our representative?

aasǎa sámák   to volunteer

    míi phǎj jâak aasǎa sámák   Is there anybody who wants
    bɔɔ?   to volunteer?

M-2

sɔɔjlỹa	help, assist
míi, phùakháw si paj sɔɔjlỹa khácàw	Yes, we will go help them.
pákan, khwáam pɔɔpháj	guarantee, safety
míi, phùakháw si pákan khwáam pɔɔtpháj khɔ̌ɔŋ khácàw	Yes, we will guarantee their safety.
láajŋáan	report
míi, phùakháw si hɛ̄t láajŋáan hâj phɔ̄n	Yes, we will make reports to him.
wáaŋ phɛ̌ɛnkaan	lay out a plan
míi, phùakháw si pen ρhǔu wáaŋ phɛ̌ɛnkaan	Yes, we will lay out the plan.
khùapkhúm	supervise
míi, phùakháw si khùapkhúm khácàw	Yes, we will supervise them.
hâj khám nɛ?nám kɛ̄ɛ khácàw	give them advice
míi, phùakháw si hâj khám nɛ?nám kɛ̄ɛ khácàw	Yes, we will give them advice.

M-3

paj sɔɔjlўa khácàw	to go help them
bɔɔ míi phǎj si paj sɔɔjlўa khácàw	There is no one to go help them.

pákan khwáam pɔ̀otpháj khɔ̌ɔŋ khácàw	to guarantee their safety
bɔɔ míi phǎj si pákan khwáam phɔ̀otpháj khɔ̌ɔŋ khácàw	There is no one to guarantee their safety.

hɛ̄t láajŋáan hâj phə̀n	to make reports to them
bɔɔ míi phǎj hɛ̄t láajŋáan hâj phə̀n	There is no one to make reports to them.

hâj khám nɛ́? nám kɛ̄ɛ khácàw	to give them advise
bɔɔ míi phǎj hâj khám nɛ́?nám kɛ̄ɛ khácàw	There is no one to give advice to them.

C-1

A. míi phǎj si paj sɔɔjlўa láaw bɔɔ?   Is there anybody that is going to help him?

B. míi, khɔ̂j si paj sɔɔjlўa láaw   Yes, I will go help him.

C-2

A. míi phǎj jâak títtaam   Is there anybody who wants
   khāāw nìi bɔɔ?   to keep up with this news?

B. míi, láaw jâak títtaam   Yes, she wants to keep up
   khāāw nìi   with this news.

A. míi phǎj jâak aasǎa sámák   Is there anybody who wants
   bɔɔ?   to volunteer?

B. bɔ̄ɔ, bɔ̄ɔ míi phǎj   No, nobody does.

NOTES

1) The verb míi may have Sentence Complements when it occurs
   without NP (Subject).

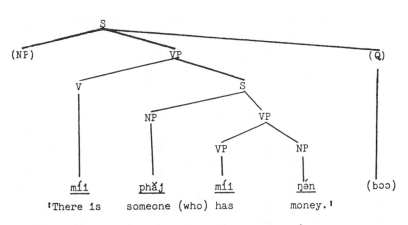

'There is   someone (who) has   money.'

The indefinite pronoun phǎj 'someone, anyone' (as contrasted
with the question word phǎj 'who') can not occur as NP (Subject)
except in included sentences.

403

APPLICATION

1. Translate the following sentences into English:

(a) bɔɔ míi phǎj jâak paj nám láaw phɔwāā lǒt láaw bɔɔ dii

(b) phǝn thǎam wāā míi phǎj jâak ʔɔk paj bàan nɔɔk bɔɔ

(c) láaw wàw wāā míi lǎaj khón jâak hían kaan tɛ̀ɛm hùup tɛ̄ɛ
    wāā diaw nîi khɔ̀j njáŋ bɔɔ hěn phǎj máa

(d) khácàw jâak hùu wāā si míi phǎj paj bɔɔ lʝy bɔɔ míi,
    thâawāā bɔɔ míi phǎj paj láaw si paj phūūdiaw

(e) khácàw jàan wāā si bɔɔ míi phǎj sǒncaj khácàw cʝŋ bɔɔ
    aw máa

(f) lǒt láaw bɔɔ dii cʝŋ bɔɔ míi bɔɔlīsát daj jâak hǎp pákan

(g) jūū nǎj sáthǎan thùut améelīīkan míi phǎj dàj pháasǎa
    wîatnáam bɔɔ?

(h) bɔɔ míi phǎj hâj khám nɛ̄ʔnám kɛ̄ɛ láaw, láaw cʝŋ hɛt phít

---

Answers: 1(a)Nobody wants to go with him because his car is
          not good. (b)They asked if anybody wanted to go out
          to the countryside. (c)He said there were lots of
          people who wanted to learn how to paint, but so far
          I haven't seen any of them. (d)They wanted to know
          if anybody was going or not. If nobody is going,
          he'll go alone. (e)They were afraid that nobody
          would be interested, so they didn't bring them.
          (f)His car is no good, so no company wants to insure
          it. (g)Is there anyone at the American Embassy that
          knows Vietnamese? (h)There was no one to advise her,
          so she did wrong.

(i) thâawāā bɔɔ míi phǎj bɔ̌ɔk tháaŋ láaw, láaw âat cáʔ lǒŋ
tháaŋ kɔɔ dàj

(j) khɔ̌j bɔɔ hùu wāā pen njǎŋ cɣ̄ŋ bɔɔ míi phǎj hâj khwáam
sǒncaj náj lỳaŋ nìi

(k) njáŋ bɔɔ míi phǎj máa hǎa khɔ̌j bɔɔ? bɔɔ, njáŋ bɔɔ míi

(l) bɔɔ míi phǎj máa pásúm láaw léəj khìt wāā mỳy nìi bɔɔ
mɛ̄ɛn pásúm

Answers: (i) If there is no one to tell him the way, he may
get lost. (j) I don't know why nobody is interested
in this situation. (k) Hasn't anyone come to see me
yet? No, not yet. (l) Nobody came to the meeting,
so he thought the meeting wasn't today.

405

CYCLE 82

M-1

nàmmán thīī dàj máa câa mǔu
the oil that we get from a pig

  háw ə̀ən nàmmán thīī dàj
máa câak mǔu wāā jāaŋdaj?
    What do we call the oil that we get from a pig?

nàm thīī dàj máa câak mâakkìan
liquid that we get from an orange

  háw ə̀ən nàm thīī dàj máa
câak mâakkìan wāā jāaŋdaj?
    What do we call liquid that we get from an orange?

nàm thīī dàj máa câak háŋphə̌ŋ
liquid that we get from a bee hive

  háw ə̀ən nàm thīī dàj máa
câak háŋphə̀ŋ wāā jāaŋdaj?
    What do we call liquid that we get from a bee hive?

nàm thīī ɔ̀ɔk máa câak taa
liquid that comes out of the eyes

  háw ə̀ən nàm thīī ɔ̀ɔk máa
câak taa wāā jāaŋdaj?
    What do we call liquid that comes out of the eyes?

thùut thīī pen thāhǎan
an envoy who is in the military service

  háw ə̀ən thùut thīī pen
thāhǎan wāā jāaŋdaj?
    What do we call an envoy who is in the military service?

kápuu thīī aasǎj jūu náj thālée
crabs that live in the sea

  háw ə̀ən kápuu thīī aasǎj
jūu náj thālée wāā jāaŋdaj?
    What do we call crabs that live in the sea?

406

paa <u>thɪɪ</u> aasǎj <u>jɯɯ</u> náj <u>nàm</u> cŷyt   fish that live in fresh water

    háw əən paa thɪɪ aasǎj jɯɯ
    náj nàm cŷyt wāa jāandaj?

        What do we call fish that
        live in fresh water?

M-2

<u>nàmmán</u> <u>mǔu</u>   lard

    háw əən nàmmán thɪɪ dàj máa
    câak mǔu wāa nàmmán mǔu

        We call the oil that we get
        from pigs, lard.

<u>nàm</u> <u>mâakkłaŋ</u>   orange juice

    háw əən nàm thɪɪ dàj máa
    câak mâakkłaŋ wāa nàm
    mâakkłaŋ

        We call the liquid that we
        get from oranges, orange juice.

<u>nàm</u> <u>phə̂ŋ</u>   honey

    háw əən nàm thɪɪ dàj máa
    câak háŋphə̂ŋ wāa nàm phə̂ŋ

        We call the liquid that we
        get from a bee hive, honey.

<u>nàm</u> <u>taa</u>

    háw əən nàm thɪɪ ɔ̀ɔk máa
    câak taa wāa nàm taa

        We call the liquid that comes
        out of the eyes, tears.

<u>thùut</u> <u>thāhǎan</u>   a military attaché

    háw əən nàm thɪɪ pen
    thāhǎan wāa thùut thāhǎan

        We call an envoy who is in
        the military service, a
        military attaché.

<u>kápuu thālée</u>   sea crabs

   háw əən kápuu thīī aasǎj   We call crabs that live in
   jūū náj thālée wāā kápuu   the sea, sea crabs.
   thālée

<u>paa nàmcŷyt</u>   freshwater fish

   háw əən paa thīī aasǎj   We call fish that live in
   jūū náj nàm cŷyt wāā paa   fresh water, fresh-water fish.
   nàmcŷyt

C-1

   A. háw əən nàm thīī dàj máa   What do we call liquid that
     cāak mâakkìaŋ wāā jāaŋdaj?   we get from an orange?

   B. háw əən nàm thīī dàj máa   We call the liquid that we
     cāak mâakkìaŋ wāā nàm   get from an orange, orange
     mâakkìaŋ   juice.

C-2

   A. paa nàmcŷyt mēēn njǎŋ?   What is fresh-water fish?

   B. paa nàmcŷyt mēēn paa   Fresh-water fish are fish
     thīī aasǎj jūū náj   that live in fresh-water.
     nàmcŷyt

ໃນບົດຮຽນບົດນີ້ແລະບົດຕໍ່ໄປ ນັກຮຽນກໍມີແຕ່ຈະຝຶກຫັດກົດຮ້ອງກັບການຈຸດຫາເອົາໃຈຄວາມໝາຍຂອງ
ຄຳ ຕລີການປະກອບຄຳໃນພາສາລາວ. ຍ້ວມີອັກຫລາຍວັຫກວານຢູ່ ທ່ານລອວດັດມາສອນຊະເຈົ້າຖົນກຸ!

NOTES

(Cycles 82-85)

Cycles 82-85 all might be called 'Word definition' cycles,
since each of them illustrates a different way of defining
words in Lao. There are other ways that are not included
in these cycles. You are encouraged to discover them. You
may do so by asking your instructor for the definition of
any new words you may encounter in your reading or elsewhere.
Avoid asking for English translations of Lao words.

CYCLE 83

M-1

aaj

háw èən khón thII aaj jɯɯ
lỳaj lỳaj wāā jāāŋdaj?

shy

What do we call a person
who is always shy?

khàan

háw èən khón thII khàan jɯɯ
lỳaj lỳaj wāā jāāŋdaj?

lazy

What do we call a person
who is always lazy?

jàan

háw èən khón thII jàan jɯɯ
lỳaj lỳaj wāā jāāŋdaj?

afraid

What do we call a person
who is always afraid?

túa? túa?

háw èən khón thII túa? jɯɯ
lỳaj lỳaj wāā jāāŋdaj?

lying

What do we call a person
who's given to lying?

409

<u>lǎk</u>   stealing

    háw ə̀ən khón thɪ̄ɪ lǎk   What do we call a person
    jʊ̄ʊ lyàj lyàj wāā jāāŋdaj?   who's given to stealing?

<u>kooŋ</u>   cheating

    háw ə̀ən khón thɪ̄ɪ kooŋ jʊ̄ʊ   What do we call a person
    lyàj lyàj wāā jāāŋdaj?   who's given to cheating?

M-2

<u>lýym</u>   forgetful

    háw ə̀ən khón thɪ̄ɪ lýym   We call a person who's given
    jʊ̄ʊ lyàj lyàj wāā khón   to forgetting, a forgetful
    khɪ̂ɪ lýym   person.

<u>bǎj</u>   grumbling

    háw ə̀ən khón thɪ̄ɪ bǎj jʊ̄ʊ   We call a person who's given
    lyàj lyàj wāā khón khɪ̂ɪ   to grumbling, a grumbler.
    bǎj

<u>khɪ̂ɪ thɪ̄ɪ</u>   stinginess

    háw ə̀ən khón thɪ̄ɪ khɪ̂ɪ   We call a person who's given
    thɪ̄ɪ jʊ̄ʊ lyàj lyàj wāā   to stinginess, a stingy persoɪ
    khón khɪ̂ɪ thɪ̄ɪ

<u>khúj</u>   bragging

    háw ə̀ən khón thɪ̄ɪ khúj   We call a person who's given
    jʊ̄ʊ lyàj lyàj wāā khón   to bragging, a bragger.
    khɪ̂ɪ khúj

máw

    háw əən khón thīī máw
    jɯɯ lỳaj lỳaj wāā khón
    khîi máw

drunk

    We call a person who is
    always drunk, a drunkard.

hâj

    háw əən khón thīī hâj
    jɯɯ lỳaj lỳaj wāā khón
    khîi hâj

crying

    We call a person who's given
    to crying, a cry baby.

M-3

khón khîi khūk

    khón khîi khūk mɛ̄ɛn
    khón nɛ́ɛwdaj?

jailbird

    What's a jailbird?

khón khîi phàj

    khón khîi phàj mɛ̄ɛn
    khón nɛ́ɛwdaj?

cardsharp

    What's a cardsharp?

khón khîi jaa

    khón khîi jaa mɛ̄ɛn
    khón nɛ́ɛwdaj?

opium addict

    What's an opium addict?

khón khîi phānjàat

    khón khîi phānjàat mɛ̄ɛn
    khón nɛ́ɛwdaj?

sickly person

    What's a sickly person?

khón khîi thùut

    khón khîi thùut mɛ̄ɛn
    khón nɛ́ɛwdaj?

leper

    What's a leper?

khón khîi lâw   alcoholic

   khón khîi lâw mɛɛn khón   What's an alcoholic?
   nɛɛwdaj?

M-4

títkhǔk juu samšə   is in and out of jail

   khón khîi khǔk mɛɛn khón   A jailbird is a person
   thîi títkhǔk juu samšə   who is in and out of jail.

lîn phàj pen kaan phānán   plays cards for money

   khón khîi phàj mɛɛn khón   A cardsharp is a person
   thîi phàj pen kaan phānán   who plays cards for money.

tít jaafīn   is addicted to opium

   khón khîi jaa mɛɛn khón   An opium addict is a
   thîi tít jaafīn   person who is addicted
                                 to opium.

dʉ̌ym lâw lǎaj kəən paj   drinks to excess

   khón khîi lâw mɛɛn khón   An alcoholic is a person
   thîi dʉ̌ym lâw lǎaj kəən   who drinks to excess.
   paj

bɔɔ sabaaj juu samšə   always sick

   khón khîi phānjàat mɛɛn   A sickly person is a person
   khón thîi bɔɔ sabaaj   who is always sick.
   juu samšə

C-1

    A. háw əən khón thīī aaj   What do we call a person who
       jūū lỳaj lỳaj wāā   is always shy?
       jāāŋdaj?

    B. háw əən khón thīī aaj   We call a person who is
       jūū lỳaj lỳaj wāā khón   always shy, a shy person.
       khîi aaj.

C-2

A   A. khón khîi khūk mɛ̄ɛn khón   What's a jailbird?
       nɛ́ɛwdaj?

    B. khón khîi khūk mɛ̄ɛn khón   A jailbird is the person
       títkhūk jūū samšə.   who is in and out of jail.

C-3

    (Students ask questions then instructor confirms. Example:)

    1. S: háw əən khón thīī khàan   T: mɛ̄ɛn lɛ̀ɛw
          jūū lỳaj wāā khón khîi
          khàan, mɛ̄ɛn bɔɔ?

    2 S: háw əən khón thīī kin   T: bɔ̄ɔ mɛ̄ɛn.
          jūū lỳaj lỳaj wāā khón
          khîi kin, mɛ̄ɛn bɔɔ?

413

CYCLE 84

M-1

<u>hētwlak klawkáp màj</u>   works with wood

   háw әәn k̠hón thīī hētwlak   What do we call a person
   klawkáp màj wāā jāāŋdaj?   who works with wood?

<u>pɛɛŋ lōt</u>   fixes cars

   háw әәn khón thīī pɛɛŋ   What do we call a person
   lōt wāā jāāŋdaj?   who fixes cars?

<u>hētwlak klawkáp fájfàa</u>   works with electricity

   háw әәn khón thīī hētwlak   What do we call a person
   klawkáp fájfàa wāā jāāŋdaj?   who works with electricity?

<u>púk hỹan</u>   builds houses

   háw әәn khón thīī púk   What do we call a person
   hỹan wāā jāāŋdaj?   who builds houses?

<u>pɛɛŋ móoŋ</u>   repairs watches

   háw әәn khón thīī <u>pɛɛŋ</u>   What do we call a person
   móoŋ wāā jāāŋdaj?   who repairs watches?

<u>tii khám</u>   makes things out of gold

   háw әәn khón thīī tii   What do we call a person
   khám wāā jāāŋdaj?   who makes things out of
                                    gold?

<u>tii lék</u>   makes things out of iron

   háw әәn khón thīī tii   What do we call a person
   lék wāā jāāŋdaj?   who makes things out of
                                    iron?

M-2

sāaŋmàj

  háw əən khón thīī hētwìak
  kīawkáp màj wāa sāaŋmàj

a wood worker

  We call a person who works
  with wood, a wood worker.

sāaŋ pɛɛŋ lōt

  háw əən khón thīī pɛɛŋ lōt
  wāa sāaŋ pɛɛŋ lōt

car mechanic

  We call a person who fixes
  cars, a car mechanic.

sāaŋ fájfàa

  háw əən khōn thīī hētwìak
  kīawkáp fájfàa wāa sāaŋ
  fájfàa

an electrician

  We call a person who works
  with electricity,
  electrician.

sāaŋ púk hýan

  háw əən khón thīī púk
  hýan wāa sāaŋ púk hýan

house-builder

  We call a person who builds
  houses, a house-builder.

sāaŋ pɛɛŋ lék

  háw əən khón thīī pɛɛŋ
  móoŋ wāa sāaŋ pɛɛŋ móoŋ

a watch repair man

  We call a person who repairs
  watches, a watch repair man.

sāaŋ tìi khám

  háw əən khón thīī tìi lék
  wāa sāaŋ tìi lék

a blacksmith

  We call a person who makes
  things out of iron, a blacksmith.

sāaŋ tìi khám

  háw əən khón thīī tìi khám
  waa sāaŋ tìi khám

a goldsmith

  We call a person who makes
  things out of gold, a
  goldsmith.

M-3

sǎaŋ tátphǒm   a barber

    sǎaŋ tátphǒm mɛɛn phūu   What does a barber do?
    thīī hɛt njǎŋ?

sǎaŋ kɔɔ sâaŋ   a builder

    sǎaŋ kɔɔ sâaŋ mɛɛn phūu   What does a builder do?
    thīī hɛt njǎŋ?

sǎaŋ thāajhùup   a photographer

    sǎaŋ thāajhùup mɛɛn phūu   What does a photographer do?
    thīī hɛt njǎŋ?

sǎaŋ tátkhȳaŋnūŋ   a tailor

    sǎaŋ tátkhȳaŋnūŋ mɛɛn phūu   What does a tailor do?
    thīī hɛt njǎŋ?

sǎaŋ tháasǐi   a painter

    sǎaŋ tháasǐi mɛɛn phūu   What does a painter (workman)
    thīī hɛt njǎŋ?   do?

sǎaŋ tɛ̀ɛm   a painter

    sǎaŋ tɛ̀ɛm mɛɛn phūu thīī   What does a painter (artist)
    hɛt njǎŋ?   do?

sǎaŋ pàn   a modeller, potter

    sǎaŋ pàn mɛɛn phūu thīī   What does a modeller do?
    hɛt njǎŋ?

M-4

thɪ̄ɪ tát phǒm pen	knows how to cut hair
sāāŋ tátphǒm mɛ̄ɛn khón thɪ̄ɪ tát phǒm pen	A barber is a person who knows how to cut hair.
kɔɔ sâaŋ pen	knows how to build
sāāŋ kɔɔ sâaŋ mɛ̄ɛn khón thɪ̄ɪ kɔɔ sâaŋ pen	A builder is a person who knows how to build.
tát khỹaŋnūŋ pen	knows how to tailor
sāāŋ tátkhỹaŋnūŋ mɛ̄ɛn khón thɪ̄ɪ tát khỹaŋnūŋ	A tailor is a person who knows how to make clothing.
thāājhùup pen	knows how to take pictures
sāāŋ thāājhùup mɛ̄ɛn khón thɪ̄ɪ thāājhùup pen	A photographer is a person who knows how to take pictures.
tháasǐi pen	knows how to paint
sāāŋ tháasǐi mɛ̄ɛn khón thɪ̄ɪ tháasǐi pen	A painter is a person who knows how to paint.
tɛ̀ɛmhùup pen	knows how to paint pictures
sāāŋ tɛ̀ɛm mɛ̄ɛn khón thɪ̄ɪ tɛ̀ɛmhùup pen	A painter is a person who knows how to paint pictures.
pàn sɪ̌ŋ khɔ̌ɔŋ dùaj dindâak pen	knows how to mold things with clay
sāāŋ pàn mɛ̄ɛn khón thɪ̄ɪ pàn sɪ̌ŋ khɔ̌ɔŋ dùaj dindâak pèn	A modeller is a person who knows how to mold things with clay.

417

C-1

    A. háw èən khón thɪɪ hɛ̄twȋak
       kȋawkáp màj wāā jāāŋdaj?

    What do we call a person
    who works with wood?

    B. háw èən khón thɪɪ hɛ̄twȋak
       kȋawkáp màj wāā sāāŋmàj

    We call a person who works
    with wood, a woodworker.

C-2

    A. sāāŋ tátphǒm mɛ̄ɛn phʊ̄ʊ
       thɪɪ hɛ̄t njǎŋ?

    What does a barber do?

    B. sāāŋ tátphǒm mɛ̄ɛn khón
       thɪɪ tátphǒm pen.

    A barber is a person who
    knows how to cut hair.

C-3

    (Student asks a question and instructor confirms: Example:)

    1. S: háw èən khón thɪɪ khúakin   T: bɔ̄ɔ mɛ̄ɛn
         pen wāā sāāŋ khúakin,
         mɛ̄ɛn bɔɔ?

    2. S: háw èən khón thɪɪ hɛ̄t   T: mɛ̄ɛn lɛ̀ɛw
         kɛ̀əp pen wāā sāāŋ
         tátkɛ̀əp, mɛ̄ɛn bɔɔ?

418

CYCLE 85

M-1

paj hóoŋhían

    háw ə̀ən khón thīī paj
hóoŋhían wāā jāāŋdaj?

goes to school

    What do we call a person
who goes to school?

sýksǎa

    háw ə̀ən khón thīī sýksǎa
wāā jāāŋdaj?

is studying at a high level

    What do we call a person
who is studying at a high
level?

thɔɔŋthīaw

    háw ə̀ən khón thīī thɔɔŋthīaw
wāā jāāŋdaj?

travelling

    What do we call a person
who is travelling?

pùn khón ɏyn

    háw ə̀ən khón thīi pùn khón
ɏyn wāā jāāŋdaj?

robs other people

    What do we call a person who
robs other people?

sŷypsǔan

    háw ə̀ən khón thīī sŷypsǔan
wāā jāāŋdaj?

investigates

    What do we call a person
who investigates?

rōp sək

    háw ə̀ən khón thīī rōp sək
wāā jāāŋdaj?

fights in a war

    What do we call a person
who fights in a war?

tɛɛŋ phéeŋ

    háw ə̀ən khón thīī tɛɛŋ
phéeŋ wāā jāāŋdaj?

composes songs

    What do we call a person
who composes songs?

M-2

<u>káp hýabin</u>   pilots a plane, a pilot

    háw əən khón thīī káp   We call the person who
    hýabin wāā nākbin   pilots a plane, a pilot.

<u>khĭan pỳm, nākkhĭan</u>   writes books, an author

    háw əən khón thīī khĭan   We call the person who writes
    pỳm wāā nākkhĭan   books, an author.

<u>tènlám kēŋ</u>   dances well, a dancer

    háw əən khón thīī tènlám   We call the person who dances
    kēŋ wāā nāktènlám   well, a dancer.

<u>māk ʒɔk phácon pháj</u>   likes to go out and face danger

    háw əən khón thīī māk ʒɔk   We call the person who likes
    phácon pháj wāā nākphácon-   to out and face danger , a
    pháj   daredevil.

<u>hɔɔŋ phéeŋ kēŋ</u>   is good in singing

    háw əən khón thīī   We call the person who is
    phéeŋ kēŋ wāā nākhɔɔŋ   good in singing, a singer.

<u>tiimúaj kēŋ</u>   boxes well

    háw əən khón thīī tiimúaj   We call the person who boxes
    kēŋ wāā nākmúaj   well, a boxer.

M-3

nākdontrii	musician
nākdontrii mɛɛn njǎŋ?	What's a musician?
nākwīthǎnjáasâat	scientist
nākwīthǎnjáasâat mɛɛn njǎŋ?	What's a scientist?
nākkaanthùut	diplomat
nākkaanthùut mɛɛn njǎŋ?	What's a diplomat?
nākkaanmýaŋ	politician
nākkaanmýaŋ mɛɛn njǎŋ?	What's a politician?
nākkíláa	athlete
nākkíláa mɛɛn njǎŋ?	What's an athlete?
nāknǎŋsŷyphím	journalist
nāknǎŋsŷyphím mɛɛn njǎŋ?	What's a journalist?
nākthòot	prisoner
nākthòot mɛɛn njǎŋ?	What's a prisoner?

M-4

| lên dontrii kɛ̄ŋ | plays music well |
| nākdontrii mɛɛn khón thīī lên dontrii kɛ̄ŋ | A musician is a person who plays music well. |

421

sýksǎa khònkhwàa tháaŋ dàan
wǐthǎnjáasâat

studies and carries out research
in the field of science

nǎkwǐthǎnjáasâat mɛɛn khón
thǐɪ sýksǎa khònkhwàa tháaŋ
dàan wǐthǎnjáasâat

A scientist is a person who
studies and carries out
research in the field of
science.

pen càwnâathǐɪ tháaŋkaan jɑɑ
nájj sathǎanthùut

official in the embassy

nǎkkaanthùut mɛɛn khón thǐɪ
pen càwnâathǐɪ tháaŋkaan
jɑɑ nájj sathǎanthùut

A diplomat is a person who
is an official in the
embassy.

lǐn kaanmýaŋ

works in politics

nǎkkaanmýaŋ mɛɛn khón thǐɪ
lǐn kaanmýaŋ

A politician is a person who
works in politics.

lǐn kíláa

plays sport

nǎkkíláa mɛɛn khón thǐɪ
lǐn kíláa

An athlete is a person who
plays sports.

khǐan khǎaw lóŋ nǎŋs̃yyphím

writes for a newspaper

nǎknǎŋs̃yyphím mɛɛn khón
thǐɪ khǐan khǎaw lóŋ
nǎŋs̃yyphím

A journalist is a person who
writes for a newspaper.

títkhʉk

is imprisoned

nǎkthòot mɛɛn khón thǐɪ
títkhʉk

A prisoner is a person who
is imprisoned.

422

C-1

    A. háw èən khón thīī paj hóoŋhían waā jāāŋdaj?

    What do we call a person who goes to school?

    B. háw èən khón thīī paj hóoŋhían waā nākhían

    We call a person who goes to school, a student.

C-2

    A. háw èən khón thīī kháp hýabin waā jāāŋdaj?

    What do we call a person who pilots a plane?

    B. háw èən khón thīī kháp hýabin waā nākbin

    We call a person who pilots a plane, a pilot.

C-3

    A. nākdontrii mɛɛn njăŋ?

    What's a musician?

    B. nākdontrii mɛɛn khón thīī lên dontrii kɛŋ

    A musician is a person who plays music well.

C-4

(Student asks question and instructor confirms. Example:)

    1 S: háw èən khón thīī tátphŏm waā nāktátphŏm, mɛɛn boo?

    T: bɔɔ mɛɛn

    2 S: háw èən khón thīī sadɛɛŋ lākhŏon waā nāksádɛɛŋ lākhŏon

    T: mɛɛn lɛ̀ɛw

S.E. ASIAN LANGUAGE INSTRUCTION
. . . from Hippocrene

BASIC COURSE INSTRUCTION—These full-length courses provide intensive instruction through dialogues, response drills, and glossaries. These volumes are reprints of courses used successfully by the U.S. Foreign Service Institute.

CANTONESE
$16.95 • 0-7818-0289-X

LAO
$19.95 • 0-7818-1389-6

BEGINNER'S SERIES—Essential grammar and vocabulary are provided allowing students to progress quickly. The goal is to provide readers with knowledge to travel independently, and speak, understand, read and write essential words.

BEGINNER'S JAPANESE
$11.95 • 0-7818-0234-2

HIPPOCRENE HANDY DICTIONARIES—For the traveler of independent spirit and curious mind, this practical series will help you to communicate, not just to get by. Common phrases are conveniently listed through key words. Pronunciation follows each entry and a reference section reviews all major grammar points.

CHINESE
$8.95 • 0-87052-050-4

KOREAN
$8.95 • 0-7818-0082-X

JAPANESE
$8.95 • 0-87052-962-5

THAI
$8.95 • 0-87052-963-3

HIPPOCRENE MASTER SERIES—This teach-yourself language series, now available in seven languages, is perfect for the serious traveler, student or businessman. Imaginative, practical exercises in grammar are accompanied by cassette tapes for conversation practice. Available as a book/cassette package.

MASTERING JAPANESE

0748	ISBN 0-87052-923-4	$14.95 BOOK
0932	ISBN 0-87052-938-8	$12.95 2 CASSETTES
1102	ISBN 0-87052-141-1	$27.90 PACKAGE

(All prices subject to change.)

TO PURCHASE HIPPOCRENE BOOKS contact your local bookstore, or write to: HIPPOCRENE BOOKS, 171 Madison Avenue, New York, NY 10016. Please enclose check or money order, adding $5.00 shipping (UPS) for the first book and $.50 for each additional book.